DEMOCRACY
AND DICTATORSHIP
IN SOUTH ASIA

DEMOCRACY AND DICTATORSHIP IN SOUTH ASIA

Dominant Classes and Political Outcomes in India, Pakistan, and Bangladesh

Robert W. Stern

PRAEGER

Westport, Connecticut
London

Library of Congress Cataloging-in-Publication Data

Stern, Robert W., 1933–
  Democracy and dictatorship in South Asia : dominant classes and political outcomes in India, Pakistan, and Bangladesh / Robert W. Stern.
    p. cm.
  Includes bibliographical references and index.
  ISBN 0-275-97041-8 (alk. paper)
    1. South Asia—Politics and government.   2. Democracy—South Asia.   3. Dictatorship—South Asia.   I. Title.

  DS341 .S75 2001
  320.954—dc21   00-039172

British Library Cataloguing in Publication Data is available.

Library of Congress Catalog Card Number: 00-039172
ISBN: 0-275-97041-8

First published in 2001

Praeger Publishers, 88 Post Road West, Westport, CT 06881
An imprint of Greenwood Publishing Group, Inc.
www.praeger.com

Printed in the United States of America

The paper used in this book complies with the
Permanent Paper Standard issued by the National
Information Standards Organization (Z39.48-1984).

10 9 8 7 6 5 4 3 2 1

For Barbara, Jenny and John, Jack and Issey,
Annie and Malcolm, Gabriel and Eloise,
Cathy and Tony, Ed and Georgia, Ben and Sam

That's All Folks!
Bugs Bunny

Contents

Acknowledgments

To subcontinental friends, colleagues, and even perfect strangers, for their patience and guidance my debts are staggering. Among those to whom I am most indebted, but who, I hasten to add, are in no way responsible for what I have made of my debts, are the following. In India, as ever, my dear friend and colleague Ravinder Kumar. My notion of coalitions of dominant classes emerged from a conversation with Barun De, then of the Maulana Abul Kalam Institute of Asian Studies, Calcutta. His colleague, Ranabir Sammadar, was also particularly helpful, as were Rajet Kanta Ray and Suranjan Das of the University of Calcutta. Prabat P. Ghosh and his colleagues at the Asian Development Research Institute, Patna, and, particularly, Shaibal Gupta introduced me to the political world of Laloo Prasad Yadav. Mammen Matthew of the *Hindustan Times* was also instructive. In Patna, too, Yuvaraj Deva Prasad and his colleagues at the A. N. Sinha Institute of Social Studies were hospitable and helpful. Anjoo and Priyankar Upadhyaya made me welcome at Banaras Hindu University and introduced me to their colleagues in the Faculty of Social Sciences. I am grateful to them, and particularly to Promod Kumar Tiwari. In Lucknow, Ram Advani kindly and gently steered me in the right directions. G. P. Misra and his colleagues at the Giri Institute of Development Studies, Lucknow, were helpful as was Asit Banerji. Having forgiven me for misspelling his name in an earlier work, Ranbir Singh helped me to understand the intricacies of *panchayati raj* during my visit to Kurukshetra. P. S. Verma and his colleagues at the Political Science Department, Panjab University, Chandigarh, made me sing for some very good Punjabi suppers. Chandrikar was particularly helpful. I am grateful for the insights of Atur S. Dhesi and H. K. Puri at the Guru Nanak Dev University at Amritsar and for the friendship of Gurdev Singh.

Over the Wagah Crossing, in Lahore, I have on several occasions been the recipient of Akmal Hussain's great generosity of mind and spirit. Sajjad Nasir and his Political Science colleagues at the University of Punjab, Lahore, were most helpful, as was Rafique Ahmad of the university's Centre for South Asian Studies. My thanks also to Hamid A. K. Rai and his colleagues in the Political Science Department at Government College, Lahore. Najjam Sethi, Arif Nizami of *The Nation*, and Athar Masood and his colleagues at *Jang* were also helpful. On the other side of the subcontinent, I have debts to Cristopher Kenna, then First Secretary of the Australian High Commission, for his help and hospitality. The eminent development economist Rehman Sobhan and Talukder Maniruzzaman, Kamal Ahmed, and their colleagues in the Political Science Department at Dhaka University have been some of my tutors in Bangladeshi politics, past and present. Other tutorials came from Mabub Ullah, Muzaffer Ahmed, M. Mufakharul Islam, Anisuzzaman, and members of the Bangladesh Institute of Development Studies, particularly Atiur Rahman and Bimal Kumar Saha.

At home, in Sydney, Morris Morley has been, as ever, a particularly patient listener and a source of good advice and criticism. Macquarie University was, as ever, generous in its support of my work.

DEMOCRACY
AND DICTATORSHIP
IN SOUTH ASIA

1

Dominant Class Coalitions: The Argument and Its Historical Contexts

Torn from cloth of the same civilization, the societies of India, Pakistan, and Bangladesh are more like one another than they are like those of any other countries. They share the same cultural and historical heritages of Islamized Hinduism and Hinduized Islam. Most Pakistanis and the vast majority of Bangladeshis belong to ethnolinguistic groups that are also Indian. Also, and crucial to this study, India is the larger part and Pakistan and Bangladesh the smaller parts of what was until 1947 the same British Indian empire—for a century at least, and for two centuries in parts of the subcontinent.

Yet over the past fifty years of independent statehood, parliamentary democracy has been developing in India, whereas in Pakistan it has never been more than a masquerade and its players in Bangladesh have yet to understand it as other than a zero-sum game. Why? This book is my effort to suggest some answers. It is largely a work of synthetic scholarship. Much of the data in it is known or readily knowable. Only their combination into a coherent argument is original to this synthesis. Like most attempts to answer complex questions, mine takes the form of a proposition, an argument. The answers it provides are certainly not definitive. But they are, I think, substantial. My argument is about history; or rather, histories. It structures this study and integrates its parts into a whole. In this introduction, and particularly for my readers who are not South Asia specialists, I present that proposition within its broad historical contexts of British India and of independent Indian, Pakistani, and Bangladeshi statehood. Along the way, I have signposted particular events that are germane to my argument. So, this chapter will, I hope, both introduce my argument and put in context the particular histories in the chapters that follow.

Summarily, and subject to considerable elaboration as we go on, the argument that I propose is this:

During the nineteenth and twentieth centuries, indirectly and directly in reaction to British imperialism, Indian Muslims and Hindus imagined and invented their religious "communities" and "communal" nationalisms, separate and distinct from one another.[1] This is where our story begins. From the first decade of the twentieth century, the British Government of India—the Raj—in collaboration with Indian politicians began a process of institutionalizing this "communalism" in the political systems that they were developing on the subcontinent.

In these systems, Indian nationalism first appeared as an alliance of "communal" nationalisms: in the Lucknow Pact of 1916 between Muslim and Hindu politicians and the anti-imperial "communal" accord of 1920–22 between the Muslim Khilafat Movement[2] and the Indian National Congress's Non-Cooperation Movement. Later, leaders of the Congress Party would revise their depiction of Indian nationalism as multi-"communal" or "secular" and insist on the acceptance of Congress's credentials as the representative organization of this revised nationalism. But while Congress had a handful of Muslim leaders, outside the North West Frontier Province—a special case—it never had a constituency of ordinary Muslims. And most of the human and material resources that had gone into Congress's making were distinctly Hindu.

The organization that claimed to be Congress's Muslim counterpart, the All-India Muslim League, denied the existence in India of any multi-"communal" or secular nationalism and claimed to be the representative organization of the Muslim "nation." The "communal" conception of subcontinental nationalism reappeared in the "transfer of power" negotiations of the 1940s between Congress, the Muslim League, and the British government. In the carnage that preceded and accompanied the subcontinent's partition in 1947, "communalism" was given terrible witness. It has never disappeared—neither from India, nor Pakistan, nor Bangladesh, not from their domestic politics nor in their relations with one another. With modifications over the years, "communalism" has remained a constant ingredient in the *masala*[3] of subcontinental politics.

Not only via the course of "communalism"—although it was a major route—India inherited from the Indian National Congress of British India a politically dominant coalition of classes whose composition and organization have been friendly to the continuing development of parliamentary democracy. Pakistan's legacy was a politically dominant coalition of classes in its western provinces whose composition and lack of organization impeded the development of parliamentary democracy before East Pakistan seceded in 1971 and impede it still. As political actors in Pakistan's eastern province, a Bengali coalition friendly to the development of parliamentary democracy had the ironic effect of ensuring its nondevelopment in Pakistan. Since 1971, the development of parliamentary democracy in Bangladesh has been dogged by its legacies of twenty-four years as Pakistan's subordinate province, its year-long secessionist war of liberation, and the disorganization and disorientation of its coalition of dominant classes. Yet unlike its counterpart in Pakistan, this coalition poses no structural barrier to the development of parliamentary democracy in Bangladesh.

Three things, at least, ought to be noted regarding this argument.

First, "class" should be understood in Max Weber's terminology: Thus, "'classes' are not *communities*; they merely represent possible and frequent bases for *communal* action." "Class" refers to "any group of people . . . in the same class situation," whether or not they are conscious of being members of that class.[4] In discussing subcontinental society, it is particularly important to distinguish between "class" and "consciousness." Consciousness is often an attribute of "community." It is quite normal for people in the same class situation to behave in the same way but to be primarily conscious of their castes and religious "communities." For example, cultivating proprietors of different castes will exploit landless laborers of their own or different castes in the same ways; however, both proprietors and laborers—the exploiters and the exploited—of the same or different castes will continue to regard these as their "communities."

Second, my argument relates to *politically* dominant coalitions of classes: to coalitions of groups of people in the same class situation who are dominant in their political systems. They need not, for example, also be dominant in their social or economic systems. This is an ordinary anomaly of parliamentary democratic society and a facilitator of its acceptance by groups that are socially or economically powerful. "Dominant castes" of well-to-do farmers, Brahmin, and other twice-born[5] castes, for example, no longer dominate, as they once did, the provincial politics of northern India. But their ritual status and wealth continues to command the deference of their neighbours in contexts other than the political.

Finally, here and in the chapters that follow, I have put in quotation marks all my references to imagined and invented "communities". Analogous to national "communities," these are largely the products of ideologies and their dissemination by various media, and by political mobilization and institutionalization. They are not the communities of ordinary human interaction, which play so large a part in the lives of the subcontinent's people and ought to be distinguished in some way from them. They need to be distinguished in particular from those communities based on ties of kinship, in which most people of the subcontinent live most of their lives, face-to-face and day-to-day: extended families, lineages, *jatis,* caste group fragments. Both communities and "communities" are relevant to the discussions that follow, but in different ways.

BRITISH INDIA

The British initially came to India in the early seventeenth century as a state trading monopoly, the British East India Company. Its commercial ups and downs—and there were many of them—are of no interest here. The company began to trade in the seventeenth century, during the heyday of the Mughal empire. The Mughals were the last and greatest of the Turkish and Afghan Muslim dynasties, and their fragments, which, from the beginning of the thirteenth century, conquered most of northern India and ruled it for the next half-millennium. From the beginning of the eighteenth century, in the chaos that attended the Mughal empire's disintegration, the company became a major political actor. By the middle of the century, it possessed an extensive Indian domain, particularly in the northeast, radiating from its port and capital at Calcutta and that city's Bengali-speaking hinterland. By 1818, the company's armies had defeated their French and Indian rivals and made Britain the subcontinent's dominant political power. In 1843 and 1849, the company made the last major additions to its Indian empire, Sindh and Punjab.

As the company's captains had convinced themselves of the great boon to India of British imperialism, the Indian Mutiny of 1857 came as a surprise and a shock. The mutiny began in units of the company's army and spread to sections of the civilian population in northern India. Its participants were both Hindu and Muslim. The stated and ostensible objectives of their leaders were to rid India of British rule and restore to rightful authority the Mughal emperor, whose *gaddi* (throne)[6] the company had usurped and whose *izzat* (public honor) it had degraded. Virtually confined to Delhi's Red Fort, the emperor had been retained by the company as its pensioner and figurehead. After a year of hard fighting and considerable brutality on both sides, the Mutiny was finally suppressed and the emperor ignominiously exiled to Rangoon.

India was officially made an imperium of the British government in 1858. The change was largely formal. Most of India's commerce was already in the hands of private traders. By mid-century, Westminster had embraced "free trade" and, in effect, transformed the company into the British government's agency for ruling its Indian empire. There were, however, political changes of substance that followed the Mutiny's suppression and British considerations of its causes.

In the Mutiny's postmortems, an underlying criticism of the company's policies were that they were politically uninformed or inadequately informed. For example, the company's pre-Mutiny policy of annexing the domains of Indian princes was in retrospect generally regarded as a serious error, provocative of opposition and arising from political ignorance and arrogance. Not only with regard to the princes, but in general, imperial hierarchs post-Mutiny began to factor into their decision-making informed judgments of its possible or probable, desirable or undesirable political effects on particular groups of their Indian subjects. Which groups should or would be favored by which decisions? To what ends? Which groups should or would be brought together or driven apart by which political decisions? To what ends? What were the fissure lines in Indian society—between British and princely India, between Hindu and Muslim "communities," between caste Hindus and "scheduled castes"[7]—and how could they be used for imperial maintenance? For the captains of empire, the Mutiny crystallized their understanding of imperial maintenance as a political no less than an administrative task. "Divide-and-rule" is this understanding's caricature. It distorts the truth, but embodies its germ.

In the era of the imperial European nation-state, the Raj was the agency of British imperialism in India. Compared to the imperialism of its contemporaries, it was relatively competent and humane. But it was not a charitable enterprise. Its raison d'être was to serve British interests, although, to be sure, these were multiplex and sometimes contradictory: The British Government of India had its own interests vis-à-vis those of the government in London; their separate departments had interests vis-à-vis those of other departments; decisions taken at bureaucratic heights were sometimes ignored on the ground or merely gave prudent sanction to ground realities; in relation to India, British enterprises at home had interests vis-à-vis each other and British enterprises in India; and so forth.

But these are the trees of bureaucratic and industrialized political systems in general, and they should not obscure our view of the Raj's forest. It was a field for exploitation. Its exploitation was a British national enterprise sanctioned by parliament, meant to serve what its politicians understood to be British "national interests" and the interests of their sectional constituencies, and entrusted in India to the keeping of the right sort of Britons. The relationship of political superiority–subordination that pertains in general between imperial "guardians"[8] and their native subjects was supplemented and reinforced in India by relationships of cultural and "racial" distance and disdain. In 1835, Thomas Babington Macaulay imagined a class in India who were Indian only "in blood and colour, but English in taste, in opinions, in morals and in intellect."[9] It was apparently to this imagined class that Queen Victoria gave her promise of the British future in India. In her proclamation of 1885, the queen declared:

that in so far as may be, our subjects, of whatever race or creed, be freely and impartially admitted to offices in our service, the duties of which they may be qualified by their education, ability and integrity duly to discharge.[10]

Macaulay's famous "minute" antedated theories of "scientific" racism that were gaining currency and respectability at mid-century, and the queen's proclamation was clearly uninformed by them. The queen's promise would have to be broken by her loyal servants in order to preserve her empire. Compounded with the cultural ingredients of what Edward Said has popularized as "orientalism"[11] and which had long been part of the British perception of Indian "others,"[12] racism was put into the service of legitimating the rule of Europeans over culturally and racially inferior Asiatics. No more or less self-serving than any other ideology, orientalism, in general, and racism, in particular, were used to maintain the monopoly by Britons of the upper, decision-making, well-paid prestigious echelons of empire and the supremacy and exclusivity of their Anglo-Indian[13] society. Macaulay's class of Indians was a fiction. In fact, Indian-ness was etched in "blood and colour," and educated Indians could not be trusted to run an empire, much less a British empire in British interests. Marriage between

Britons and Indians was socially and professionally tabooed, and the progeny of mixed marriages either passed into British Indian or Indian caste society or were categorized and segregated as Eurasians, neither British nor Indian. Above the congeries of Indian races, the British were a race apart, particularly gifted by nature in head and heart to rule according to "law and system" and by their custodianship of a higher, European civilization—Christian, at once morally and intellectually superior, and committed to a civilizing mission in Asia.[14] Anglo-Indians were the "new race of Asia."[15] Bureaucratic competence and discipline were attributes of superior race. The British in India were a "ruling race."

> God of our fathers, known of old,
> Lord of our far-flung battle-line,
> Beneath whose awful hand we hold
> Dominion over palm and pine—[16]

Less poetically, it was an empire that, certainly from mid-century, excluded Indians from its higher social, political, and ideological reaches.[17] Yet, if the British were to rule India effectively and economically, they needed not merely the passive acquiescence of ordinary Indians, but the active collaboration of Indian elites. The Raj had to make friends and influence people in India. What friends and what people? Of necessity and prudence, the cooperation of some Indians had to be enlisted in the housekeeping and routine administrative chores of empire, at least. But which Indians, and under what terms of employment, and at what cost?

Ironically, the British were least fond and most suspicious of the group of Indians that had for the longest time provided them with many, if not most, of their subordinate collaborators. The Hindu professional middle classes—upper caste, literate, numerate, and disproportinately Bengali—were most of the cogs in the bureaucratic machinery that ran the empire and services ancillary to its running—the law, in particular. Post-Mutiny, the Raj's dependence on the educated middle classes for imperial maintenance grew as the empire's bureaucracies expanded and came to be operated increasingly in English and by Indians who had been university-educated in English. These were the people who took Victoria at her word, who at the turn of the century, and increasingly thereafter, demanded equal access with Britons to posts and postings in superior imperial bureaucracies. They also demanded legislative councils in which they could represent their own interests and act on them. They insisted on being treated no longer as mere subjects and subordinate servants of the empire, but as important stakeholders in it. In a word, they were intrinsically "seditious." They aspired to govern the Indian empire, on parity at least with Britons, or, failing that, to be rid of it.

Their largest and most enduring organization was the Indian National Congress. Begun largely as their interest group in 1885, it came under the leadership of Mahatma Gandhi from 1920 as a nationalist movement in opposition to the authoritarian regime of foreigners. Although it had virtually no Muslim constituency, Gandhi defined Congress's nationalism in multi-"communal" terms. In composition and organization, Congress was friendly to the development of parliamentary democracy. Initially, the major partners in its coalition were Hindu professional men and landed peasants. They were joined from the late 1930s by leading "merchant princes". Organizationally, Gandhi married a nascent Indian nationalism to pervasive and long-lived provincialism and localism.

The Bengali component of the politically aspiring Hindu professional middle class were the *bhadralok* of chapter 3. They were overwhelmingly high-caste, middle- to upper-class Hindus. Their economic base was on the land, where they were landlords and moneylenders to a peasantry that was largely Muslim. They were also Bengal's social elite, the core of its professional middle class and its intelligentsia. To the British, the *bhadralok* were, par excellence, collaborators who aspired to be competitors, if not usurpers. The British scorned them: "competition-wallahs," mere clerks—*babus,* the Monkey-People of Kipling's *Jungle Book*, Sir Alfred Lyall's "half civilised *avocasserie*, that bane of all British India."[18] Behind the scorn, however, there was apprehension. The earliest articulators of a Hindu Indian nationalism were *bhadralok* litterateurs. From the Congress's founding, *bhadralok* were major participants in it. Bengal was a breeding ground of "sedition," nonviolent and violent. Between 1905 and 1911, Hindu Indian nationalism had its first *cause célèbre* and its first victory in Bengal.

To Muslims, who were Bengal's majority "community," the *bhadralok* were not only rent and debt collectors, but concocters of an Indian nationalism that was exclusively Hindu and often explicitly anti-Muslim. The British were only untrustworthy friends; the *bhadralok* were enemies. From this enmity and with British assistance, there emerged in Bengal among Indian Muslims their only coalition of dominant classes friendly in composition and organization to the development of parliamentary democracy. Like Congress, it was a politically organized coalition of professional men and land-holding peasants. By the late 1930s it threatened every *bhadralok* interest. In 1905, when the *bhadralok* were Bengal's dominant class, they opposed the partition of their province as an imperial scheme to divide and rule. When their dominance was threatened in 1947 by organizations of their province's Muslim majority, the *bhadralok* were the most enthusiastic supporters of Bengal's partition.

After initially having seen behind the Mutiny the hand of the Muslim landed nobility of northern India, the *ashraf*,[19] and exacted their victor's condign revenge, the British began from the last decades of the nineteenth century to court these Muslims of good family and some property. The wooing was prompted by fear and hope. A fear was that the Muslim hoi polloi, almost a quarter of the subcontinent's population, would continue to be misled by their *ulama*[20] to Islamic fanaticism, and thus remain unreconciled to the Raj. Popular movements that coupled Islamic puritanism and opposition to British imperialism had from the early decades of the nineteenth century anathamatized the company *raj* as an illegitimate regime of infidels. The hope was that a reconciliation might be effected if Muslim landlords, the British-sponsored "natural leaders" of Muslim peasants, were offered the Raj's grace and favor. A fear was that the Muslim professional classes would align themselves with their Hindu counterparts in the Indian National Congress. The hope was that they would not—that if they, too, *as Muslims* were offered imperial grace and favor, they would share a common interest with Muslim landlords in its enjoyment and their loyalty to the empire. British grace and favor was legislated for Muslims of the professional and landlord classes in the India Act of 1909, and in all subsequent acts of British "constitutional reform" (see chapter 2).

Although Muslim landlords in Bengal were empire loyalists, they were few and far between and were generally outside the coalition of politically dominant classes that was taking shape among Muslims. In Punjab (the second Muslim majority province in British India), on the other hand, the dominant class was great landlords, and among these the Muslim landlords of the west were the greatest. The Punjab Land Alienation Act of 1900 was ostensibly aimed at protecting "agriculturalists," in general, from the predations of urban moneylenders and rentiers. The underlying political rationale of the act was to ally the interests of great landlords with those of the Raj. Less directly than "constitutional reforms" and the 1905 partition of Bengal, but no less in effect, the Land Alienation Act favored the interests of Muslim elites and disfavored those of their Hindu counterparts. Briefly, most of the "agriculturalists"—the "agriculturalists" who lent money, and the "agriculturalists" who were great landlords—were Muslims. While Sikh and Hindu landlords and "agriculturalists" profited from the act, most of Punjab's urban moneylenders, rentiers, and troublesome *vakils*[21] (lawyers) and all of the province's Congressmen were Hindus.

Particularly notable in Punjab, the wooing of Muslim landlords overlapped the Raj's post-Mutiny strategy of courting the favor of substantial landlords, in general, and promoting them as the "natural leaders" of Indian society. For foreign imperial rulers of peasant societies throughout Asia, there were economies in the patronizing of landlords. Contented landlords could use their political, economic, and ideological authority over the countryside to keep their peasants politically quiescent. In Punjab, landlords even served as recruiting agents for the British Indian Army. If there were landlords to attend to the collection of a large number of tenants' rents, then the imperial government could observe the countryside's exotica with anthropological detachment and concentrate on the collection of revenue from small numbers of landlords and the maintenance of domestic order sufficient for its collection. In eighteenth-century plain English, the company entitled its district officers "collectors." Post-Mutiny, the British attempted to reduce their dependence on the educated middle classes by various and vain attempts to recruit the sons of the landed "aristocracy"[22] to imperial service.

The most dramatic manifestation of the Raj's entente with these landlords was the virtual cessation post-Mutiny of any further British annexations of the territories of the empire's most substantial landed magnates, the princes, more than

500 *maharajas* and *nawabs*. Some were the scions of ancient dynasties, some of recent usurpers, others were placed on their *gaddis* by the British government itself.[23] Their territories varied in size from peninsular India's Hyderabad, two-thirds the size of France, to scores of principalities in Kathiawar,[24] each of only a few villages. Together, these "princely states" comprised about a third of the empire's area, and their subjects made up about a quarter of its population. In return for being neither deposed nor dispossessed by the "paramount power," the princes submitted in feudal form as vassals of the British monarch.

In bureaucratic substance, princes and their principalities were sorted like peas and graded into "gun-salute" categories of twenty-one, nineteen, seventeen, fifteen, and so on down the line. Then they were suitably incorporated into the bureaucratic empire as charges of the Government of India's Political Department. In two vain attempts in the twentieth century, the British government tried to make the princes into a political bloc at the empire's centre, as a bulwark against the forces of Indian nationalism. Some princes made a better fist of their clientage than others, and some flourished. But so dependent had they become on Delhi's patronage that by 1947, when most of their states "acceded" to the jurisdiction of a Congress government that wanted no client princes, they could be pensioned off and their territories integrated into the Indian Union in about two years.

For the future of parliamentary democracy in India, the dependence on imperial patronage of landlords, in general, and princes, in particular, was significant, if not crucial. It meant that as Congress became increasingly oppositional during the twentieth century, increasingly well organized in the countryside, and increasingly uncompromising in its demand for *swaraj*,[25] substantial landlords—the Raj's most dependent and dependable allies—became increasingly unavailable and undesirable as members of Congress's coalition of classes. Orchestrated by Mahatma Gandhi, Congress's recruitment of its constituency in the countryside was largely of land-holding peasants, and in alliance with peasant communities and community associations. Nothing, I believe, contributed more crucially to India's parliamentary democratic future than the absence of great landlords in the pre-Independence Congress coalition.

Other than in eastern Bengal, the legacy to Pakistan of imperial favor to Muslims of good family and some property was the nondevelopment of a popularly based, well-disciplined, and well-led political party and the development of a coalition of dominant classes of professional men and landlords that was unfriendly to the future of parliamentary democracy. That coalition dominated the factions both of the multi-"communal," Muslim landlord-dominated National Unionist Party in Punjab and the All-India Muslim League in northern India. But for a few years of Muslim League unity under its Quaid-i-Azam (great leader), Mohammad Ali Jinnah, in the 1940s, both it and the Unionist Party existed only in factions. Neither had landed peasants as coalition partners. Peasants were the clients and dependents of the Unionists' landlords. It was not until the 1940s that Muslim peasants in Punjab and northern India were rallied to the League, and then not as coalition allies but rather as adherents to a resonant political–religious–"communal" ideal captured in the League's slogan of "Pakistan." It was in Bengal that landed peasants were partners in the Muslim coalition of politically dominant classes. Ironically, this presence, in what was to become East Pakistan, of a coalition of dominant classes friendly to parliamentary democracy, experienced in its politics, and representative of Pakistan's ethnolinguistic majority became the insuperable obstacle to the establishment of parliamentary democracy in Pakistan. The Bengali coalition of professionals and landed peasants threatened all the interests of all the members of the ruling nondemocratic coalition in West Pakistan—heirs to the empire's "Punjab tradition"—and eventually led to Pakistan's dismemberment in 1971.

Finally, before and after the subcontinent was partitioned and the republics of India and Pakistan were created, the Hindu "merchant princes" who owned most of India's big business houses and their smaller, but aspiring, Muslim counterparts joined their respective, "communally" separate coalitions of dominant classes. That was the best that they could do. Given the post-Independence life expectancy, in either India or Pakistan, of the princely states, investment in them was, at best, risky. Neither Hindu nor Parsi[26] industrialists would throw in their lot with Muslim Pakistan. To Muslim industrialists, Pakistan was a promised turf of their own, free of competition from the great Marwari and Gujarati *baniyas*.[27] India's great Hindu and Parsi capitalists were thus integrated into a coalition friendly to the establishment of parliamentary democracy. Muslim capitalists, largely from northern India and Gujarat, reestablished themselves as Muhajirs (émigrés) in West Pakistan, where they were culturally and linguistically more at home than in Bengal. With Punjabi elites, Muhajir capitalists entered into and fortified the antidemocratic coalition of dominant classes that was West Pakistan's legacy from the Raj. With the encouragement and support of the government of Pakistan, Muhajir capitalists became major participants in the economic exploitation of east Bengal and, thus, contributors to its disaffection and secession to become Bangladesh.

INDEPENDENT STATEHOOD

Thus, the paths that were laid down in British India have pointed toward different political destinations for India, Pakistan, and Bangladesh.

India

Unencumbered by the weight of landlords, India's coalition of dominant classes took Congress into independent India as its "one dominant party" and used it in the 1950s to lay the foundations for parliamentary democracy, not only at India's centre, but crucially, in its countryside. Four of Congress's measures were of particular significance for India's parliamentary democratic future.

First, Congress maintained itself as India's "one dominant party." Elections, "free and fair" by international parliamentary democratic standards and based on adult franchise, were held regularly for parliament and state legislative assemblies. All over India, opposition parties were formed and reformed in competition against Congress. But, with one notable exception,[28] Congress always won. Its election victories, however, always for parliament and generally for state legislative assemblies, were based on pluralities rather than majorities of the vote. In a first-past-the-post electoral system, the majority of votes were scattered among a considerable number and wide ideological range of opposition parties. Thus, the implicit threat to Congress hegemony lay in coalitions of opposition parties. In prudence, Congress had to be sufficiently sensitive to opposition, particularly on social issues, to preclude such coalitions from forming and attracting defectors from its own ranks.

This situation prevailed at the state level until 1967 and at the Centre (the central government) until 1977, where it revived briefly and precariously from 1980 to 1989. It is useful to think of these decades, particularly the earlier ones, as a period of transition from the elite parliamentary politics of British India's provincial assemblies to the Indian parliamentary democracy of today. It was a period of learning the parliamentary democratic "rules of the game": for Indian politicians, for aspiring politicians, and, particularly, for the great mass of hitherto unenfranchised and politically quiescent Indian voters. For many of these the notion of political power emerging from the sum of ballots in ballot boxes rather than from the prerogative of those who were divinely or otherwise ordained to rule was exotic. The alternatives for India in the calculations of its first prime minister, Jawaharlal Nehru, and his colleagues in these years immediately after Independence was "Congress or Chaos." I think that they were partially right. The other-than-Congress alternatives to chaos were, on the one hand, the imposition of an authoritarian order, as in Pakistan, or, on the other—but likely to produce the same result—the apparently chronic instability of coalition government at India's Centre. Such instability is, at least, tolerable today, but it is unlikely to have been so during the 1950s and 1960s.

In the 1960s and 1970s and since, at its Centre and in its states, India has regularly passed what I regard as the acid test for a parliamentary democracy. If defeated in a free and fair election, will its party in power surrender it? Congress—India's party in power from 1947, in command of all the Indian state's instrumentalities and resources, the party of India's struggle for independence and of its founding fathers—wherever and whenever defeated at the polls surrendered power. To date, the most blatant threat to India's parliamentary democracy was Prime Minister Indira Gandhi's assumption of "emergency" powers between 1975 and 1977. Yet, however reluctantly, she, too, when her Congress was voted out of power, surrendered it.

Second, subject to direction from the party's "high command," state Congresses legislated measures of land reform that confirmed the ownership rights of land-owning cultivators and transferred the ownership of land from noncultivating landlords to their cultivating tenants-in-chief—that is, cultivators who paid rent to noncultivating landlords. Ceilings were established on landownership. Land above these ceilings was meant to be "resumed" by the states and redistributed among the landless. Otherwise, they were meant to be protected under the law: by the legislation of minimum wages for agricultural labor and maximum shares from sharecroppers, for example. This was the usual pattern of land reform. It was most effective in redistributing tenurial rights and in eliminating noncultivating "intermediaries"—landlords and their rent-collectors—between the farmer and the state. In practice, land reforms in India redistributed little land and gave little protection to the landless. Landlords were generously compensated for their losses of rent and permitted to retain for their "personal cultivation" the maximum acreage allowable under land ceiling legislation. They were thus discouraged from aggregating as landlord classes in opposition to Congress, although there were legal challenges. *Benami*[29] holdings and transfers of land were commonplace and generally overlooked by state authorities.

The variation on this strategy of land reforms appropriate to princely states was to treat their rulers with great generosity, thereby discouraging them from rallying their coteries of land-holding noblemen. India's principalities were then integrated into states of the Indian Union where the usual pattern of land reform was applied.

The effects of these reforms relative to parliamentary democracy was to free a critical mass of the better-off peasantry from the political, economic, social, and ideological direction of their landlords. Had they remained subject to their landlords, parliamentary democracy in India would have become a charade, as it is in Pakistan. But the competitive dynamic inherent in parliamentary democracy was largely confined within Congress. Many of its better-off rural constituencies also belonged to regionally "dominant castes," thus coupling economic with social power. In a word, they represented the village "haves." The effects of land reforms were more to reassure them and to pay Congress's pre-Independence debts to its coalition partners of landed peasants, rather than to serve the interests of the countryside's "have-nots." Parliamentary democracy's competitive dynamic began to break from its Congress confines only with the collapse of its "one-party dominance."

Third, legislative assemblies with substantive constitutional powers were established in the states. They soon came under the control of the beneficiaries of land reforms—now "farmers," cultivating proprietors, no longer "subject cultivators," no longer peasants. They legislated to protect their interests and suppress the interests of the countryside's underclasses: subtenants, sharecroppers, and agricultural laborers. Legislation passed in the states also enabled cultivating proprietors to expand their interests into nonfarming enterprises: small business, professional, and bureaucratic employment. Rural underclasses, though granted universal franchise and paper protection by land reform legislation, nonetheless remained subject to cultivating proprietors: clients to patrons. Since1967, however, these subordinate groups have increased their presence and influence in parliamentary politics, particularly at the state level, but also at the Centre. They have sought through politics to redress their grievances, assert their interests, and influence state instrumentalities, particularly of coercion, direct and indirect. But it is unlikely that there will in the future be any more redistribution of land than there has been in the past. The resources most widely redistributed by the Indian political system in recent years have been political power and social honor

Finally, the redistribution of social honor has taken place primarily through the system of parliamentary politics. From *panchayats* (village councils) in the countryside, through state legislative assemblies, to the Lok Sabha,[30] parliamentary democracy provides arenas in which hierarchies are being determined more and more by political muscle rather than by "sacred" caste status or economic class. Needless to say, in India as elsewhere political capital can readily be built from status and wealth. But in recent years those with little of either have used their numbers and their organization to enter the political arena as major players. Thus, throughout India the "dominant castes" that ruled the roosts of state politics have largely been displaced by coalitions of lesser castes known collectively as "other backward classes" (OBC).

A major and doubtlessly vital component in this redistribution of social honor has been the Government of India's programs of compensatory discrimination, better known by the American euphemism, "affirmative action." Since the adoption of its constitution in 1950, the Indian Union has provided a comprehensive system—from schooling to educated employment—whose intended beneficiaries have been "scheduled castes and tribes." "Scheduled castes" is the name first given in British India to that congeries of several hundred unrelated castes all over India who are stigmatized by their neighbors as "untouchable." Members of their castes live and work in virtually every Indian village as the poorest of the poor and, in caste terms, the lowest of the low—the bottom strata in one of the world's best articulated and most ancient and enduring systems of social inequality. Combined with constitutional and legal prohibitions against the practice of untouchability, compensatory discrimination was meant to destroy it. It has not done so. However, in recent years, educated untouchables, as politicians and bureaucrats, have taken to flexing untouchable muscle in parliamentary democratic arenas, raising the political consciousness of their untouchable constituents, ameliorating some of their hardships, and redressing some of their grievances in the countryside. Understandably, the competitive dynamic of parliamentary democracy in India that has worked so well for OBC has worked less well and more slowly for less numerous and less well-resourced untouchables. But no one doubts that it is working. One symbolic indication of this is the name that untouchables have given to themselves as a group: "Dalits"—the oppressed. Not birth but depression has degraded them.

Pakistan

Unlike India, Pakistan inherited from its British imperial past no political party that was nationwide, popularly based, or reasonably well disciplined and organized. In the United Provinces of British India, where the Muslim League was most popularly based as the party of "Pakistan," the great majority of its peasant followers remained in their Indian villages and became residents of the Indian state of Uttar Pradesh. They were never partners in a political coalition in any case, but, rather, adherents to a political–religious–"communal" slogan. Ironically, in view of subsequent events, the Muslim League in what was to become Pakistan was best organized in eastern Bengal. But the Bengali League's vision of "Pakistan" was quite different from Jinnah's. In western Pakistan, most notably in its core, western Punjab, the Muslim League had virtually no presence until the 1940s. There, the ruling "party" was the Punjab National Unionist, an inter-"communal" coalition of landlord factions. Sensing the irresistibility of "Pakistan," many of its Muslim members changed their party labels accordingly in the 1940s and retained their dominance on the land.

Mohammad Ali Jinnah died in 1948. The Muslim League in West Pakistan barely survived his death. Without a political party in the west capable of replacing the imperial government, the "Punjab tradition" of British India was resurrected and replicated during the 1950s under local management: a regime of bureaucrats, back-stopped by a disciplined army and supported by landlords who ruled a subject, politically quiescent peasant population.

The ruling civil servants were largely Punjabis and Muhajirs. But for a smattering of Pathans, the army and its commanders were Punjabis. Most of the great landholdings were in Punjab, but the landlords of Sindh and the tribal chiefs of Baluchistan and the North West Frontier Province were, no less than Punjabi landlords, masters of subject populations. Muslim "industrialists"-cum-traders, who were mostly Muhajirs, emigrated to West Pakistan and with leading bureaucrats, generals, and landlords formed their new country's coalition of politically dominant classes. This was a subcontinental variant of "the marriage of iron and rye"—the archetypical antidemocratic alliance of dominant classes.[31]

East Pakistan, the eastern districts of Bengal, was the alliance's milch cow, its "colony." The rulers of West Pakistan predicated their program of industrialization on their exploitation of the east's material and human resources. Denied access to political power and to an equitable distribution of the state's resources and scorned by their country's rulers for their "Hindu language" and the unauthenticity of their Islam, Pakistan's Bengalis became increasingly disaffected and increasingly well organized, resolute, and united in their disaffection. During Pakistan's first few years, there were some leading Bengali politicians in the Muslim League, but, as politicians in general, they became redundant under a regime of bureaucratic authoritarianism. In the 1954 provincial elections in Bengal, a left-leaning United Front of political parties decimated the League in East Pakistan. The elections' results were nullified by the bureaucrats and generals of the west's coalition of dominant classes. The hegemony of its resurrected and refurbished "Punjab tradition" was then nationalized in an unequivocally authoritarian Pakistan. To Pakistan's rulers, authoritarianism was not only their preferred system but the only one available to tie the two wings of their country together. Pakistan had had no nationwide political party that might have mediated between the interests of key groups in its eastern and western wings.

More and more socially homogenized—by intermarriages, investments of industrialists in land, and landlords in industry—and emboldened and enriched by power and wealth and resolved to keep them in their grasp, Pakistan's coalition of dominant classes was resolute in its opposition to parliamentary democracy. Was it not a potentially hazardous instrument, capable of transferring political power to Bengali leftists? And, through them, even to the peasants of western Pakistan? In its opposition to parliamentary democracy, Pakistan's coalition of dominant classes enjoyed the explicit support of its "official" *ulama* and the implicit support of its great friends in Washington and Beijing.

East Pakistan's secession in 1971, to become Bangladesh, brought no lasting change to either the membership or the political inclination of Pakistan's coalition of dominant classes, and no more of parliamentary democracy than its occasional show—from 1970 to 1977, and from 1988 to 1999. Anything more than a show is unlikely in the absence of a free peasantry in what is still largely a peasant society. There is little chance of the vast majority of "have-nots" using parliamentary democracy to reallocate to themselves some of the wealth or status or power enjoyed by the tiny minority of "haves." In effect, there have been no reforms that redistributed land tenure, much less land, in Pakistan, and its landlord-dominated national and provincial assemblies are unlikely to consider seriously, or at all, any such reforms in the foreseeable future. Nor are any of their coalition partners, and nor is Pakistan's current military ruler, General Pervaiz Musharraf.

For a few years now and then, behind the facade of parliamentary democracy—but for most of Pakistan's history, as now, in plain sight—the army, a force of little political consequence in India, has been the dominant partner in Pakistan's coalition of dominant classes. It is the protector of Pakistan's "national interests" and the arbiter of its internal conflicts. The army has never been a force for economic development in Pakistan, or for social change, much less for parliamentary democracy. The increasing Islamist influence in its officer corps is unlikely to change this. Whether on the throne or from behind it, the army and its intelligence agency have always determined Pakistan's foreign policy, particularly with regard to Afghanistan and to India via Kashmir. The domestic consequences of these foreign-policy determinations have been considerable—in the lack of resources for economic development, for example. What has come to be known as the "Kargil War"[32] and General Musharraf's subsequent coup indicate unequivocally that that sine qua non of parliamentary democracy—an army subordinate to the ministers of an elected parliament—is no more the case in Pakistan in 2000 than it was half a century before.

Bangladesh

Under the Raj, Bengal was the only region in Muslim India in which there was a dominant political coalition of professionals and landed peasants (*jotedars*). First as the Krishak Praja Party in the 1930s and then as the Bengal Provincial Muslim League, the coalition was brought together by its partners' mutual hostility to the Hindu *bhadralok,* who were not only the province's major "intermediaries" on the land but dominated its urban professions as well. Thus, in what was to become East Pakistan, there was a coalition of dominant classes, similar to Congress's, friendly in composition and organization to the establishment of parliamentary democracy. It was a coalition whose organization and ethnolinguistic constituency, the largest in Pakistan, virtually ensured that parliamentary democracy would be used to serve Bengali interests. That certainty hardened the ruling classes of West Pakistan in their opposition to parliamentary democracy, and doomed its establishment in Pakistan.

After a year's war of liberation, in which the Indian army played no small part, East Pakistan seceded to become the Republic of Bangladesh in 1971. But twenty-four years of factionalized rebellion against West Pakistan's rule and the dislocation of a war of secession fought by armed factions disabled Bangladesh from establishing its parliamentary democracy. The political leader of the combined factions—which demanded, at first, provincial autonomy for East Pakistan, and then, in response to violent repression by Pakistan's army, independence—was Sheikh Mujibur Rahman, the "Father of the Nation." Mujib aimed to turn his party, the Awami League (AL), into a Bangladeshi copy of India's Congress, and to establish a parliamentary democracy under the AL's "one-party dominance." But while Congress came to power as a party well-enough disciplined to be in control of its state's instrumentalities, the AL did not, and Bangladesh's bureaucracy and army existed only in factions. Having failed to establish its parliamentary democratic "dominance," Mujib tried to reconvert the AL into an instrument that would support his personal dictatorship. In 1975, he was assassinated in a military coup.

From 1975 until 1991, there were any number of coup attempts by various factions in Bangladesh's factionalized military, and two relatively stable regimes, both led by generals—Ziaur Rahman until his assassination in 1981 and Hossain Mohammad Ershad until his deposal in 1991. Both reinvented themselves as civilian politicians and created parliamentary democratic facades behind which they ruled. Confronted by massive and escalating opposition to his regime, overflowing the streets of Bangladesh's towns and cities and virtually paralyzing the state's capacity to function, Ershad was forced to resign. Bangladesh's first bona fide parliamentary democratic elections since 1971 were held shortly thereafter. The major party in the winning coalition was the BNP (Bengal National Party), founded by Ziaur Rahman and led by his widow. In Bangladesh's second and most recent democratic election in 1996, the BNP was defeated at the polls, left office, and surrendered power. The dominant party in the winning coalition was the AL, led by Mujib's daughter, Sheikh Hasina Wajed. She is Bangladesh's prime minister at the time of writing.

Parliamentary democracy has a toehold in Bangladesh. Its position is certainly insecure, but, I think, not without some promise of becoming secure. Unlike India, Bangladesh has had no tutelary period of transition from elite parliamentary politics to parliamentary democracy. But unlike Pakistan, parliamentary democracy is regarded as *the* legitimate form of government by virtually all politically aware and participant groups of the population, except for the Islamists. Their position in Bangladeshi politics is much as it is in Pakistan's: weak at the polls but strong in the bazaars and on the streets. From all indications, the army has returned to its barracks indefinitely, and not only literally but politically. It was never the political force in Bangladesh that it was and is in Pakistan.

Unlike parliamentary democracy in India, its development in Bangladesh has been stunted by its urban-centeredness, its lack of a rural base. The *jotedars*, as a class, have been virtually absorbed into the white-collar urban population, and the vast majority of the peasantry are impoverished. On the other hand, that class most entrenched in their opposition to the development of parliamentary democracy in Pakistan—great landlords—are nonexistent in Bangladesh. Most active in Bangladeshi politics are the various factions of university students. Their relationship to parliamentary politics is anomalous. But for their Islamist factions, students would be first to man the barricades in defense of parliamentary democracy. Yet like student movements elsewhere, its Bangladeshi variant is, in the moral certitude and elitist romanticism of its participants, inherently antidemocratic. In particular, student factions in Bangladesh engage in armed battle with one another and provide the "musclemen" for the political parties that sponsor them. Student movements are both cause and effect of the BNP's and AL's proclivity to confront one another less as parliamentary democratic competitors than opponents in a zero-sum political battle. They have not yet resolved the conflicts that dog Bangladesh's short but troubled past. However, they have made some headway in agreeing on rules of the parliamentary democratic game appropriate to the present. I suspect that the businessmen whose concerns dominate both parties will in the interests of domestic law and order help to facilitate further agreement.

NOTES

1. My initial debt here is to Benedict Anderson, *Imagined Communities*, revised edition (London: Verso, 1991). But it must be made explicit that the religious "communities" in India that were *imagined* by ideologues became *inventions*: they took form and manifested themselves in politics.

2. The Khilafat Movement was organized after the First World War to protest against the dismantling of the Ottoman empire and the possible deposal by the British of its sultan/caliph. The Ottoman caliph was regarded by India's Sunni Muslims as the Prophet's temporal and spiritual successor (see chapter 2).

3. Literally, a mixture of ingredients. A very Indian term, it is used mostly in cooking, but its use is often extended. "Masala movies," for example, Bollywood's staple, have in their recipes varying quantities, preparations, and mixtures of much the same ingredients.

4. *From Max Weber: Essays in Sociology*, translated, edited, and with an introduction by H. H. Gerth and C. Wright Mills (New York: Oxford University Press, 1958), chap 7; emphasis added.

5. Twice-born castes are those who claim, and whose claim is generally accepted, to belong to the upper three categories—brahman, kshatriya, and vaishya—of the *varnadharma*, Hinduism's "sacred" ordering of human society.

6. Literally, a cushion.

7. One of a number of British euphemisms for castes that were regarded in their villages as untouchable.

8. Following Plato, a term used by Philip Mason, under the pseudonym Philip Woodruff, *The Men Who Ruled India,* 2 vols. (New York: Schocken, 1964).

9. From Thomas Babington Macaulay's 1835 "Minute on Education," quoted in Burton Stein, *A History of India* (Oxford: Blackwell, 1998), pp. 265–266. Macaulay's argument, accepted by the company's directors, was that such a class could be created through English-medium higher education in European science and literature. It is worth noting that the minute is predicated on the assumption of Europe's cultural superiority but not on the "racial" superiority of Europeans—that came later.

10. Quoted in P. E. Roberts, *History of British India under the Company and the Crown*, 3rd edition, completed by T. G. P. Spear (London: Oxford University Press, 1958) p. 384.

11. Edward Said, *Orientalism* (New York: Random House, 1979).

12. Again, from the quotable poet, essayist, biographer, and historian Macaulay's 1835 "Minute on Education"—"a single shelf of a good European library was worth the whole native literature of India and Arabia." Stein, *History of India.*

13. In imperial India, "Anglo-Indian" referred particularly to those Britons who lived and worked, sometimes for generations, in India as well as to their society. Post-independence, the name has been appropriated by the people who were known in imperial India as "Eurasians."

14. The French were wont to refer to their imperial adventure as *la mission civilisatrice,* but the sentiment was not peculiar to them. For example, after the Spanish–American War of 1898, the great litterateur of British imperialism, Rudyard Kipling, urged the United States to take up 'the white man's burden' in the Philippines.

15. Alfred C. Lyall, "The Rajput States of India," *Asiatic Studies*, Vol. 1 (London: John Murray, 1899), pp. 265–301. Of lesser literary distinction than Macaulay, Lyall was a biographer, essayist, and poet. He was also an imperial hierarch.

16. Rudyard Kipling, "Recessional."

17. Princes were a partial, but only partial, exception to the rule.

18. Lyall, "The Rajput States," p. 263.

19. This is one meaning of *ashraf*; it has other meanings as well (see chapter 2).

20. Muslim divines: rather than being clerics, they are legists—doctors of Islamic holy law.

21. Frequently used pejoratively.

22. Many "aristocrats" were really successful adventures and/or landed plutocrats.

23. The *nawabi* of Tonk in Rajputana, for example, was settled on the freebooter Amir Khan Pindari by the company in c.1818 in the hope that he would confine himself to exploiting peasants rather than preying on princes.

24. Peninsular Gujarat. Mahatma Gandhi was a native of one of these mini-principalities, Porbandar.

25. Literally, our own rule. A legacy of the Hindu revivalist organization, Arya Samaj, it was used by Gandhi and Congress to mean "freedom" and to leave open the question of

whether that "freedom" would be inside or outside the British empire. Since independence in 1947, the Republic of India has been a member of the (British) Commonwealth.

26. The Indian Parsis claim descent from the Zoroastrians, who fled Persia after it was conquered by Arabs in the eighth century CE. They are prominent in Indian commerce and industry, particularly in Mumbai. The Tatas, a Parsi family, own and manage the largest and most diversified and progressive family conglomerate of industries in India.

27. Businessmen, or castes whose traditional occupation is trade or moneylending. The name is sometimes used disparagingly: "What can you expect of a *baniya*?" Mahatma Gandhi belonged to a *baniya* caste, and M. A. Jinnah was known to have referred to him on occasion as "that wretched *baniya*."

28. A communist government was elected in the southern state of Kerala in 1957.

29. Literally, in a false name. Landlords and farmers evaded statutory ceilings on land ownership by listing some of their holdings under the names of relatives and clients.

30. The lower house of the Indian parliament; literally, the people's council.

31. The reference is to the classic antidemocratic alliance between an established landlord class and an emerging industrial bourgeoisie. Specifically, it refers to the "marriage" that was contracted through the German naval expansion program and presided over by Admiral Alfred von Tirpitz at the turn of the century. The program was a landmark in Germany's state-sponsored industrialization. It increased the power and influence of industrialists in a state otherwise dominated by titled landlords. It opened a naval officer's career for the sons of the bourgeoisie in the great imperial enterprise that depended for its success on sea power. For the great rye-producing landlords, naval expansion was coupled with tariff protection from agricultural imports and a reassertion of Prussian militarism. "Through the demagogic exploitation of popular nationalism" the German monarchy solidified, at the expense of social democrats, its support in a community of interests between aristocracy and plutocracy. Hans-Ulrich Wehler, *The German Empire*, translated by Kim Traynor (Leamington Spa: Berg Publishers, 1985), p. 168.

32. After the region in Kashmir in which the fighting was centered.

2

"Communalism" and Coalitions of Dominant Classes

The imagining and inventing of Indian "communalism" took place in two more or less sequential stages that we can designate—with some arbitrariness, but for the sake of getting on with it—broadly as religious and secular. Only as analytical categories, however, can these be kept distinct. In "communalist" theory and practice, they overlapped at any number of points and at times merged into one another. With this in mind, it is possible to say, no less arbitrarily and not at all surprisingly, that popular "communalism" nurtured by religious was largely religious and that elite "communalism" nurtured by secular elites was largely secular and elitist. Muslim and Hindu groups, often in hostile reaction to one another, shared in the imagining and inventing of "communalism." It was institutionalized in British Indian politics by the Raj with the collaboration of Indian politicians from both "communities."

My underlying argument in this chapter is that "communalism" gave initial shape to the composition and organization of the different coalitions of classes that were to dominate the politics of India and Pakistan. Thus, the development of parliamentary democracy in India, its tentative development in Bangladesh, and its nondevelopment in Pakistan received their impetus from "communalism" in British India.

There are three sections to this chapter. The first is devoted to a discussion of popular religious "communalism" and British contributions to it, which were largely inadvertent and unintentional. The second treats the invention of elite secular "communalism" and the impetus given to it by the imperial policy of "balance and rule." In collaboration with Indian politicians, it institutionalized "communalism" in the political system of British India. Central to this institutionalized "communalism" and to the parliamentary democratic future of the subcontinent were "reservations and weightage" for Muslim politicians. These are the centerpiece of the concluding section, "Coalitions of Dominant Classes and the Legacies of 'Reservations and Weightage'." "Communalism's" particular histories in Punjab and Bengal, and their contributions to the histories of coalitions of dominant classes in India and Pakistan, are the subjects of chapter 3.

POPULAR RELIGIOUS "COMMUNALISM"

The historian Bipan Chandra calculates that from 1763 to 1856 there were "more than forty major rebellions [against British rule in India] apart from hundreds of minor ones." But, while "massive in their totality," they were "local in their spread and isolated from each other": in effect, peasant jacqueries and tribal uprisings, parochial in their causes and their effects.[1] Neither ideologically nor organizationally did they constitute an anti-imperialist *movement or movements.*

In the Land of Infidelity

The earliest anti-imperialist movements on the subcontinent were of Muslims qua Muslims who rejected British imperial rule because they believed that it was, *as such,* an insult to their faith. These movements were led by *ulama*. They were the "community's" most evident "natural leaders," before the British—in the hope of curtailing their leadership—moved to patronize Muslim grandees. Muslim anti-imperialist movements of the early nineteenth century numbered their followers in the hundreds of thousands of ordinary believers. The movements were pan-local in sentiment and only less so in organization or action. They were informed and energized, first, by coherent late-Mughal, pre-British movements of Islamic reform, and, second, by a comprehensive ideological challenge to the legitimacy of the British East India Company's government

These early nineteenth-century movements inevitably combined the ideologies of religious anti-imperialism and Islamic puritanism. We are reminded that religion and politics are "inseparab[le] . . . categories in Islamic thought."[2] Certainly, subcontinental "communities " were not the invention of *ulama* alone. They were subsequently reinvented and elaborated by Hindu "communalists." But the construction of "communalism" as a coherent, well-articulated Indian ideology originated with *ulama*.

They took from Islam itself the basic religious–political concepts of "communalism." Thus, Indian Muslims were members of an *ummah,* a "community" of believers, united by their faith to Muslims the world over *and separated by it from Indian nonbelievers.* For believers, the basic political divisions of the world were separated into *dar al-Islam,* places in which the *ummah's* faith was secure, and *dar al-harb,* the land of infidelity, in which that faith was threatened. Under British rule, India had become *dar al-harb.*

The mobilization of an anti-imperialist movement by Muslim divines and grounded in Islam was inherently—in India, at least—puritan and, as such, separatist. The leaders of Muslim anti-imperialism in India were champions of an exclusivist Abrahamic[3] faith. As they mobilized the faithful against a government of infidels, *ulama* necessarily defined the faithful as those who were true to their faith—and to their faith *alone.* Their "community" was bound in faith to oppose the regime of a British Christian "other" whose government was repugnant to Islam. But no less crucially and of far more enduring consequence, the *ummah* was bound in faith to be separate from a Hindu "other," and wary of it: an agglomeration of idolaters and the carriers of a demonstrably contaminating idolatry, demeaning to the faith and the faithful.

This imagining of the "community's" religious leaders notwithstanding, we must note the mundane reality that Indian Muslims, no less than Hindus, belong to a multitude of different communities. They speak the mother-tongues and use the languages of their Hindu neighbors. Like them, too, Muslims belong to communities that are integral parts of multi-"communal" village societies: kinship-based, separate from one another, and hierarchically arranged. Elsewhere, I have called these quasi *jatis*: the Muslim equivalent, more or less, of Hindu castes. While *ulama* were beginning to imagine and invent a Muslim "community," Muslim communities were, in general, eclectic, not to say, "polytheistic," in their worship. Still, this binary divide, these two "communities," imagined and invented in the nineteenth century, was actualized in the politics of the twentieth.

"Islam has a fundamental political orientation . . . ," writes Ishtiaq Husain Quereshi. "The Muslim community is, *ideally,* an association of believers organised for the purpose of leading their lives in accordance with the teaching of their faith."[4] The ideal is reflected in Muslim history and hagiography. The Prophet and his immediate, golden-age successors—the four "rightly guided caliphs" (636–661 CE) of Sunni Islam—were conquerors and rulers. The Muslim calendar dates not from the birth of the Prophet, but from the beginning of his career as Medina's ruler

Islam's political ideal is incorporated into comprehensive bodies of law, the *shariah,* and legal systems that draw their ultimate sanction from the Quran, the word of God, and the reported teachings (*hadith*) of the seal of His prophet Muhammad. The Islamic ideal also sanctions its worldly shadow, its second-best: the Muslim regime. In Indian history, the ideal was never more closely approximated than this. A polity acceptable to Indian believers, a *dar al-Islam* de facto, was a principality or empire ruled by a Muslim dynasty: however much, above some tolerable minimum its rulers accepted or applied to their subjects the guidance and restraints of the *shariah.*

A government of Muslims may be insufficient to make of their county *dar al-Islam* de facto, but it was regarded as necessary by Muslim divines of the first half of the nineteenth century. In *The Indian Musalmans*, first published in 1871, a volume of great influence on subsequent British "communal" policy, W. W. Hunter quotes the following *fatwa* (ruling) of the "most learned Law Doctor of the age, the Sun of India . . .":

When infidels get hold of a Muhammadan country and it becomes impossible for the Musalmans of the country, and of the people of the neighbouring districts, to drive them away, or to retain reasonable hope of ever doing so, and the power of the infidels increases to such an extent that they can abolish or retain the ordinances of Islam according to their pleasure; and no one is strong enough to seize on the revenues of the country without the permission of the infidels, and the (Musalman) inhabitants do no longer live so secure as before, such a country is politically . . . [*dar al-harb*].[5]

In sympathy with such rulings, groups of Muslims felt obliged by their faith to *jihad* or *hijrah*: roughly, and subject to various interpretations, opposition or emigration. The Muslim anti-imperialist movements of the first decades of the nineteenth century, beginning from about 1818,[6] were inspired by these Islamic obligations. The oldest, largest, and most widespread section of this movement was named "Wahhabi" by British writers who mistakenly equated it with a contemporary group of puritan reformers in Arabia. That name, like others awarded by misinformed scorners—"Quakers," for example—has passed into general and predominant use. For their first decade or so, Indian Wahhabis, led by their founder and religious preceptor, Saiyid Ahmad Bareilly, were most notable for their *hijrah* from British India to the northwest frontier, and, from there, their armed *jihad* against the Sikhs—infidels, usurpers of Mughal rule, and allies of the British East India Company.

In 1831, Saiyid Ahmad Bareilly was killed in battle against the Sikhs, and his army of *mujahidin* was routed. The Wahhabis survived as an anti-imperialist movement in India. After the Sikhs' incorporation into the British empire in 1849, the Wahhabis confronted British imperialism directly with their *jihad* by other means. They extended it from Saiyid Ahmad Bareilly's short-lived Islamic republic on the Punjab–Afghanistan border—finally destroyed by British arms in the 1870s—across northern India, eastward to their headquarters in Patna,[7] through Bengal, and as far south as Hyderabad. In British India, the Wahhabis' anti-imperialism took the form of subversion and sabotage. To congregations of the faithful, Wahhabi preachers and pamphleteers anathematized British India as *dar al-harb* and admonished the faithful to have as little to do with their Christian rulers as possible. This was a *jihad* of nonviolent noncooperation, the subcontinent's first—and Muslim! More overtly "seditious," Wahhabi activists made systematic and organized efforts to subvert the loyalties of the company's Muslim soldiers.

To the Raj, the Wahhabis were at worst an irritant: they were never a threat, nor, in themselves, even a matter of great concern; a mere rabble. Of more enduring significance than their anti-imperialism was its inherent complement: Islamic puritanism. *Dar al-Islam* can be a land of the faith only if it is a land of the faithful. Only the godly, after all, are deserving of God's political dispensation. Anti-imperialism and the purification of their ordinary Indian coreligionists' Islam were sides of the same coin for the Wahhabis. They were not anti-Hindu as such, and they numbered among their soldiery and supporters some Hindus. But as a movement of religious reform, the Wahhabis were committed to the creation of a distinctly Muslim "community," free from those "polytheistic" traits that it had imbibed in its Hindu environment from "heretics in Sufistic garb."[8]

Over centuries, from the seventh century, of mingled and mingling Hindu and Muslim devotionalism and mysticism, much had been taken up. And not only from Hinduism by Muslims. Islam and Hinduism were taken up and assimilated into new religions, of which Sikhism is the largest and most vibrant survivor. *Dargahs* (tombs) of Sufi *pirs* (saints) became—and are still—places of popular Hindu worship. But this was of no great concern to Wahhabis. Their great concern was this: The vast majority of Indian Muslims lived their lives according to their faith only in part, with the other part—as large or larger—according to the faith of their Hindu neighbours.[9] M. Mujeeb quotes this example from a Bengal district gazetteer of 1908:

In the Chittagong District [of eastern Bengal], Pir Badar [who is believed to reside in the seas and rivers and to protect mariners from shipwreck] was venerated as their guardian saint by Hindu as well as Muslim sailors. When they started on a voyage by sea or river, they invoked him saying, "We are but children, the [Pir] is our protector, the Ganges is on our head. O Five Saints, O Badar, Badar, Badar!"[10]

"O Five Saints," indeed! To Wahhabis, this Hindu invocation was a curse on Muslim lips. Islam has no "guardian saints." There is only God. Muslims must believe and behave like Muslims and not like Hindus. "Polytheism" was commonplace among Bengali Muslims. Bengal was the Wahhabis' major area of proselytizing activity in British India and their principal base of support and recruitment for their *jihad* on the northwest frontier.[11] In the decades before the mutiny of 1857, the Wahhabis in Bengal made common cause with two local Muslim movements: in the west, their inspired peasant movement led by Titu Mir; in the east, the *Faraidi,* particularly under the leadership of Dudu Miyan. These two, albeit with tactical and Islamic doctrinal differences between them and with the Wahhabis, combined Islamic puritanism and Muslim "communalism" with anti-imperialism. They were well organized and led by men whom their followers esteemed to be of considerable religious standing. All three movements drew their followers from ordinary Muslim peasants and artisans. In passing and in anticipation of what was to come in the twentieth century, we might note here that the Wahhabi and *Faraidi* Movements laid the groundwork for the only enduring, organized mass movement of Muslims on the subcontinent—in Bengal.

Hunter noted that partisans of the two movements were "found side by side alike among the dead on the field of battle and in the dock of [British] courts of justice."[12] Their common enemies were the local manifestations of British imperialism and the Hindu exploitation and idolatry that imperialism nourished. British indigo planters exploited Muslim peasants, and the company's government of infidels and its soldiers supported the planters. Under the cover of British law, Hindu *zamindars* (landlords) levied cesses on their Muslim tenants to support the idolatrous worship of Hindus. Muslim tenants were prohibited from slaughtering for food or worship that living and ubiquitous Hindu idol, the cow. With the rents of Muslim peasants, Hindu landlords patronized the "superstitions" that had beguiled Bengali Muslims and corrupted their faith. The lines of class shadowed the lines of "communalism."

These early movements in Bengal of popular, Muslim religious anti-imperialism were repressed by British soldiers and law courts, and by the end of the century they had largely dissipated. Popular, Muslim anti-imperialism, however, lived on. Certainly, there were Hindu, as well as Muslim, soldiers and civilians who rose in 1857 to vindicate their religions from the perceived threat of subversion by their British Christian rulers. No less certainly, for many of these Muslims the mutiny was *jihad*.[13] The mutineers' capture of the Mughal capital, Delhi, and their proclamation of the last Mughal emperor—an enfeebled, powerless pensioner of the company—as ruler of Hindustan, gave dramatic witness to their belief, at one with Wahhabis' and *Faraidis'*, that the subcontinent could become *dar al-Islam* again only with the "renewal of Muslim political strength."[14]

From 1920 to 1922, "urban, newspaper-reading"[15] Muslims in particular took part in the Khilafat Movement of popular religious anti-imperialism. The focus of their movement was British hostility to the Ottoman Empire: before, during, and after the First World War. The Ottoman head of state, the sultan, was, in the ideology of the Sunni majority of Indian Muslims, the Prophet's *khalifa* (successor) and, as such, their "lawful Muslim leader,"[16] however titular. It was to this movement that Mahatma Gandhi attached his Non-Cooperation Movement. His attempt to ally Hindus and Muslims against British imperialism in a composite, inter-"communal" Indian *nationalist* movement failed. Ironically, the Khilafat Movement probably succeeded in reinforcing the underlying religious–"communal" foundation of Muslim politics:

the Muslim masses and lower middle classes were brought into the [Khilafat] movement . . . on a religious question. . . . They joined the movement as a matter of religiosity. The result was that [they] remained unacquainted with modern anti-imperialist ideology or . . . modern principles of political organization. . . . Instead the intrusion of [a] religious outlook into politics was legitimised and perpetuated. When the Khilafat Movement was withdrawn, hardly any nationalist residue was left.[17]

The "residue" was "communalist." In 1921, for example, Muslim tenants in what is now Kerala used the idiom and imagery of Islam in their rebellion against their Hindu landlords. In 1922, not the British, but Kemal Ataturk abolished the Ottoman caliphate/sultanate, declared Turkey to be a secular republic, and thereby brought the Khilafat Movement in India and its alliance with the Non-Cooperation Movement down with a crash. It was collapsing anyway, under the strain of containing two movements that shared a common enemy but not a common enmity. In her summary of the Khilafat movement, Gail Minault notes the capacity of Islam to mobilize ordinary Muslims as Muslims in opposition to British imperialism:

Islam as a religion and a social order contains within itself certain symbols and networks of influence which allow for the development of alternative structures of mobilization which can operate independently of the state, whether traditional or modern, whether colonial or post-colonial.[18]

To this we must add that mobilization of Indian Muslims in the name of Islam and in defense of the Ottoman *khalifa* was inherently "communal," no less than the Islamic movements of opposition to British imperialism which preceded it. All defined a Hindu no less than a British "other." After its collapse, much of the energy of the alliance between the Khilafat and Non-Cooperation Movements was released in a sharp increase throughout India during the 1920s of Hindu–Muslim, inter-"communal" violence and "riots." Their incidence has ebbed and flowed since then, but never ceased. Ironically, the enduring effect of the alliance was not to shake the empire at all, but to sharpen the "communal" divide between the alliance's erstwhile partners.

Finally, the movement for "Pakistan" from 1940 to 1947 was the last expression of Indian Muslim opposition to British imperialism and its aspiration to reestablish *dar al-Islam* de facto on the subcontinent. The "Pakistan" movement was driven both by its reaction to a waning British Raj and its fear of a waxing Hindu *rashtra* (nation). The All-India Muslim League at Lahore resolved itself, in 1940, in favor of what came to be called "Pakistan." It was, at once, a slogan for mass mobilization and a scheme, vague even in outline, for the preservation and enhancement on the post-imperial subcontinent of the political power and influence of the north Indian Muslim elite. In the last Indian provincial elections held under British aegis, in 1946, "Pakistan" carried the day for the League.

For most Muslim voters, the League "was a chiliastic movement rather than a pragmatic [or programmatic] political party." In the United Provinces (now Uttar Pradesh), "religious fervour undoubtedly played its part" in the League's electoral success. In Punjab, which the League had to win if the "Pakistan" slogan was to have any credibility, the League gained its electoral victory by making a religious appeal over the heads of the "professional [Muslim] politicians" of the Unionist Party, who were not interested in "Pakistan."[19] The partition of the subcontinent in 1947 was, at once, the end of British imperialism and, in its savagery, the culmination of "communalism," both Muslim and Hindu, in British India.

Hindu Revival

The contribution of nineteenth-century Hindu "revivalism" to "communal-ism's" imagining and inventing trailed that of the *ulamas*, but it was doubtlessly of greater effect. Muslims were, after all, a minority: "them" in almost every society. Hindus, as such, comprised about 80 percent of the Raj's subjects, and more as a proportion of the subcontinent's literate suppliers and consumers of ideologies. The Brahmo Samaj, founded in 1828 in Calcutta and carried across the subcontinent by Bengali civil servants and professionals, was the precursor of the Hindu revivalism of the late nineteenth and early twentieth centuries. The Prarthana Samaj of high-caste Bombay intellectuals followed. But these, initially reactive to imperial Christianity, were puritan in their attempts to rid Hinduism of its "excrescences"—idolatry, for example—and to square it with nineteenth-century "rationality" and "progress." They were movements less to revive than to reform a Hinduism of, by, and for its educated upper classes.

The earliest, most successful, and long-lived Hindu popular revivalist move-ment in northern India was the Arya Samaj, founded in 1875. Its founder, Swami Dayanand Saraswati, a Gujarati Brahman, "saw the need for a real *national* religion which would unify all diverging [Hindu] forces."[20] He was one of the earliest and most influential inventors of a Hindu "community." Dayanand's Hinduism combined religious puritanism with an unequivocal and baldly stated assertion that "Vedic Hinduism"—Hinduism as it was meant to be, as Dayanand derived it from its earliest sacred texts, the Vedas—was morally and intellectu-ally superior to all other religions. This claim he elaborated most extensively with regard to Islam.[21]

Superior and, therefore, separate! Ironically, Dayanand's major contribution as an inventor of the Hindu "community" was to claim for its religion an exclusiveness that had not been creedal to it but was to the Abrahamic faiths that Dayanand deplored and denigrated. Particularly after his death in 1883, Samaj leaders tried to fix the borders between Hinduism and Islam by, for example, discouraging Hindus from worshipping at the tombs of Sufi saints. But most publicly and at politics' grass roots, the Samaj sought to define the Hindu "community" and to mobilize it through popular campaigns. They were cam-paigns of imagination and invention. Samajists worked to promote, particularly by government, the use of the language that they denoted as "Hindu"—Hindi in the Devanagari script—as against the language that they designated as "Mus-lim"—Urdu in its modified Arabic script. Reality intrudes: distinguishing be-tween the two languages on the basis of their "communal" use was itself part of the work of imagination.[22] Samajists preached and pamphleteered against the slaughter of cows, particularly by Muslims as sacrificial acts of faith. They presented Muslims with a challenging enterprise that was conceptually and actually new to Hinduism, an invention, a creed that manifested itself in *shuddhi*: a movement for the "reconversion" to Hinduism of formerly Hindu caste seg-ments and lineages that identified themselves as Muslim.

Muted during his lifetime, but nonetheless explicit in Dayanand's insistence on the moral and intellectual superiority of Hinduism was his rejection of any British claims to a moral or intellectual right to rule Hindus. This "seditious" undercurrent of Hindu assertiveness in Dayanand's message was never lost on the government's secret police—the Criminal Intelligence Department—which kept tabs on the Samaj from its inception. During the last decades of the nineteenth century and the first decade of the twentieth, the Arya Samaj's anti-imperialism became more manifest, foreshadowing and shading into new Indian nationalist movements. Samajists responded worriedly to the organization of Muslim "community" interests post-Mutiny and angrily to the apparent British inclination to favor those interests. A particularly bitter pill for the middle-class, salary-earning Samajists was the British government's apparent policy of "balancing" its employment of Hindus by favoring the employment of Muslims.

As the Arya Samaj's hostility to Muslims increased, its antipathy to a British imperialism that allegedly favored Muslim interests became manifest and suffused as a Hindu ingredient into Congress nationalism, or into the Hindu nationalism of the various *sabhas* (organizations), founded or reestablished in the 1920s.[23] Most notable among these were the Hindu Mahasabha and the RSS (Rashtriya Swayamsevak Sangh, the national volunteer association). Hindu opposition to British imperialism provided a paradigm for a Hindu understanding of the antecedent imperialism of Muslims. Had not they, like their British successors, come to India as foreign conquerors, votaries, and proselytizers of a foreign religion, mandators of a foreign rule over Bharat Mata's (mother India's) authentic, "national community," of Hindus? And weren't Indian Muslims the spawn of an imperialism that in its contempt for Hinduism taxed its worshippers, killed its priests, slaughtered its cows, and sacked, desecrated, and destroyed its temples? In a word, the inventors of a Hindu "community" reinvented its Muslim "other" as a "community" that was foreign and fearsome.

Two imagined and invented "communities" born and nurtured in mutual competition and contempt by their ideologues were briefly reconciled in the Lucknow Pact of 1916. It was an anti-imperialist entente, ironically predicated on the acceptance by its Hindu and Muslim negotiators of the imperial government's political codification of "communalism" in its Morley–Minto Reforms (see below). In consonance with these reforms, the Lucknow Pact "was not based on a fusion of Hindus and Muslims into one political community: it was an agreement recognising them as two distinct communities."[24] And this was at least tacitly accepted and legitimated by none less than Indian nationalism's Mahatma, and the supremo of its the Indian National Congress. The alliance of the Non-Cooperation and Khilafat Movements followed. The Non-Cooperation Movement was supported by prominent Arya Samajists and was regarded as a Hindu enterprise by its Khilafat allies. Their movement was unambiguously Muslim, and its leaders' conception of Indian nationalism was like the Lucknow Pact's and the Non-Cooperation–Khilafat alliance's: a composite of "communal" nationalisms. The point here is this: Indian nationalism made its debut in the joint

Khilafat–Non-Cooperation Movement as an anti-imperialist alliance of religious "communities."

Along with the increase in number and severity of intercommunal "riots," the legacy of the failed Khilafat–Non-Cooperation alliance was an expansion in the activities of Hindu and Muslim organizations to distinguish their "communities" one from the other. Hindu *sabhas*, including the Arya Samaj and the Hindu Mahasabha, redoubled their efforts to "reconvert" Muslim lower castes to Hinduism (*shuddhi*) and to recast Hinduism's mosaic of communities into a "community" (*sangathanan*). Muslim organizations responded by stepping up their missionary activities and their efforts to cleanse Muslim worship of its Hindu saints (*tabligh*) and to bring Muslim communities into their imagined "community" (*tanzim*). Muslim associations reasserted an Islamic imperative for slaughtering cows, and Hindu associations reasserted a Hindu imperative for forbidding it.

Gyanendra Pandey is certainly correct that an Indian nationalism that was secular, unmediated by religious "communities," of individual citizens without regard to their "communal" or communal memberships, became the Indian National Congress's creed largely in reaction to the failure of the Khilafat–Non-Cooperation alliance, conceived and aborted in "communalism."[25] In 1928, an All Parties Conference, dominated by Congress and chaired by Motilal Nehru, drafted a constitution for an independent India which, in effect, reneged on the Lucknow Pact and rejected the legitimacy of the Morley–Minto concept of "communal" representation on which the pact was based. Motilal's son, Jawaharlal, was the great champion of a secular, "communally" unmediated Indian nationalism, from the 1937 elections in which he was Congress's leading campaigner and rhetorician until his death in 1963, after sixteen years as India's first prime minister.

The Raj and Popular "Communalism"

As for the imperial government's contribution to the construction of India's invented "communities," in 1930 one of the Khilafat Movement's erstwhile leaders alluded wryly to the "the old maxim of 'divide and rule'." "[T]here is a division of labour here," Muhammad Ali observed: "We [Indians] divide, and you [British] rule."[26] Francis Robinson's gloss on the epigram is as follows:

The fact was that the British feared the Muslims. They were thought to be the greatest threat not only to British rule in India but to the British Empire. To deal with them, government adopted special measures and made special concessions. These were aimed not at setting Muslims against Hindus, but at reconciling them [i.e., Muslims] to British rule.[27]

Similarly, Peter Hardy characterizes the British government's communal policy as "balance and rule."[28] Everyone, however, concedes that the Raj, whatever the intentions of its captains, contributed to inventing and mobilizing "communities" of Hindus and Muslims and to widening the divide between them. It would be excessively naïve to believe that this was not the intention, at least in part, of the Morley–Minto Reforms of 1906, the Punjab Alienation Act of 1900, and the partition of Bengal in 1905. But here we are concerned with the unintentional contributions of British rule to the invention of "communalism": with the production of "communalism" as an unintended by-product, a spin-off, of bureaucratic imperialism.

I have already indicated that British rule, as such, was a catalyst, first in the invention by Islam's divines of an Indian Muslim "community," juxtaposed to Hindu idolaters and opposed to a regime of infidels; then in the invention by Hindus of a Hindu "community," juxtaposed and opposed to a reinvented Muslim "community." Though still without intention, but more actively, the Raj catalyzed the invention of India's religious "communities" by its official perception of India and the mode of its governance.

In the British view of it, India, as such, was a geographical expression. Its 250 million souls, in 1911, were a vast congeries of extended families, lineages, clans, subcastes, castes, caste groups, and tribes metamorphozing into castes, tribes, tribal groups. Each of these was invariably factionalized, as were the almost half a million villages scattered across the subcontinent in which 90 percent of the population lived. In areal concentrations, there were literates in a score of written languages, most in different scripts, and vast populations of illiterates who spoke hundreds, if not thousands, of dialects. There were superior and inferior races: "martial races" in Punjab, "the soft, weak populations which swarm in . . . tropical low lying regions."[29] In the countryside there were princes, great landlords, land-holding peasants, landless laborers, swidden cultivators. In the cities there were "merchant princes," lawyers and editors, *babus* (clerks), factory workers, mendicants, and lumpen. And, of course, apart from the two major ones there were different religious "communities": Christians, Sikhs, Parsis, Buddhists, Jains, Jews, "animists"—and within each one of them, any number of divisions and sects.

Bewildering in number and complexity, these categories cut across one another. Peasants of the same village were of different castes; peasants and their prince might be of the same caste; members of the same caste might belong to different religious "communities"; members of different religious "communities" spoke the same language; speakers of the same language belonged to different "races"; members of different "races" . . . and so forth.

It was the Raj *alone* and its modalities—railroads, post, and telegraph, the "steel frame" of its bureaucracy—that gave the subcontinent its coherence as a political entity: not a nation, certainly, but an empire. In order to rule it, a small number of British "guardians,"[30] atop a vast bureaucracy, had to know and understand the melange that constituted their empire. From 1872, they took decennial censuses and annotated them, they compiled gazetteers and surveys, and they produced an endless flow of reports and observations, official and "demi-official," up the chain of command to the imperial capital and down to district officers and resident agents in princely courts. They produced a library of special studies, many still read and used as references by scholars: Tod on Rajputana, Darling and Ibbetson on Punjab, Hunter on Muslims, Lee-Warner on the princely states, O'Malley and Hutton on caste, Anstey on economic development, Baden-Powell on village communities, Wheeler and Marshall on the Indus valley civilization, Keith on Sanskrit literature, Moreland on Muslim India, Radcliffe-Brown on Andaman Islanders, Maine on ancient legal systems, and, in addition, a spate of political histories and memoirs.

Whatever could be measured by British measurers was measured: not only land and crops, road and railroad mileage, the lengths of rivers and depths of harbors, literacy and schooling, but the qualities of "race." For example, the crania of one large cultivating caste—the Jats, a caste that spans the "communities" and is of particular interest to us—"are of tolerably fair size and shape, often elongated, altogether a lower type than the Brahman skull."[31] Indians could be categorized according to "race."

Particular categories pass in and out of fashion, but bureaucrats and scholars— and some of the best British officers in India were both—categorize. Categories impose intellectual order on the randomness of things. From official British categorizations in India, there were two effects at least—and not only on "communalism," although that is our concern here. First, things that were liquid, contextual, multilayered, indeterminate were reified, tabulated, named. Communities whose religious beliefs and practices varied widely but who professed or were thought to profess adherence to Islam or to some of the myriad manifestations of Hinduism were aggregated and divided into census categories, "communities": "Hindus" and "Muslims" and their reified subcategories, "Brahmins" and "Shiahs," for example. And these "communal" and sub-"communal" reifications were broadcast by the empire's railroads, its newspapers, its post and telegraph, its authors and their publishers. Second, because the *sarkar's* (government's) categories were meaningful to it and affected its dispensation of goods and services and of grace and favor, these categories created meanings for the *sarkar's* categorized subjects. After 1909, politicians who belonged to communities that were categorized as Muslim could, for example, contest in provincial assembly constituencies that were reserved for Muslims. Politicians who belonged to communities that were categorized as non-Muslim could not. After 1900, Punjab townsmen who were categorized as belonging to "agricultural tribes" could own land. Their neighbors who were categorized as belonging to "non-agricultural tribes" could not.

The British certainly knew that their "communal" categories were mixed bags. Much of our information about the "polytheism" and religious inclusiveness of ordinary people who called themselves Muslims, for example, comes from imperial gazetteers.[32] But for a foreign government attempting to impose a bureaucratic empire on a multitude, at once exotic and diverse, mixed bags were better than none—particularly if those placed in them could be convinced to behave as though they belonged there. Thus, for the Muslim "community" whose invention it refined, patented, and installed in India's political system, the Raj could recognize the "natural leadership" of compliant great landlords rather than contentious *ulama*. I think also that the British were probably predisposed as Christians to share with Muslims their common Abrahamic tradition's perception of religion as an exclusive "community" of believers, however much ordinary folk who "belong" to the "community" or profess its beliefs err in its proper observance.

ELITE SECULAR "COMMUNALISM"

When, for reasons that will become clear, the British addressed themselves directly to "communalism," it was initially to invent and patronize an alternative "natural leadership" of the Muslim "community." "Communities" (and communities) have leaders. We take that for granted. They are the people with whom politicians deal. But the "natural leaders" of the Muslim "community" and its inventors, the *ulama*, were generally (though not universally) unamenable to dealing with the British. The *ulamas'* inclinations were to Islam's "fundamental political orientation," to dichotomize polities according to their regimes as *dar al-Islam* or *dar al-harb,* and to plant the Raj in the latter category. If a policy of "balance and rule" was meant to reconcile the Muslim community to Pax Britannia, the British would have to promote as their collaborators a Muslim "natural leadership" alternative to the *ulamas'*. The obvious choice was the *ashraf*: literally, the "nobility" (although it does have other meanings, that is its meaning here). These *ashraf* were, in the idiom of the times, men of "good families"—in particular, good families of landed wealth in the Muslim heartland of northern India and Punjab. Many were families of the former service gentry of Muslim courts and families that succeeded and emulated these *gens de la robe*.

Francis Robinson is certainly correct: The British policy post-Mutiny of reconciling India's Muslims to British rule was predicated on fear: of Islam's political imperative, of an *ulama*-led rabble of mutinous Indian Muslims, of unreconciled Muslims in the expanding British empire outside India. Hunter had warned that unless British policy took particular note of Muslim disaffection, there was:

danger that the entire Muhammadan *community* will rapidly be transformed into a mass of disloyal ignorant fanatics, on the one hand; with a small class of men highly educated in a narrow fashion, high[ly] fanatic [i.e., *ulama*], on the other . . . exercising an enormous influence over their ignorant fellow Muhammadans.[33]

But in India, fear and danger marched with opportunity. Opportunity lay in catering to the interests of the *ashraf*. Originally their holdings were of alienable land grants, and/or they were collectors of land revenue. The *ashraf* were made land-*owners* by the Raj—"landlords," as we understand the term, and landlords subject to British law and protected by it. Dependent and dependable landlords were particularly useful to the Raj. It was managed by a handful of British foreigners. They knew, of course, that peasants, whatever their religious "community," were the largest occupational and social groups in the empire, and the major producers of its income. But much of Indian peasant life, however well explored by its scholar-bureaucrats, was exotic to the British or was unknown. What to do? If they permitted Indian landlords to exercise their customary ideological, political, and economic control over the multitude of their peasant tenants and dependents, then the British needed only to exercise their revenue-collecting authority over a handful of compliant landlords.

As administrative servants, the *ashraf* demonstrated their "loyalty" to the Raj. Immediately after the Mutiny, the British inclination had been to see the hand of Islam behind it, and in Delhi, most terribly, the Muslim nobility had been the objects of imperial vengeance. In spite of this, both before and after 1857, the *ashraf* were prominent in the empire's subordinate administrative services; they were considerably overrepresented as a proportion of their "community's" population in northern India and, to a lesser extent, in Punjab. They were stake-holders of the empire: "we have the support of the comfortable classes" of Muslims, Hunter asserted, "men of inert convictions and some property, who say their prayers, decorously attend the mosque, and think very little about the matter."[34]

But, post-Mutiny, the *ashraf's* stake came under threat—and not from the Raj, but from its Hindu subjects, Brahmans and Bengali *babus*.[35] Now officially an imperial government, and chastened by the Mutiny, the Raj looked to the support of its wise, wealthy, and well-born "native" subjects. It asked for their services in municipal and provincial councils. More and more, it selected the higher grades of Indian civil servants by competitive examinations administered to the graduates of its English-medium universities in India; and more and more, the Muslim stake in the Raj was put at risk.

Muslims competed at a disadvantage for positions on municipal and provincial councils against more numerous, better-educated, and wealthier Hindu Brahmins, *babus* and *baniyas*. Under the new rules of competition for government jobs, the *ashraf* stood little chance against Hindu "competition-wallahs," who were more numerous in universities then their Muslim counterparts and were better educated both in English and in modern vocations useful to the Raj. If the British were successfully to reconcile the Muslim "community" to British rule, it would have to protect and encourage the interests of the *ashraf*—the "community's" "natural leaders," so designated by the Raj—its "comfortable classes," against Hindu competition.

The World of Sir Saiyid Ahmad Khan

In this protective enterprise, the Raj enjoyed not merely the collaboration but the guidance of one of the remarkable men of the time, a *sharif*,[36] Sir Saiyid Ahmad Khan. He was born in 1817, the son of a north Indian Mughal service gentry family of Afghan pedigree but declining assets. In 1839, he entered the company's subordinate judicial service, was conspicuously loyal during the

Mutiny, and retired with honor in 1876. However, his most notable achievements—including the founding of what was to become the Aligarh Muslim University—his great renown, and his knighthood followed his retirement.

In a word, Saiyid Ahmad was the secularizer of Muslim "communalism" and the initial negotiator of its entente with the British. He was a modernist religious reformer who argued that Islam was compatible with "progress" and modernity, and that Muslims could live an Islamic life in British India. He argued in the language of religion. But his concern was with the secular welfare of the Muslim "community," and particularly of its good families.

The Raj was in India to stay. The Mutiny's failure had settled that. Muslims would have to make do—not even with a second-best regime of Muslim princes, but with a least-worst regime of British Christians who tolerated Islam. Indeed, although it was the wont of Sir Saiyid and his British collaborators to grieve for the Muslims as a "community" that had "fallen behind in the race of life under British rule,"[37] it was only in Bengal that Muslim good families were "backward"—unwilling or unable to compete for British India's educational and employment opportunities. In northern India and Punjab, Muslim backwardness was a myth. There, as I have indicated, the *ashraf* had already made the best of a bad bargain. Sir Saiyid's concern was to keep it best, to protect and enlarge the *ashraf's* vested interest in the Raj, to guard their stake against Hindu encroachment. This was an enterprise of two parts.

First, Muslim good families had to be convinced, or more likely, reassured, that serving the British government was not the high road to infidelity. They had to prepare their sons for government service and the professions by giving them an education that was, at once, respectful of Islam and relevant, through its English medium, to the preparation of its students for respectable and remunerative employment in British India. Only through their knowledge of the Raj's business and by their active participation in it could Muslims of good family serve their "community's" interests, and their own. Education was the key. Sir Saiyid was at one with Hunter. The Aligarh Muslim University is Sir Saiyid's enduring monument. Education was essential—but, by itself, insufficient.

Second, sufficiency was in the hands of the Raj. Education might be made sufficient only by the Raj's assurance of its particular solicitude for the welfare of Muslim good families. By the last quarter of the nineteenth century, an increasing number of Muslim boys were being educated as Sir Saiyid wanted them to be. But that was not sufficient, nor would it ever be. They would always be outnumbered by literate and numerate Hindus, who were more advanced in English-language university education for professional employment and more attuned to it. For places on municipal and provincial councils, Muslims would always be outnumbered by English-educated Hindus and overwhelmed by the money power of Hindu *baniyas*. In each following generation, as fathers were succeeded by their sons, the Hindu advantage would increase, as would the Muslim disadvantage. If the British wanted to reconcile the Muslim "community" to their rule, they would have to shelter its good families from Hindu competition. The way to do that would be to reserve places in government service for Muslims and to reserve constituencies for Muslim members and their electors in provincial assemblies and municipal councils. In addition, the importance of Muslims as a "nation" merited the weighting of these reservations in positive disproportion to the size of the "community's" population.

As it had been under the Mughals, India was an empire. It had never been and was not a nation, a conviction that Sir Saiyid shared with the British. The British empire in India was comprised of "two nations" at least; more exactly, of a Muslim "nation"—the "community" reinvented for political purposes, a *millet*[38]—and an agglomeration of Hindus and others. Because India was not a nation, the Indian National Congress, founded in 1885, was and could never be more than a faux nationalist organization. It was not even an organization of the Hindu "community," but largely of upper-class Brahmins, *babus* and *baniyas*. Much less did it represent the Muslim "nation" or its interests. Sir Saiyid cautioned Muslims against joining it. Even more, he advised them to eschew political action altogether and rely on the British to protect Muslim interests[39]—or, more exactly, the interests of Muslim good families.

But why should the British do so? Hunter had worked it out: because the *ashraf* were the accepting and acceptable "natural leaders," or could be made so, of a fearful one-fifth of the empire's population as yet unreconciled to their political fate and still susceptible to an *ulama* call for *jihad*. The other bird to be killed with the same stone was the Hindu professional middle classes. They were increasingly restive under the Raj, because of its "orientalism,"[40] its autocracy, and the limited opportunities it offered to Indians for professional employment and advancement. Sir Saiyid's implicit offer was an *ashraf* guarantee of the Muslim "nation's" loyalty in return for special British protection of its good families' interests.

"Constitutional Reforms"

The deal was struck in 1906, at one of the most fateful meetings in British Indian history. A delegation of Muslim dignitaries, mostly great landlords, led by one of the greatest, the Aga Khan, and encouraged by British officers, presented the viceroy, Lord Minto, with an "address."[41] In it they expressed their appreciation of the "incalculable benefits conferred [on India] by British rule" and pledged the "unswerving loyalty [of Muslims] to the Throne." No word of *dar al-harb* here! In return, these grandees requested reserved places for Muslims, with "weightage," in government service and on all representative assemblies, from district boards to the viceroy's council.

The request was granted in the Morley–Minto Reforms. It was incorporated into law by the India Councils Act of 1909 and perpetuated in law by the British parliament's two subsequent omnibus India acts of 1919 and 1935. These acts of "constitutional reform" established two precedents that are relevant here.

First, Indians were to be members of imperial and provincial legislative councils: in 1909, selected in indirect election; from 1919 and thereafter, directly by an electorate that was restricted in size by property and educational qualifications. These qualifications were reduced over the years, and at the last election held under imperial aegis in 1946, the electorate had grown to roughly one-quarter of the empire's adult population. Increasingly, Indian elections were contested by movements organized as political parties, most notably Congress and, later, the Muslim League. In provincial—though not in imperial—councils, and subject to imperial veto, the power of Indian legislators and their parties also grew.

Second, from 1909 to the end of the Raj, most Muslim members of legislative councils were selected from constituencies reserved to Muslims voters; also, in those provinces where Muslims were a minority, which was most of India, Muslim representation on councils was disproportionately weighted. Provincial governments, which were the major providers of government jobs to Indians, began reserving and weighting a portion of these for Muslims even before the Morley–Minto Reforms, and the practice became general. By 1937, British reforms had gradually transferred provincial legislative power to an Indian elite of property and education, but in two constituencies: a "reserved" one for Muslims, a "general" one for Hindus.

During the 1940s, it became increasingly certain that the British would leave India, and that the future of the Indian Muslim "community" would have to be determined in negotiations with the Hindu Congress. The latter was likely to succeed the Raj in most of the subcontinent, but not all. Leaders of the Muslim League, most notably Mohammad Ali Jinnah, bid for an important part of it by holding open the possibility of Muslims protecting their future by means other than reserved and weighted constituencies in provincial assemblies. These, after all, gave the "community" only an assured and somewhat enlarged minority of seats in Muslim minority provinces. By producing a contented Muslim class of good families, reservations and weightage also disinclined them from assuming the political leadership of the Muslim "nation" against the threat of Congress's Hindu "nationalism" or a Congress–British entente.

For surrendering their reserved and weighted constituencies, what Jinnah and other Muslim politicians wanted in return were Muslim League ministries virtually assured in Muslim-majority provinces, most notably in Punjab and Bengal. Post-Independence, Muslim-majority and Hindu-majority provinces would be tenuously incorporated into an Indian confederation in which the constitutional balance of power was held in its provinces or in a middle-level federation of provinces. Coupled with a strong and determined Muslim representation at the empire's center, a Muslim majority province that supplied India with most of its soldiery and guarded its marches in the west and another that contained its major industrial city and seaport in the east—Calcutta—would together assure that Muslim interests were protected throughout the confederation. Or, if not, its

Muslim majority units would secede from the confederation, or threaten to do so. This was more than likely the "Pakistan" that Quaid-i-Azam Jinnah preferred.

The Muslim League was more united and active under the Quaid's leadership than it had ever been, revived by its collaboration with the British during the Second World War and by its discovery of "Pakistan." Jinnah was a secularist. His fear was not the specter of *dar al-harb* in an independent Hindu-majority India, but the possible harm that it might inflict on the mundane interests of a legally or constitutionally unprotected Muslim minority. Jinnah was an Indian nationalist—but of the old school. His was the nationalism of an alliance between two "communities" defined by religion. He was one of the signers of the Lucknow Pact. Jinnah preferred to have matters settled by elites. He turned his back on the alliance between the Khilafat and Non-Cooperation Movements. His distrust of mass politics had not yet been overcome by his ambition to lead them.

To Jinnah, as to Sir Saiyid Ahmad, India was home to "two nations," and any constitution for an independent India would have to accommodate them as such. He denied, not without evidence, the validity of Congress's claim to secularism and saw it as a screen behind which Muslims would be subjected inevitably to a regime of the Hindu majority. After Partition, this became a Pakistani article of faith. It was prefigured in pre-Partition India, our concern here, by the results of the 1937 and, particularly, the 1946 elections. While Congress had a handful of Muslims among its leadership, neither it nor the concept of a secular Indian nationalism—and not for want of "mass-mobilization" campaigns—enjoyed a Muslim constituency.

An Indian confederation was unacceptable to Nehru and others whose vision was of an Indian Union that was secular and strong at its Centre. British governments—still aspiring to their country's return to great-power status postwar, and thus interested in keeping India and, particularly, the Indian army intact—sent two parliamentary missions to Delhi, in 1942 and 1946, in the hope of negotiating an Indian confederation. It was the only form of Indian unity acceptable to Jinnah. Congress would have none of it. Partition, in 1947, was then inevitable, and Jinnah got the "moth-eaten" Pakistan that he more than likely did not want.

DOMINANT CLASS COALITIONS AND THE LEGACIES OF RESERVATIONS AND WEIGHTAGE

Again, "communalism" was not a British invention. British India's political machinery was. It was a construct of "constitutional reform." Installed in the machinery and critical to its functioning was "communalism." Its particular device was reservations and weightage. They were the way in which people were represented in the provincial assemblies and municipal councils of British India. From these nodes, the subcontinent's political systems and their institutionalized "communalism" developed in tandem and became legacies for political development in India and Pakistan.

The legacies with which we are concerned are those that relate to the development or nondevelopment of parliamentary democracy. We are particularly concerned with the relationship between the political foundations laid in British India and the organization and class composition of the political parties that were subsequently built in India and Pakistan. Our basic assumption is that political parties play a "crucial role in making [parliamentary] democracy viable or not under very similar economic and social structural conditions . . ."[42]—that is, those of India and Pakistan.

Legacies for India

Into the making of Congress had gone the legacy of Hindu "communalism" and the rejection of Muslim "communalism." But the legacies of reservations and weightage were less to facilitate party-building in India than to inhibit it in Pakistan. Their facilitation of party-building in India was directly through their contribution to positioning the Congress Party's ancestor, the Indian National Congress, as a party of opposition in British India. It was in opposition to British imperialism that Congress grew into a political party. As such, it was pressed to cultivate the organization and discipline of the imperial government that it opposed. On these political attributes, the factionalized Congress's hold was not always or in all cases firm. But it was firm enough to carry Congress over into independent India as its one dominant, nationwide, ruling political party, and to maintain it as such for two decades. Less directly, reservations and weightage for Muslims contributed to making the Hindu-dominated Congress a party free of the patronage of great landlords.

Although it was, for its first decade or so, little more than an interest group of the professional middle classes, effusive in its declarations of loyalty to the Crown, the Indian National Congress carried the germ of "sedition" from its inception. Its earliest resolutions proclaimed its opposition to two pillars of the empire. It opposed the intentional monopolization by Britons of India's superior civil services—and thereby the political dominance of Britons in the subcontinent's bureaucratic empire. It opposed the regular expenditure of about 40 percent of the Raj's budget on its Indian army—a critical component of imperial Britain's armed force, available for worldwide deployment, but largely paid for out of Indian revenues. By the turn of the century, no later than Curzon's viceroyalty, Congress was generally regarded by the British as the Hindu party opposed to the government.

The Morley–Minto Reforms and the 1905 partition of Bengal nudged Congress further in the direction of anti-imperialism. The Raj was playing the Muslim card in a game of divide-and-rule. It was being contemptuous of Indian nationalism. It was discriminating against Hindus. "Balance and rule"—a variation, however subtle, of divide-and-rule—was a new pillar of empire. Reservations and weightage were its capital. Congress opposed reservations and weightage—except when that master of lateral thinking, Mahatma Gandhi, appropriated them for a few years to prop up the anti-imperialist alliance of Muslim *khilafatists* and Hindu noncooperators.

To some extent, reservations and weightage were the Muslim part of a more comprehensive imperial maintenance strategy that began to develop a decade or so after the Mutiny. The first aim of this strategy was to reduce the Raj's dependence on the subordinate services of the increasingly restive and demanding Hindu middle classes—the upper-caste professional men who made the empire a going concern: bureaucrats, lawyers, engineers, surveyors, doctors, journalists. British patronage for the English-language education of the sons of Muslim good families followed. The second aim was to ally the Raj with the "natural rulers" of the Indian countryside—the great landlords, including, of course, the greatest, the princes. "Chiefs' colleges" were built to educate their sons to loyalty and noblesse oblige, and special civil-service cadre and cadet corps were formed to reinforce the lessons. The Punjab Alienation of Land Act of 1900 was, to a degree, particular to Punjab, but in general it was part of this strategy. For those in search of its monument, Aitchison College in Lahore will do.

As the most dependent and dependable allies of the Raj, great landlords were, in general, unavailable as recruits to Congress. And their unavailability increased as Congress's opposition became more strident and unequivocal, at least until the 1940s, when the writing was clearly on the wall. Great landlords are almost everywhere the great opponents of parliamentary democracy—and, of particular concern to us, in Pakistan. Due largely to Gandhi's efforts, Congress's recruits and allies in the countryside were land-holding peasants—those inveterate enemies of noncultivating great landlords. As subsequent "constitutional reforms" reduced educational and income requirements for enfranchisement, the political importance and assertiveness of land-holding peasants increased. In 1920, Gandhi reorganized Congress in unilingual Pradesh (provincial) Congress Committees to reach out to land-holding peasants in their ethnolinguistic clusters, usually castes and caste groups. And he provided them with a strategy of conflict and conflict resolution which did not threaten their landholdings.

Congress threatened neither the expropriation of land nor the taking of rent. It recruited petty landlords. It was not inviting to great landlords, its non-allies, but it was not particularly menacing to them either, or even to the princes. Mahatma Gandhi's anti-imperialist strategy of "non-violent non-cooperation," *satyagraha*, was calculated to keep Congress's struggle against imperialism from becoming a class war. Only after the 1937 elections did Congress begin to organize front groups in the princely states. In general, these *praja mandals* (people's societies) were as moderate in opposition to their princely regimes as Congress was in opposition to the Raj. Post-Independence, the integration of the princely states into the Indian Union was accomplished with great generosity to the deposed princes. Revolution-from-below was abhorrent to Congress's "high command." Its revolution was from above: the installation in post-Independence India by English-educated, professional middle-class politicians of a parliamentary democratic system dominated at India's Centre by them and, in its provinces, too, by them in alliance with land-holding peasants. Although reformist in practice, the system was revolutionary in its underlying, essential assumption of a political equality among citizens, an assumption foreign and exotic to customary, pervasively hierarchical Indian society, and—as we shall see—subversive of it.

From the late 1930s, and particularly during the imperial sunset of the 1940s, Congress's coalition of professional men and landed peasants was readily joined by India's Hindu "merchant princes." They were the subcontinent's big businessmen and its Hindu philanthropists. They had little sympathy with a political system that overrepresented Muslim interests, patronized great landlords, and, thus, favored an agricultural economy for India. Colonial rather than comprador capitalists,[43] India's industrialists were pushed during the Great Depression by discriminatory British policies against them and in favor of British industry: the official pound sterling/rupee rate of exchange, for example. They were pulled by Congress's conduct of provincial government from 1937 to 1939: stable, disciplined, financially responsible, law-abiding, and committed to the maintenance of domestic order, the protection of property, the discouragement of "labor unrest," the purchase of *swadeshi* (Indian-manufactured) goods, and a proper respect for the money power of big business. The Bombay Plan of 1944, endorsed by the paterfamilias of virtually every major industrial house in India, signed them into the alliance. The plan envisaged big business's collaboration as government's junior partner in the industrialization of independent India.

Apart from their Hindu attraction to the Mahatma, Marwari and Gujarati industrialists[44]—the largest in India—were reassured by his opposition, and that of the Congress's dominant right wing, even to democratic socialism, much less "bolshevism." Gandhi's choice of Jawaharlal Nehru as his heir was less reassuring. Nehru's association with the Congress left wing and his leanings toward socialism were worrisome. But they could be discounted in favor of his secularism. Though friendly to Muslims in general, Nehru was unshakeable in his opposition to reservations and weightage for their gentry. He was in general agreement with the Bombay Plan, and his enthusiasm for industrialization was no less than the industrialists' and far more than Gandhi's. Finally, the Mahatma's faith in Nehru's political soundness was unshakeable. As the 1940s wore on, it became increasingly apparent that Congress would succeed the Raj not only in British India, but in that third of the subcontinent that was ruled by its client princes. In the 1930s, there had been an increase, "not altogether negligible," of industrial investment in the princely states, where there were no trade unions and hardly any labor legislation, and princely investments in British India's big business were probably "constant and significant."[45] But unlike the British, Congress had no use for princes, and they were unlikely to survive a Congress *raj*. So an Indian alliance of an established landlord class and an emerging industrial bourgeoisie—the classic antidemocratic alliance—was not an option, and, while they may not have been democrats, joining the Congress coalition was Hobson's choice for India's "merchant princes."

The industrial working classes—and, particularly, "labor unrest"—were of great concern to their employers, of course. But urban working classes were a negligible influence in either the development or nondevelopment of parliamentary democracy in British India. They were occasionally assertive in their own interests and occasionally mobilized for political activity—by Congress and Congress-sponsored trade unions, among others. But before 1947 no more than 5 percent of the empire's population was dependent on "organized industry."[46] It was largely concentrated in two or three cities in a subcontinent nine-tenths of whose population lived in villages and country towns. British strategies of imperial maintenance and nationalist strategies that challenged them were centered in the countryside.

While Muslims were notably absent from the Congress coalition or its constituency, there were always among Congress's leaders a sufficient representation of prominent Muslim professionals. It could therefore stake its claim to be an anti-imperialist, *Indian* nationalist movement rather than a party of Hindu Brahmins and *babus*. Moreover, its official view of India's future was as a "secular" state. It would neither favor Muslims nor discriminate against them. But Congress was largely a Hindu organization, and it neither generalized a common anti-imperialist cause with Muslim middle-class professionals nor secured a base among Muslim land-holding peasants—except on the northwest frontier, a special case. A Muslim constituency attached itself to Congress only post-Independence, and then—with unfortunate consequences—in clientage, a "vote-bank."

Pakistan's Legacy

For Pakistan, the legacies of institutionalized "communalism," in general, and reservations and weightage, in particular, were a Punjab-centered, nationally dominant coalition of classes that were in composition unwilling and in organization unable to develop a parliamentary democracy.

In northern India, landlords and well-to-do professional men, sometimes of the same *ashraf* families, were the primary beneficiaries of reservations and weightage. As service gentry of the expired Muslim dynasties of northern India, the *ashraf* incorporated in their families administrative experience and land-holding—converted to land-*owning* under British law. Reservations and weightage reinforced this incorporation and inhibited the political dissociation from landlords of men who had come to their professions from middle-class families. Thus, unlike the Hindu middle classes, which formed the mainstay of a coalition friendly to the development of parliamentary democracy, the Muslim professional middle classes—particularly their more successful members—aligned themselves with great landlords. Together they shared the benefits of reservations and weightage. Reservations and weightage gave Muslim professional men a vested interest in being Muslim.

The organization, such as it was, of these Muslim elite was the All-India Muslim League. From its founding in 1906, and for most of its career, the Muslim League was not even a party of notables—only an agglomeration of notables' factions. In some places, they were pastimes of a handful of urban gentry; in other places, the vehicles of locally competitive landlords. In many places, the League was virtually nonexistent: in Punjab, critically, until the 1940s. Leaguers who competed for reserved and weighted seats in provincial assemblies did so from constituencies whose electorates, restricted in size by property and educational qualifications, were small. Candidates depended for their success much less on their nominal connection to some party than on their access to the endorsements and patronage of great landlords and/or great *rais*—eminent townsmen who were frequently landlords as well. In 1937, it was to these local magnates that the Muslim League lost most of the constituencies reserved for Muslims in northern India.

Those elections were held under the India Act of 1935. Following the Montague–Chelmsford Reforms of 1921,[47] the "constitutional reform" of 1935 furthered the course of Indian politics toward becoming provincial and rural, as well as "communal." Because of its organizational tenuousness, the All-India Muslim League—unlike the Indian National Congress—could provide no countervailing centripetal force to the provincializing of Indian politics. In what was to become West Pakistan—the Muslim majority districts of western Punjab, Sindh, Baluchistan, and the North West Frontier—the League was virtually nonexistent. In what was to become East Pakistan—the Muslim majority districts of eastern Bengal—the provincial League was at odds with the Quaid.[48] The class coalitions that dominated Muslim politics differed from province to province. Crucially, in Punjab, landlords were the major partner in the coalition of dominant classes that took the League's label in the 1940s. In Bengal, the coalition of classes that dominated Muslim and League politics was an anti-landlord alliance of urban professionals and land-holding peasants.

Reservations and weightage were a disincentive for northern India's Muslim landlords and moneyed professional men to recruit ordinary Muslims to their coalition and no incentive for these Muslims to seek recruitment. Why should a coalition of dominant classes—one of whose partners was great landlords—seek to recruit peasant allies? When access to political resources, provided by reservations and weightage, increased the *izzat* of landlords and, probably, their customary power in the countryside? When the *ashraf's* British benefactors, who were the givers of reservations and weightage and could, as well, be their takers-away, were haunted by the specter of politically mobilized Muslim peasants, of *mujahidin*? Jinnah, who both deplored reservations and weightage and made the most of them, understood that they disinclined the Muslim elite from seeking the political alliance of their ordinary coreligionists. As for unenfranchised Muslim peasants: Why should they seek to ally themselves with "natural leaders" whose economy was predicated on the exploitation of their peasantry? What benefits could the vast majority of Muslims, poor and illiterate, anticipate from reservations and weightage?

North Indian Muslim elites were disinclined from associating themselves with the Hindu-dominated Congress, which opposed reservations and weightage. Conversely, north Indian Muslim elites were inclined by reservations and weightage to make their peace with the imperial government. Not through their own organizational efforts, but through the calculated grace and favor of the British government, did northern India's Muslim notables enjoy their political privileges and the benefits that flowed from them. Sir Saiyid understood that the Raj's gifts were more likely to flow to Muslims of good family in appreciation of their political inactivity rather than as a consequence of their political activity. These Muslims were recognized as "natural leaders" in appreciation and anticipation of their not leading anyone or anything. Their loyalty was demonstrated by their inactivity and their tacit and self-interested cooperation in ensuring the political inactivity of their "community." The reunification of Bengal in 1911 distressed the Muslim grandees of northern India. But to put their reservations and weightage at risk by organizing themselves in opposition to the British and in support of the nascent professional middle class of their "communal" brethren in Bengal was on no agenda of any clique that called itself the Muslim League.

To be sure, the Khilafat Movement was organized by a Muslim elite in opposition to British imperialism. But these were men of the "New Party"—run-of the-mill lawyers, journalists, and *ulama*—whom Robinson distinguishes by class from the great landlords and moneyed professionals who led the "Old Party." "Party" is a misnomer. Both "old" and "new" were aggregations. Neither was a "party." The Khilafat Movement had no organizational connection with the All-India Muslim League, and it eclipsed it as the Muslim "party" during the 1920s. However tenuously, the *khilafatists* were connected to Congress by a complementarity of interests in opposition to the entente between men of the "Old Party" and their imperial benefactor. The Khilafat Movement was in the Indian Muslim tradition of popular, religious "communal" anti-imperialism. Until the movement for "Pakistan," that popular tradition was largely unconnected to the elite, secular, collaborationist, reservation- and weightage-driven "communalism" that initially inspired "Pakistan." By and large, the anglophile leaders of the "Old Party" abstained from participating in the Khilafat Movement. Jinnah, for one, would have none of it. The "Old Party" survived the *khilafatists* and reestablished their dominance of Muslim politics in northern India.[49]

During the "Pakistan" Movement, the inclination of the Muslim upper classes to collaborate with the Raj reasserted itself, and a newer strategy of balancing the Raj against Congress came to the fore. Jinnah, as balancer, was favored by a grateful empire's patronage in return for his support in the Second World War. He benefited from the fears of provincial Muslim politicians that Congress's ambition was to control postwar India from its Centre. He became the Quaid-i-Azam—the great leader—of India's Muslim "community" by his successful manipulation of "Pakistan" as a slogan of great emotional resonance but no specific reference to any clearly defined or generally understood prospective reality. Thus, for a few years during the 1940s, the Quaid overcame the centrifugal force of reservations and weightage. Outside of Bengal—a critical exception—Jinnah unified the Muslim League under his leadership. He became the "sole spokesman" for a party of notables that with momentary success brought together under its green banner Muslim elite and popular "communalism."

It was the togetherness of a movement rather than the unification of a party. For want of popular Muslim organization, and perhaps as a matter of choice, Muslim League politicians in British India popularized "Pakistan"—hastily, in a five-year countdown to the "transfer of power"—not by recruiting into their coalition ordinary Muslims, but, rather, by appealing to their demonstrable religious anti-imperialism and puritanism. Religious and secular "communalism" merged, however briefly. "Pakistan" would be a resurrected *dar al-Islam* de facto. It would be free of Hindu idolaters and moneylenders. Its enemy and the enemy of the faithful was not the British Raj but the Hindu Congress. These were the messages carried by Muslim students and divines to Muslim villagers and townspeople.[50] They joined the Muslim League in considerable number during the 1940s, particularly in northern India, and voted overwhelmingly for Muslim League candidates in the 1946 elections. But they were nonetheless a constituency of adherents to a religious–political–"communal" ideal that had been sloganized rather than the alliance partners of the dominant Muslim coalition.

For a century until Partition, the history of the Muslim upper classes was of collaboration with the British in return for secular benefits. For more than a century until Partition, the history of the Muslim lower classes, led by their *ulama*, was of opposition to British imperialism in return for the rewards of heaven. "Pakistan" brought them together, but in no political party alliance. There was never in pre-Independence India a

great [Muslim] nationalist party [like the Congress]: firmly rooted in each province, organised down to town and village level, long involved in local causes, and manned by politicians with much experience both in reconciling differences and in subordinating them to their party's higher purpose.[51]

If Ayesha Jalal is correct, the "Pakistan" that Jinnah wanted, as opposed to the Pakistan that he got, was predicated on a new, prospective complementarity of interests between the British government and the Muslim "community's" leaders: for the one, an Indian army intact; for the other, the capacity to threaten the dissolution of an Indian confederation that was unheedful of Muslim interests.[52] Once in the Pakistan that Jinnah got, the Muslim League that he unified began to fragment. Even as an association of notables, it barely survived the Quaid's death in 1948.

In the next chapter, I detail the contributions of the different coalitions of dominant Muslim classes in British Punjab and Bengal to the nondevelopment of parliamentary democracy in Pakistan. I conclude this chapter with a few paragraphs to connect those particular legacies to the legacy of reservations and weightage.

In Muslim-majority Punjab, the power of great Muslim landlords was assured less by reservations and weightage than by their position on the ground, as lords of their tenants and dependents. The "Punjab tradition" of authoritarian imperial administration encouraged the rule of landlords in the countryside, and their rule was given legislative sanction, in effect, by the Punjab Land Alienation Act of

1900. The National Unionist Party was formed in 1923 by an inter-"communal" group of landlords—Muslims, Sikhs, and Hindus—to protect their interests by collaborating with the British administration in the implementation of the act. The Muslim landlords of Punjab were disinclined to "Pakistan" or to sharing their power with Muslim professional men of the towns—or with Jinnah. When Pakistan was formed in 1947, the economically and socially dominant class in its western wing, soon to become a major partner in its coalition of politically dominant classes, was the great landlords. Their centrality in Pakistan's "marriage of iron and rye" is an enduring political legacy from the Raj.

During the century's first decade, the north Indian *ashraf's* self-interested, lukewarm-at-best support for the Bengali Muslim middle class's campaign to retain the Muslim-majority province of East Bengal left it with a sense of having been betrayed—and to Sir Saiyid's bogey: the Bengali *babu*, the Hindu *bhadralok*! Many of the same Bengali Muslims sensed further betrayal in the Lucknow Pact of 1916. According to the pact's formula for "communal" representation, the north Indian *ashraf* and their allies agreed to increase the number of provincial assembly constituencies reserved for them in their Muslim-minority provinces at the cost of reducing the number of provincial assembly constituencies reserved for Muslims in Muslim-majority provinces. The Muslim upper classes of Punjab were probably unaffected by the arrangement, so great was their power on the land.

The Bengali Muslim middle class feared that it would be affected. It need not have—for whatever it lost to the Lucknow Pact, the coalition of professional men and landed farmers which dominated Muslim politics in Bengal, from 1937 certainly, gained in organization. Unlike Muslims anywhere else in India, they organized to make the most of reservations and weightage—first in the Krishak Praja Party, then in the Bengal Provincial Muslim League. And in spite of the overwhelming control by Hindus of Bengal's commerce, industry, professions, and professional training institutions, the coalition that dominated Muslim politics in Bengal put together the only provincial government in British India that was popularly supported by Muslims.

There is, however, a sting in the tail. By leading the only coalition of dominant classes among Indian Muslims that was friendly to the development of parliamentary democracy, the Muslim middle class of Bengal contributed to the early demise of parliamentary democracy in Pakistan. In brief, the coalition of dominant classes in Muslim Bengal was an impediment to the development of parliamentary democracy in Pakistan because it threatened the hegemony of the nationally dominant, antidemocratic coalition of classes in West Pakistan.

NOTES

1. Bipan Chandra et al., *India's Struggle for Independence* (New Delhi: Penguin, 1989), p. 44; Muin-ud-Din Ahmad Khan, *History of the Fara'idi Movement in Bengal, 1818–1906* (Karachi: Pakistan Historical Society, 1965).

2. A. C. Neimeijer, *The Khilafat Movement in India, 1919–1924* (The Hague: Martinus Nijhoff, 1972), p. 171.

3. Judaism, Christianity, and Islam all trace the origins of their faith to God's revelation of Himself to the patriarch Abraham of the Book of Genesis.

4. Ishtiaq Husain Qureshi, *The Muslim Community of the Indo-Pakistan Subcontinent, 610–1947* ('S-Gravenhage: Mouton, 1962), pp. 84, 270; emphasis added.

5. W. W. Hunter, *Indian Musalmans* (Republished Delhi: Indological Book House, 1969), p. 134.

6. Muin Ud-Din Ahmad Khan, "Research into the Islamic Revivalism of the 19th Century and Its Effect on the Muslim Society of Bengal," *Social Research in East Pakistan*, edited by Pierre Bessaignet (Dacca: Asiatic Society of Pakistan, 1960).

7. Then in the British province of Bengal, now the capital of the Indian state of Bihar.

8. The reference is to irregular Sufi orders and freelancers whose mysticism was unbounded by Quranic revelation: that the prophetic line that began with the patriarch Abraham ended with the Seal of the Prophets, Muhammad, for example. Qeyamuddin Ahmad, *The Wahhabi Movement in India,* 2nd revised edition (New Delhi: Mahohar, 1994), p. 43.

9. M. Mujeeb, *The Indian Muslims* (New Delhi: Munshiram Manoharlal, 1985), Part I.

10. Ibid, p. 15. *Pir*, also *Sheikh*, are titles for Sufi divines.

11. Muin Ud-Din Ahmad, "Research."

12. Hunter, *Indian Musalmans,* p. 92.

13. Eric Stokes, *The Peasant Armed: The Indian Revolt of 1857*, edited by C. A. Bayly (Oxford: Clarendon Press, 1986), pp. 87–88.

14. Freeland Abbot, *Islam and Pakistan* (Ithaca, NY: Cornell University Press, 1968), p. 86.

15. Gail Minault, *The Khilafat Movement: Religious Symbolism and Political Mobilization in India* (New York: Columbia University Press, 1982), p. 77.

16. Khan, *History of the Fara'idi Movement.* Only after eastern Bengal became part of Pakistan, and as such, *dar al-Islam* de facto, did the *Faraidis,* by then a small sect, resume congregational Friday prayer, suspended for more than a century because of British rule.

17. Bipan Chandra, *Nationalism and Colonialism in Modern India* (Hyderabad: Orient Longman, 1979), p. 260; emphasis added.

18. Minault, *The Khilafat Movement,* p. 211.

19. Peter Hardy, *The Muslims of British India* (Cambridge: Cambridge University Press, 1972), pp. 238–239. See also Kalim Siddiqui, *Conflict, Crisis and War in Pakistan* (London: Macmillan, 1972), chap. 2.

20. Quoted in Shiv Kumar Gupta, *Arya Samaj and the Raj (1875–1920)* (New Delhi: Gitanjali Publishing House, 1991), p. 18; emphasis added.

21. Kenneth W. Jones, *Arya Dharma: Hindu Consciousness in 19th-Century Punjab* (Berkeley, CA: University of California Press, 1976).

22. For example: The great Hindi novelist of pre-independence India, a Hindu, Dhanpat Rai (1880–1936), who wrote under the pen-name Munshi Premchand, wrote many of his novels and short stories in Urdu.

23. Gupta, *Arya Samaj*, and K. C. Yadav and K. S. Arya, *Arya Samaj and the Freedom Movement*, Vol 1, 1875–1918 (New Delhi: Manohar, 1988).

24. Niemeijer, *The Khilafat Movement in India,* p. 67.

25. Gyanendra Pandey, *The Construction of Communalism in Colonial North India* (New Delhi: Oxford University Press, 1992).

26. Quoted in Niemeijer, *The Khilafat Movement in India,* p. 163.

27. Francis Robinson, *Separatism among Indian Muslims: The Politics of the United Provinces' Muslims 1860–1923* (Delhi: Oxford University Press, 1994), pp. 131–132.

28. Hardy, *Muslims*.

29. Alfred C. Lyall, "The Rajput States of India," *Asiatic Studies*, Vol. 1 (London: John Murray, 1899), p. 263.

30. The term is used most consistently and admiringly by Philip Mason, under the pseudonym Philip Woodruff, *The Men Who Ruled India*, 2 vols. (New York: Schocken, 1964).

31. M. A. Sherring, *The Tribes and Castes of Rajasthan*. An offprint from *Hindu Tribes and Castes*, first published in 1881 (Delhi: Cosmo Publications, 1974), p. 73.

32. Cited in Mujeeb, *Indian Muslims*, pp. 12–25.

33. Hunter, *Indian Musalmans*, p. 141; emphasis added.

34. Ibid., p. 136.

35. Literally, a term for "father," but used descriptively—and sometimes derisively—for clerk, "a mere clerk"; in this context, an educated Bengali.

36. The singular of *ashraf*.

37. Quoted in Hardy, *Muslims*, p. 122.

38. In its "modern Turkish meaning," nation. John L. Esposito, editor and chief, *Oxford Encyclopedia of the Modern Islamic World*, Vol. 3 (New York: Oxford University Press, 1995), p. 107.

39. In this regard, he differed from the other great secularizer of Muslim "communalism," his contemporary, Amir Ali.

40. "Orientalism," as Edward Said uses it in his book of that title (London: Routledge, 1978), describes an orientation to the inferior "other"—much in vogue among the British in India, but generally benign—which includes race, but other indications of inferiority as well: an inferior religion, culture, language, literature, science, history of achievement, and so forth.

41. Quoted in Ram Gopal, *Indian Muslims: A Political History, 1858–1947* (London: Asia Publishing House, 1959), pp. 329–335.

42. Dietrich Rueschemeyer, Evelyn Huber Stephen, and John D Stephens, *Capitalist Development and Democracy* (Cambridge: Polity Press, 1996), p. 287.

43. Chandra, *Nationalism*, chap. 5.

44. "Marwari," derived from Marwar, modern Jodhpur, is a term applied to businessmen, originally migrant from what is now the state of Rajasthan.

45. Claude Markovits, *Indian Business and National Politics, 1931–1939* (Cambridge: Cambridge University Press, 1985), pp. 3, 165.

46. Vera Anstey, *The Economic Development of India* (London: Longmans, Green and Co., 1957), p. 62.

47. Named for the secretary of state for India, Edwin Montague and the viceroy, Lord Chelmsford; often contracted to Montford Reforms.

48. Yunus Samad, *A Nation in Turmoil: Nationalism and Ethnicity in Pakistan 1937–1958* (New Delhi: Sage Publications, 1995).

49. Robinson, *Separatism*.

50. Siddiqui, *Crisis*.

51. Francis Robinson, "Origins," *Foundations of Pakistan's Political Economy: Towards an Agenda for the 1990s*, William E. James and Subroto Roy, eds. (Karachi: Oxford University Press, 1992), pp. 33–34.

52. Ayesha Jalal, *The Sole Spokesman: Jinnah, the Muslim League, and the Demand for Pakistan* (Lahore: Sang-e-Mel Publications, 1992).

3

Punjab and Bengal

My objectives here are to sketch the establishment in composition and organization of the various coalitions of politically dominant classes in the British provinces of Punjab and Bengal and to position these coalitions in relation to the political future in Pakistan and India.

In 1947, most of what became Pakistan's provinces were the western districts of Punjab and the eastern districts of Bengal. Together, they contained over 80 percent of Pakistan's population. Pakistan's political future was largely determined in these provinces. What was to become most of the Indian states of Punjab and Haryana were the eastern districts of Punjab. The western districts of Bengal became the Indian state of West Bengal. Less than 15 percent of India's population lives in these states. The political future of India's states was largely determined at its Centre.

The contrast is striking. Pakistan's legacies from its imperial past were two mutually hostile, provincially centered coalitions of dominant classes, different in composition and organization, and mutually hostile: the one nationally dominant and well-served by bureaucratic authoritarianism, the other disaffected and ill-served by the absence of parliamentary democracy. In India, vast and socially complex, there were, of course, provincial differences in the composition and organization of politically dominant classes. But there was an overarching similarity. It was the product of the Congress Party: legatee of the Raj, master of the state's instrumentalities, politically dominant at India's Centre and in virtually all of its states, and in composition and organization dominated by a coalition of classes that was friendly to the development of parliamentary democracy.

PUNJAB

The political system of British Punjab had a name: the "Punjab tradition." It was a synergy of the authoritarianism of British bureaucrats and the domination of a peasant society by indigenous landlords. Between them there was a complementarity of interests in a politically quiescent peasantry. Insulated by the "mediation" of their landlords from the troublemaking of political "agitators" and "seditionists," the sons of Punjabi peasant families of "martial race" were eminently suitable recruits for the Indian army. With imperial support for their *izzat* and their incomes, Punjab's great landlords enhanced their ideological, economic, and political control over the Punjabi countryside. Largely for reasons that I have already hinted at in the introduction to this chapter, the "Punjab tradition" survived in Pakistan but not in India.

"Martial Races"

"*Jai Jawan, Jai Kisan!* [Hooray for the soldier, hooray for the peasant!] The Jats of Punjab celebrate themselves!" To their British rulers, no less, Punjab was the homeland, par excellence, of soldiers and peasants, of peasant soldiers—of the Indian army.

Britain derived no greater benefit from its subcontinental empire than the Indian army. It added substantially, perhaps crucially, to Britain's imperial land forces. It mitigated for Britain's rulers the political, social, and economic costs of recruiting or, worse, conscripting a large standing army at home to secure its vast empire overseas. Indian soldiers fought in every foreign British war from the Crimean in 1854–56. The Indian army fought in Afghanistan, Abyssinia, China, Burma, Somaliland, and South Africa. They fought Turks at Gallipoli and in Mesopotamia and William II's German army in France and Flanders. They fought Italians and Hitler's German army in North Africa and Italy. They fought Japanese in Singapore and Burma. The Indian army fielded a million and a half men for the First World War and two and a half million for the Second. Between wars, virtually all the Indian army's financial costs—in total, the largest charges by far on the Government of India's budgets—were met from Indian revenues. During imperial war times, whenever and wherever they happened to be, a substantial portion of the army's financial costs were met out of Indian revenues.

These costs included the salaries and pensions of its officer corps, which was exclusively British until 1917 and substantially British thereafter. At all times, the Indian army was a major market on the subcontinent for British goods. In India, it guarded the marches against the restiveness of Afghan tribesmen and an obsessive British fear of Russian invasion. Less problematically, it provided the *ultima ratio* for the authoritarian regime of a British civil bureaucracy.

The *jawans* of the Indian army were carefully selected, long-term enlisted recruits rather than hastily assembled, short-term conscripts. By 1914, almost half of them were recruited from Punjab's "martial races." In the Raj's post-Mutiny taxonomy of Indian "races," these were peasant castes and "communities," particularly from the temperate zone's northwest, the progeny of warriors and the fathers of sons who were physically fit, "high-spirited and intelligent, independent but respectful, straightforward, honest, manly. . . ."[1] They were drilled to be loyal to "King and Country," and this was not without effect. But British officers certainly understood that, to Indian soldiers, George V was a remote and foreign king-emperor and his country was not theirs. Theirs was a mercenary army. The British put it together and held it together by contriving, with considerable success, to conflate their soldiers' inculcated loyalties to their regiments and battalions with their primordial loyalties to their castes and religious communities, their villages, and their families. "Single-class" regiments and battalions were recruited not only from the same caste and "communities," but from the same subcastes and communities, the same groups of villages, the same families. Regimental recruiting parties visited villages with the orientation though not the ostensible disinterestedness of social and physical anthropologists.[2] They enlisted *jawans* who were hostages to their families' and villages' military fortunes—the flow of pensions to their old soldiers and money-order remittances from their serving sons, their reputations as reliable suppliers of soldiers "true to their salt." From the 1880s, honorably retired Punjabi soldiers and their families were eligible to apply for land grants in the canal colonies of western central Punjab—a considerable reward for faithful service!

Mediating between British officers and Indian soldiers on the one hand, and between them and their communities on the other, were Viceroy's Commissioned Officers, *jemadars* and *subedars*, a subordinate officer class of Indians, up-from-the-ranks, speaking the same languages and from the same "classes" as the men they led—at once, company officers and village and community elders. The army mediated between the British government and Punjab's religious "communities." The military's fondness for Jat Sikh soldiers, for example—and *keshadhari* Sikhs,[3] at that—was doubtlessly a support for Sikh orthodoxy and an impediment to the reabsorption of Sikhism into the Hinduism from which it had begun to emerge in the sixteenth century. The many Sikh regimental memorials carved into the marble walls and floors of the Golden Temple at Amritsar, the Sikh's premier house of worship, God's Court,[4] are testimony to the mutually supportive relationship between the *khalsa* (the Sikh "community") and the army. The Punjab government's solicitude for the great landed *sajjada nashins*, the heirs of Sufi saints, doubtlessly facilitated the army's recruitment of Muslim Jats. Finally, these and other "martial races" were not only a resource *from* Punjab, but a perceived resource *in* it. What if the Russians did invade? Punjab lies on the invasion route from central Asia. If contented, a peasantry of "martial races," many of whose men were trained at arms, were likely to impede such an invasion. Discontented, they might well facilitate it.

"Agriculturalist Tribes"

No less than the empire's investment and involvement in Punjab's military manpower resources and in the "martial races" that provided them was the Raj's investment in Punjab's agricultural resources and in its "agriculturalists."

Its great investment was in the canal colonies of western Punjab. Between 1885 and 1947, British engineers irrigated approximately 4 million hectares in the *doabs*, the countryside, between three of Punjab's five eponymous rivers.[5] It cost billions of rupees, but it turned a virtual wasteland into the greatest revenue-producing, most prosperous, and commercially productive agricultural area on the subcontinent. It was the Raj's masterwork of modern irrigation—its monument, at once, to its benevolence and to its awesome capacity to direct the flow of great rivers, to master the earth itself. "Look on my works, ye mighty. . . ."[6] Monuments are political statements.

And it was on political criteria, at least in part, that the Raj dispensed its benevolence. With only limited success, it granted land specifically for the breeding of horses and camels to serve the army. But, generally, British benevolence was meant to nurture the social status quo. Except for Rajputs, "more accustomed to fight than to till,"[7] the peasant proprietors of "martial races" were also considered to be conscientious and industrious farmers. Most of the canal colonies' "squares of land" were granted to them. The government settled them in villages where it attempted to replicate, as far as possible, the social order of the villages of eastern and central Punjab from which the settlers had migrated. The canal colonies were to be used not to undermine but to fortify the existing social structure of rural Punjab.

It was also the structure of British rule in Punjab. Canal colony lands were not distributed to Punjab's landless "menial" castes, for example. That would have disturbed the social order. Canal colony lands were granted to honorably retired old soldiers, "yeoman" (well-to-do farmers), great landlords, and *sajjada nashins* of Muslim shrines. Apart from peasant proprietor grantees, many of these were neither conscientious and industrious farmers, nor farmers at all. Many of them did not settle in the canal colonies, but became their absentee rentiers. They were granted canal colony lands not to farm but to fortify the structure of British rule. If they were great landlords of great political influence, and in danger of losing their lands, government even provided courts of wards to rescue them from their profligacy and mismanagement.[8] Thus:

in parts of the Punjab, society was still semi-feudal in character, and there were obvious advantages [to the government] in propitiating the landed gentry with valuable grants of land; and the hope was cherished that this would help to restore the influence of a class which had been seriously impaired by recurring partitions of family estates *and by the rise to power of a prosperous and educated middle class in the towns.*[9]

It was this class of townsmen whom the British government feared in Punjab as in India generally. In Punjab, they threatened to undermine the social order on which British rule was based. It will not surprise observers of European anti-semitism that the threat was personified in the figure of "the moneylender": the urban, Hindu *sahukar*.

In 1886, S. S. Thorburn, a British civil servant, published "his remarkable book" *Mussalmans and Money-lenders in the Punjab*. Its title is significant. Muslims, who formed almost 60 percent of rural Punjab, were its moneylenders' greatest debtors; their urban creditors were mostly Hindus of the "trading castes." A decade later, Thorburn submitted his *Report on Peasant Indebtedness and Land Alienation to Money-Lenders in Parts of the Rawalpindi Division* (of northern Punjab). Both "vividly depicted" the increasing dominance of urban moneylenders over the countryside. "Exhaustive official enquiry . . . established beyond a doubt that the moneylender was slowly eating his way into the heart of the village." In the decade from about 1875, the yearly average of contracted mortgages more than trebled and the area under mortgages more than doubled. The head of Punjab's provincial government, its lieutenant-governor, was distressed. "Transfers of land were proceeding in all districts in an increasing ratio, and in many with dangerous rapidity."[10]

Thorburn's government addressed the danger, in its Alienation of Land Act of 1900. The act was the Raj's compromise in Punjab with its earliest and most profound contribution to the development of capitalist agriculture in its subcontinental empire: the general application of the rule of a "free market" in agricultural land. Like most regimes, the Raj was informed by ideologies. But like most successful regimes, it would not be led by them. Again, in its imperial context, the Alienation of Land Act was of a piece with contemporary British attempts to reduce the bureaucratic empire's dependence on educated Hindu middle classes: to reinvent India's landlords as its "natural leaders" and to "balance" in imperial favor the interests of Muslim good families against those of their Hindu counterparts.

The Alienation of Land Act divided Punjab's population into "agriculturalist tribes" and "non-agriculturalist tribes." For various reasons, including Muslim sensitivities, "tribe" was preferred to "caste." The Islam of its Prophet tolerated tribes. Castes were, by Muslim definition, Hindu. In Indian reality, however, there were Muslim castes, and caste—Hindu, Muslim, and Sikh—was the act's dividing line between "agriculturalists" and "non-agriculturalists." Simply, the act barred families that were officially deemed to be of "non-agriculturalist" castes from acquiring agricultural land, either through purchase or through debt forfeiture. These "non-agriculturalist," "trading castes" were overwhelmingly Hindu. Subsequent amendments to the act, many in reaction to the agricultural depression of the interwar years, protected "agriculturalists" from being sued by professional moneylenders for arrears, and from their claims on the tools, animals, and legacies of "agriculturalists."

The complex of issues that motivated the Land Alienation Act are well summarized in Van den Dungen's compendium of a survey on the question of land alienation taken among his officers by Punjab's lieutenant-governor in 1888–89:

The landowners . . . represented a political force in the country; and they were being displaced by moneylenders, men of no political significance. The landowning tribes were the foundation of British rule; they had a vast superiority in numbers; they supplied the man-power for the native army; they were the hereditary proprietors of the soil; they were, in many cases, war-like with traditions and a history; they were sturdy, courageous and independent; and if discontented and given an opportunity they would fight. . . . On the other hand, the trading castes contributed nothing to the stability of the state and little to its revenues. Their numbers were insignificant and they were feeble in spirit and physique. They were both feared and despised by the landowners whose social inferiors they had often been before British rule. Far from being able to fight, the trading castes required protection, so that they were a source of weakness rather than strength in time of danger And in any case, their loyalty to Government was only doubtful.[11]

In a word, then, while solicitude for Punjab's indebted "agriculturalists" was the ostensible reason for the Alienation of Land Act, underlying that solicitude were calculations of British political interests. The government feared that the indebtedness of "agriculturalists'" to urban, professional moneylenders would undermine the social system on which British rule was based. It would threaten the Raj's defense of its northwestern frontier, its access to Punjab's military manpower, and its considerable investment in the province's agriculture. I have already alluded to this rural social system. What was it, and how did it support British imperialism?

The "Mediation" of Landlords

The best answers to these questions are in David Gilmartin's masterly *Empire and Islam*:[12]

However varied the forms of local social organization that the British found as they established their rule, local organization drew widely in rural Punjab on idioms of *biradari* [brotherhood] solidarity—idioms that suggested the importance of genealogy in the construction of local systems of organization and authority.[13]

The British politicized these "idioms" and incorporated them into the imperial system, most notably by preferring in its law courts the application of personal law that was local and customary to either Hindu or Muslim injunctive scripture, and by appointing *biradari* headmen—creating them, if need be—to local administrative positions. These headmen were meant to "mediate" between, on the one hand, the peasant proprietors and occupancy tenants of their "brotherhoods" and, on the other, "higher authority." Particularly, though not exclusively, in western Punjab, that higher authority belonged to great lay landlords or great landed *sajjada nashins*, who gave economic, political, genealogical, and/or devotional direction to their dependents and "mediated" between them and the highest authority: the *sarkar* (government).

At every point in the system there were conflicts: of interests, personalities, jurisdictions. The *sarkar* was the mediator-in-chief. The moneylender fuelled the social system of rural Punjab, but was not of it. In it, as an urban rentier—resourceful and knowledgeable, however despised, a caste fellow of scheming district court *vakils*—the *sahukar* could only weaken the "idioms of *biradari*" on which the system was based: British rule, landlord dominance, and peasant quiescence:

as long as the masses were contented . . . professional agitators would be powerless; but agricultural discontent would open the ears of the people to the various forms of political organization which were coming into existence.[14]

There seems little doubt but that among Punjab's "agriculturalists" the major beneficiaries of the Alienation of Land Act were landlords, particularly the great Muslim landlords of the western districts. They were already well established when Punjab became part of British India. Generous government land grants in the canal colonies increased their establishments. The Alienation of Land Act, according to one British source, was spoken of by "The big [Muslim] landlords . . . as their economic salvation, and probably it has to some extent protected them from the results of their extravagance and made it easier to swallow up their neighbours."[15] Ironically, much of the swallowing-up was done through debt. In effect, the act took business away from the *sahukars* and gave it to the "agriculturalist moneylenders," who were generally "yeomen" and landlords. To the disadvantage of their urban competitors, "agriculturalist" moneylenders were enabled by the Land Alienation Act to risk lending up to the value of the holdings that were mortgaged to them. On default, they could do what was prohibited to the Hindu *sahukar*: foreclose the mortgage and take possession of the land. Twenty-five years after the passage of the act, the Punjab government estimated that 75 percent or more of the land mortgaged was by "agriculturalist" moneylenders.[16] "[S]ince the Land Alienation Act gave him his chance," a great landlord of the southwestern district of Dera Ghazi Khan "has sometimes doubled his acres." To the north in Muzaffargarh:

the bulk of the land is held by the rich men, who are increasing their possessions. . . . Society . . . consists of [these] land-holding squires, whose local authority is only limited by their mutual jealousies; and of their retainers and tenants, who, holding no share in the land which they till, and knowing that an appearance of wealth will lead to exaction from their feudal or spiritual masters [i.e., their *pirs*], are content to lead a hand to mouth existence.[17]

Rural indebtedness was being perpetuated by "agriculturalist" moneylenders, and there was growing inequality of landholdings in western Punjab in favor of noncultivating landlords. This was politically acceptable to the imperial government. It did not impinge upon, and perhaps reinforced, the *biradari*-based, "local loyalties of mediated authority"[18] on which British power in the Punjab was based. The government, one British officer observed, was "purposely creating a 'Junker' class" of Muslim landlords. Their "illegal acquisitions of land" and "ever growing latifundia" were unlikely to be checked because they "defend[ed] the British against . . . urban representatives in the [Punjab provincial] legislature" and "the government considered their support crucial in the passing of 'official' legislation."[19]

The Punjab National Unionist Party and the Alienation of Land Act

The National Unionist Party of Punjab, founded in 1923, had its "Junkers," no doubt: in its twenty-five-year history it had three leaders, and all were great Muslim landlords of western Punjab—and British knights. But the Unionists were less a "Junker" party, less a party at all, than an inter-"communal" interest group of "Junkers" and "Junker" factions. Whatever their individual and competitive concerns, these great landlords shared an interest, complementary with the government's, in giving legislative representation to Punjab's "local loyalties of mediated authority" and collaborating with the British in sustaining them. The Alienation of Land Act was the Unionist "charter."

Sikh and Hindu landlords were Unionist members and legislators. Sir Chhotu Ram, a Jat Hindu landlord of eastern Punjab, was with Sir Fazli Husain, a Muslim "Junker" from the west, a cofounder of the party. During the interwar agricultural depression, the Unionists and the government joined in supplementing the Land Alienation Act with additional measures to protect "agriculturalists"—*against urban, professional moneylenders*. Unionists and government jointly opposed Congress, which in Punjab was the party of urban Hindus, moneylenders, *vakils*, and "agitators." They opposed the party of Sikh revivalism, the Akalis (the Godly), as representing "communally" focused politics as opposed to the Unionists' politics which were "communally" diffuse, local, and mediated. For much the same reason, the three Muslim landlords who led the Unionists, all "communal" politicians and members of the Muslim League, opposed the entrance of the League and its "Pakistan" into Punjabi politics.

Unionists fought against and decimated the League in the 1937 provincial elections and formed the first elected government of Punjab. In the guise of Leaguers, Unionists colonized and captured the leadership of the urban-based League. In 1937, Jinnah signed a pact with the Unionist leader, Sir Sikander Hyat, that in effect gave him control over the League in Punjab. In return, Sikander agreed only to enrol Muslim Unionist legislators in the League and to recognize Jinnah as the "sole spokesman" for Muslim interests in negotiations with the British at India's Centre. It was a clear win for Sikander.

Leading up to the 1946 elections, Jinnah tried unsuccessfully to pressure Sikander's successor to rename as the Muslim League the agglomeration of his Unionist colleagues who were Muslims. Most local League leaders in Punjab's countryside were Unionist landlords who decided, for whatever reasons, to swim with the rushing "Pakistan" tide, but only to their own shore. Officially, the League campaigned to recruit mass membership and to establish local party units that were independent of local "mediatory hierarchies." But "most League leaders showed little interest" in transforming the League into a popular party. "At the local level the power of most [League leaders] continued to depend on the mediatory structures that had long served the Unionists." Indeed, most League leaders were Unionists who had changed their colors—but not their spots. In Punjab's districts: "the development of League influence . . . generally followed, not the League's propaganda campaign but the shifting pattern of district-level factions, which in turn reflected the underlying 'tribal' and mediatory structure of the . . . colonial political system."[20]

The great, landed *sajjada nashins* validated that secular "communalist," Mohammad Ali Jinnah, as an authentic champion of Islam and gave Islamic sanction to "Pakistan"—*dar al-Islam* de facto. For many of their followers, voting for the League in 1946 was thus made an obligation of faith that bonded them to the wider Muslim "community": "But these votes were still cast within the structure of a political system largely shaped by local 'tribal' idioms. Within this context, the colonial system established by the British, the battle for Pakistan was contested."[21] In the 1946 provincial elections, the League and its "Pakistan" won seventy-three of the eighty-six Muslim seats and about 65 percent of the Muslim vote.

West and East

My concern with British imperialism's legacies to Punjab's post-Partition political fortunes has shifted my narrative westward, to the germ of those legacies for Pakistan: the synergy between bureaucratic authoritarianism and landlord domination in a peasant society. It was from this germ that a coalition of dominant classes unfriendly to the establishment of parliamentary democracy grew. Now, in this section's concluding paragraphs, I must shuttle between west and east to consider the question of why such an antidemocratic coalition did *not* develop in those districts of Punjab which became a state—and in 1966, states—of the Indian Union.

To the formation of an antidemocratic coalition in Pakistan, the obvious legacies of the British regime in Punjab were the perpetuation and enlargement of socioeconomic and ideological systems that were dominated by great landlords—secular magnates and *pirs*—and the institutionalization of this domination in a political system invented and managed by an imperial government. This domination by landlords was all the more pervasive and enduring for not being binary. The pattern was not of "us" and "them." Rather, it was of an elaborate rural tapestry of dominance in which strands of dependence, habit, factionalism, patronage and clienthood, violence and coercion, inherited loyalties and hatreds, kinship and religious devotion were intertwined. In this society, landed magnates dominated not only their tenants, but their countryside. As for identifying "them," the Land Alienation Act did the job.

The political microcosm of Punjabi society was the National Unionist Party, in which landlords "represented" the interests of "agriculturalists," the vast majority of whom were peasants and about half of these, tenants. Redistributive land reform in their favor, needless to say, was nowhere on the Unionist agenda. Nor, as I have indicated, were the Unionists—except in name—a political party. To the end, in 1947, they "remained a combination of local, factional leaders—a powerful combination, it is true—but one without an independent, institutional identity in the localities."[22] Land reform was not on the Muslim League's agenda either. Nor was it a political party of any consequence in Punjab. Apart from a small and politically marginalized membership in Punjab's towns, the League was not a Punjabi party. It came to Punjab at endgame and from outside. Jinnah understood that, without Punjab, "Pakistan"—whatever "Pakistan" he had in mind—could only be a fantasy.[23] He insinuated the League into Punjab's politics by working through its landlords—and these landlords then took over the League. It entered the Punjabi countryside in the 1940s, not by building an organization, but with the combination of an apparently irresistible popular slogan—"Pakistan"—and the support of ex-Unionist landlords and *pirs* whose interests were not in resisting it. Instead, they made themselves and their "mediatory authority" available to "Pakistan" and to the League.

I argued earlier, and I will again, that land reforms, however moderate, so long as they free a critical mass of peasants from the control of their landlords, are a prerequisite to the development of parliamentary democracy in a peasant society. The organization most appropriate to negotiate land reforms that support the development of parliamentary democracy, that cater for the demands of "have-nots" while reassuring "haves," is the political party. What was to become West Pakistan had no such political party. West Pakistan's legacy from the "Punjab tradition" was the want of the one political organization that *might* have mobilized popular support for land reforms, on the back, possibly, of an appeal to have in the Islamic Republic some degree of Islamic social justice. West Pakistan was born with no political party that might have carried it over the threshold to parliamentary democracy. It had no political party that *might* have offered a political alternative to the domestication in Pakistan of the bureaucratic authoritarianism of British Punjab.

The chances of such a party coming into existence in British Punjab were reduced by the Alienation of Land Act. It not only centered politics in the "mediatory" local societies of the countryside, it opened to urban Muslims, as it closed to urban Hindus, a stake in these politics—"balance and rule," again! Essentially, the act was class-based, but it was also insidiously, politically "communal." It put a barrier between the interests of urban, middle-class Hindus and Muslims. It recruited Muslim townsmen into the "mediatory" political system of the countryside. It gave them a vested interest in being Muslim. Muslim *rais*—eminent townsmen—for example, were often landlords.

The privilege of acquiring land permanently would be denied to the educated Hindu because his membership of a trading caste ensured that he would be ranked with the money-lender; but it would not be denied to most educated Muslims for their [caste] appellations ensured, quite apart from their occupations, that they would be placed among the agricultural tribes and hence free to acquire land.[24]

Coupled with the lack of a popular political party and no land reforms, militarism was another of imperialism's legacies to Pakistan's nondemocratic future. "The rural roots of Pakistani militarism"[25] were dug by Indian army recruiters in the agriculturally infertile areas of northwestern Punjab, and dug deeper by the British policy of granting land to soldier-settlers in the canal colonies. More than 60 percent of the canal colonies went to Pakistan. Clive Dewey's suggestion is well-taken: "The deep and enduring roots which the military have sunk into thousands of Punjabi villages *may* be the key to military dominance in Pakistan."[26] The roots are of material and nonmaterial interests: salaries and pensions, opportunities for employment and advancement, training in remunerative post-enlistment occupations, markets for goods and services, identification with an organization that values manliness, *izzat,* order, loyalty, probity, devotion to duty, comradeship, cleanliness.

It is also correct that the roots of militarism were entwined with those of Punjab's "mediatory" political system. Indeed, one of the great services that "mediation" performed for its British arbiters was recruitment for the Indian army and the maintenance of a peasantry ever amenable to its sons' recruitment: "loyal," disciplined to authority, benignly Muslim, financially dependent on military service, quiescent, and apolitical. It is also correct that apart from these political roots there were none other. Militarism and "mediation" may have survived by default. Islam in Punjab did *not* as a social system "operate independently of the state."[27] Popular Islam, the Islam of landed *pirs*, exercised its political authority through "mediatory" politics. Neither was there in Punjab, nor in its immigrant Muslim League, a political party any more able to restore civilian political control over the military than it was to impose itself on the "mediatory" authority of landlords.

Invidious comparisons with India are unavoidable. Things were different in the districts of Punjab that went to India. Some of the differences were local. In neither central nor eastern Punjab were there the great landed magnates who dominated the countryside in the west. In central Punjab, Sikh society had been leveled to some extent by Punjab's last, independent Sikh prince, Ranjit Singh [1780–1839], to a society that was largely of peasant proprietors. Sir Chhotu Ram was a landlord, but the Zamandara League that he united with the Unionists was a "popular rural political organization," largely of Hindu Jat peasant proprietors.[28] In 1947, when the subcontinent was partitioned, migrants were fitted into the different patterns of land tenure that prevailed in west and east Punjab. Muslim tenants who migrated westward became tenants in Pakistan. Sikh peasant proprietors who migrated eastward became peasant proprietors in India, commonly of smaller holdings than those they had vacated, particularly in the canal colonies. The acreage vacated by Muslims in the east and redistributed to Sikh refugees was about 70 percent of the acreage vacated by Sikhs in the west, and generally of poorer quality. So the agrarian society of eastern Punjab was further leveled by Partition.[29]

Sikh Jats were perhaps the most militarized "community" in British India. But they were less enveloped in Punjab's "mediatory" politics than their Muslim caste-fellows. Their peasant proprietorship, the absence of great landed magnates in central Punjab, and, perhaps, the egalitarian élan of Jat Sikhism gave them some measure of independence. The Unionists' Sikh collaborators, the Khalsa National Party, counted for far less in the Sikh countryside than the Akalis. They were factionalized, turbulent, and opportunistic but nonetheless widely accepted as the authentic representative of Sikh "communalism," which was generally anglophobe and anti-Muslim.

The Congress Party in British Punjab was a factionalized party of urban Hindus. Nonetheless, its factions reflected, to some extent, and suffered from their national party's official non-"communalist" ideology and the solicitude for land-holding peasants on which the National Congress's rural alliances were based. As a result, the Punjabi Congress was outflanked on its Hindu front by unambiguously "communal" *sabhas,* and on its peasant front by Unionists, Akalis, and Zamandara Leaguers. Only in 1946, in popular anticipation of Punjab's impending partition and the incorporation of its eastern half in the Indian Union, did the Punjabi Congress make a creditable showing. It won almost every Hindu seat in the election for the provincial assembly: 51, up from 17 in 1937.

Congress party-building in eastern Punjab was largely a post-Partition phenomenon. It was accompanied by bitter factional warfare. To keep it in check, there were frequent interventions by the National Congress's "high command." Factional alignments and realignments among Punjabi Congressmen were recurrent, as were persistent eruptions and inexplicable subsidences of personal animosities among factional politicians. Within the Punjabi Congress there was violence and sabotage, charges and countercharges of incompetence, corruption, and worse. Almost from the beginning, the Akalis were major contributors to the tumult by demanding yet another "communal" partition of Punjab: to produce a Sikh majority state from Indian Punjab's northwestern districts. Jostling for places in the Congress *raj*-in-becoming, Congress's factions came from everywhere. The Akalis were more or less allied with Congress in 1946, or at least allied against the League, and they briefly merged into Congress in 1956. Some Hindu *sabhas,* most notably factions of the Arya Samaj, went into the Punjabi Congress. Zamandara League partisans became Congressmen after Chhotu Ram's death in 1945. During Congress's tumultuous first decades as Punjab's ruling party, its chief minister most responsible for giving the party its presence in the countryside was Pratap Singh Kairon, a Sikh and a former Unionist. He was murdered in 1965.

The underdevelopment of a Congress party in Punjab complicated its incorporation into the new Congress *raj*. But the job was done. And it was done from Delhi. At India's Centre, the Congress Party was the British Raj's true successor. True, in the sense that unlike the Muslim League government in Karachi, Congress inherited a going concern and was capable of taking over its management. Only its edges had been torn away. Nehru's government could, and in 1951 did, take an unruly Punjab under the central government's administration. The Congress government in Delhi could, and did, demand of the Indian military, including its Punjabi regiments, the continuation of its subordination to civilian government. It could and did extend Congress's coalition of dominant classes, of urban professionals and landed peasants, to Punjab. Much of the factional jostling in Punjab was over control of the coalition's levers. The system in which they operated was a rough-and-tumble parliamentary democracy. Nehru's Congress government incorporated Punjab as a state in the Indian Union and laid the same foundations for parliamentary democracy there as it did in all its states. Punjab was brought under Congress's "one-party dominance." Land reforms that favored landed peasants and were more generous to landlords than to the landless were legislated.[30] Parliamentary democracy based on adult suffrage was established at the provincial level. In 1966, the Congress government of Prime Minister Indira Gandhi acceded to the Sikh's long-standing demand for *Punjabi Suba*: in effect, the bifurcation of Punjab to create from its northwestern districts a new, Sikh-majority Punjab.[31] Nowhere in India was parliamentary democracy better established as the political system of the landed peasantry than it was in Punjab. In contrast to Pakistan, there was in India a political center committed to the establishment of parliamentary democracy. And the center held.

BENGAL

For a century and a half until 1911, when the Government of India moved its capital to Delhi, the British province of Bengal was the center of the Indian empire. Calcutta was the British empire's "second city," the capital city of the Raj, the center of British commerce and trade on the subcontinent, its great port on the Bay of Bengal, and its entrepôt to China. Before Bengal's first partition in 1905, the province comprised what are now approximately the Indian states of West Bengal, Bihar, Orissa, and Assam and the republic of Bangladesh. In 1901, the population of this 500-thousand-square kilometer province was about 80 million. Of the Indian empire's subjects, almost one in three lived in Bengal province; of these, about 60 percent were Bengali-speakers.

Most Bengalis lived and worked on the land. Agriculture was Bengal's major source of wealth and its government's major source of revenue. Bengal's was the first extensive countryside to be ruled by a hierarchy of British bureaucrats, a "steel frame" contrived to turn agricultural wealth into state revenue. The first major attempt by the British East India Company to systematize and maximize the assessment and collection of agricultural revenue was in Bengal: the Permanent Settlement of 1793. The settlement initiated and embodied the Raj's most profound and enduring change to Indian agricultural tenure. It generalized the status of agricultural land as an owned, alienable, and defeasible commodity—a good of the marketplace. The settlement was also the imperial government's first, and one of its least successful, attempts to align its interests with those of great Indian landlords—even where they had to be created.

Zamindars and *Bhadralok*

The tenurial systems of the company's predecessor regimes in Bengal were characterized by the presence of land-*holding* intermediaries of various sorts—revenue farmers, most notably—between the *raj* and its peasants. They are known, generically, as *zamindars*. In 1793, the company's governor-general, Lord Cornwallis, imagining a progressive and loyal class of Indian squires, transformed these intermediaries into land-*owners*. In British Bengal, *zamindar* came to mean landlord.[32] Over the decades, many of the original *zamindar* families, Hindu and Muslim, disappeared from the land, not least by way of a pitiless marketplace and their incapacity to cope with it. Their lands were sold, divided, mortgaged, partially resold and tenanted, partitioned among sons, partially subdivided, mortgaged and resold again, subtenanted, sharecropped, partitioned among grandsons, and so forth. No squirearchy, but a tenurial crazy quilt was the product. Over it, ownership rights were enjoyed primarily by a new class of rentiers—thousands of them, great and small, magnates and pensioners, village gentry and townspeople.

The Permanent Settlement failed as an imperial scheme to create a new class of improving squires, landed "natural leaders" loyal to the Raj. It succeeded, however, in serving the interests of a new class of rentiers. They varied widely in wealth and "culture," but they shared an economic interest in the perpetuation of the settlement's *zamindari* system. Here were the *bhadralok,* Bengal's gentle folk, one of modern India's first and most enduring dominant classes. To be sure, they were not only rentiers, but at their grass roots, that is what they were. And as a class, they behaved accordingly. But, what else were they?

Overwhelmingly, they were Hindus, as were most of Bengal's rent-collectors and moneylenders. In India, rent-collecting and moneylending are allied professions. Crucially for Bengal's history, most of their tenants and debtors were Muslims. Among Hindus, the *bhadralok* were overwhelmingly of their highest castes—Brahmins, Kayasthas, and Baidyas—and to few of them was their place in the Bengali caste hierarchy a matter of indifference. Poor *bhadralok,* their salaries supplemented by small rental incomes, eked out a livelihood as *mofussil* (countryside) schoolmasters or clerks in the city. Rich *bhadralok,* blessed with large rental incomes, lived in great town houses, prepared their sons for the ICS examination in London, flourished at the Bar, patronized factions of the Brahmo Samaj, involved themselves in municipal or university politics, wrote poetry, plays, and novels. Calcutta was their city. They were glorifiers of Bengali Hindu culture, incubators and carriers of the "Bengal renaissance" of the late-nineteenth and early twentieth centuries.

With regard to the British, the *bhadralok* incubated a love–hate relationship. An English-language education—the higher the better, and preferably in the law—was the sine qua non of upper-class *bhadralok*. The University of Calcutta was theirs. Its Hindu College was venerable: founded in 1818. The *bhadralok* resented the Raj for frustrating Victoria's post-Mutiny promise to allow qualified Indians to "be freely and impartially admitted to offices in our service." They admired the British for their science and their organization, and feared them for their power and influence. They hated the British for their racism and their disdain for "the Bengali" as effeminate and feline, and they half-believed—at once, with shame and loathing—that this British stereotype mirrored reality. The earliest articulations of Indian nationalism emerged from this ambivalence. The *bhadralok* were among its earliest articulators. It was distinctly, if not exclusively, an elite Hindu Indian nationalism.

From the mid-nineteenth century, it was articulated in the English and Bengali writings of *bhadralok* litterateurs. Of these, Bankim Chandra Chatterjee [1838–94] and Romesh Chunder Dutt [1848–1909] were among the most famous and well read. Their "historical romances" were remembered thus by the late Nirad C. Chaudhuri, that most contrary and politically incorrect *bhadralok*:

[They] glorified Hindu rebellion against Muslim rule and showed the Muslims in a correspondingly poor light. Chatterji was positively and fiercely anti-Muslim. We [boys from *bhadralok* families] were eager readers of these romances and we readily absorbed their spirit.[33]

Of ordinary Hindu peasants and artisans, the *bhadralok* were no more admiring or solicitous than they were of Muslims. The *chhotolok*, the "little people" of Bengal's villages, were caste and cultural inferiors whose Hinduism was theologically unenlightened and ritually degraded. Moreover, they were tenants, or many of them were. And in British India the *bhadralok* never wavered in support of the tenurial system that protected their rents, the Permanent Settlement. "Official [British] proposals for the extension of mass primary education in rural areas were also opposed by the Hindu *bhadralok*."[34] In much the same light of "mixed concern and contempt" as they saw their Muslim tenants, the *bhadralok* viewed their "low caste Hindu tenants." They, too, were "livestock."[35]

The "Bengal Renaissance" of the nineteenth century—a synthesis of European science, ideology, and organization with a revitalized Hinduism, and notably bereft of any Islamic influence—radiated across India from Calcutta, as did the first substantial class of native-born, English-language-educated professional men and subordinate civil servants. They incubated and dispersed the earliest imaginings of a modern Hindu Indian nationalism.

Lest this imagined nationalism capture imaginations further and wider than Bengal and its *bhadralok,* that most capable viceroy and remarkable person

George Nathaniel Curzon ordered the partition in 1905 of the sprawling Bengal province. It was bifurcated in such a way as to divide its Bengali population between a truncated Hindu-majority province in the west and a new Muslim-majority province in the east—"balance and rule!" "[O]lympian in his detachment and adamantine in his disregard of public clamour . . . ," Curzon insisted that the partition was only a "necessary administrative measure."[36]

> For forms of government let fools contest.
> Whate'er is best administered is best.[37]

The Bengali imaginers of an Indian nation correctly disbelieved Curzon's insistence and deplored the authoritarian sentiment that motivated it—at least insofar as the authority was not theirs. They were not democrats. Theirs was a conflict in deadly earnest between the Hindu Indian nationalism of their invention, a sapling of imagined roots, and a viceroy who was set upon uprooting it. Partition was anathematized at massive rallies in Calcutta. It spawned a "pistol cult"[38] among young Bengalis intent upon assassinating British officials and thereby asserting their "manliness" against the British caricature of Bengali "effeminacy." Partition inspired a boycott of British cloth that gave the movement its name and its slogan: *swadeshi*, things of our own country. Bengal's partition was the first *cause célèbre* of Hindu Indian nationalism defined as Indian nationalism. Its definers, propagandists, and organizers were overwhelmingly upper-class and high-caste Hindu professionals, and they were disproportionately Bengali.

The partition of Bengal in 1905 was the *bhadralok's* political moment. Curzon had blundered, overplayed the "balance-and-rule" card. For any empire that relied heavily for its management on the benign indifference of its peasants and the collaboration of their betters, the *swadeshi* movement presaged a threat. In 1911, at his splendid "Delhi Durbar," George V announced the Government of India's capitulation. The Bengali-speaking areas of Bengal would be reunified as one province. Like patriotism, nationalism can be—and has as often as not been—the refuge of scoundrels and self-seekers. But, whatever its underlying definition, its Hinduness, whatever particular *bhadralok* interests were hidden behind its banners and obscured in its sloganeering, Indian nationalism—a quarter-century after the Indian National Congress's first meeting—confronted the imperialism that denied its existence, and won.

It was a particular victory for the *bhadralok*. Under the banner of Indian nationalism, they regained for their Calcutta its provincial dominance[39]—dominance as *the* Bengali cultural center and over government service, education, commerce, and the practice of law. They protected the Permanent Settlement's *zamindari* system. From the early decades of the twentieth century, the British government began to turn some of the empire's housekeeping functions over to municipal councils and provincial assemblies. Their memberships were increasingly Indian, mostly Hindu, and increasingly empowered and selected by an expanding electorate. In effect, the reunification of Bengal protected the Hindu *zamindaris* of eastern Bengal from the regulation of a government of Muslim populist politicians in a new Muslim-majority province.

Apart from the *bhadralok,* the only other group articulate in its support of Bengal's reunification were the Marwaris.[40] These were expatriate, Hindi-speaking traders from what is now Rajasthan. They were *baniyas,* Hindu and Jain: the latter were members of what, in effect, has become a Hindu sect.[41] It was not Bengalis but Marwaris who were Calcutta's Indian "merchant princes." And they too had interests in eastern Bengal, most notably in jute production, which they were loath to entrust to a Muslim government in Dacca (now Dhaka). The Marwaris, it is fair to say, are among the most Hindu of Hindus.

A Muslim Coalition

In the *bhadralok* scheme of things, Muslims, were doubly damned: retrospectively, as the conquerors and defilers of Hindu India and the villains of *bhadralok* historical fiction; contemporaneously, as the enemies of their Indian nationalism, supporters of partition, and allies of the British. After 1905, "a cold dislike for the Muslim settled down in [*bhadralok*] hearts, putting an end to all real intimacy of relationship."[42] For about a decade after 1911, Bengal's dominant class alliance was of *bhadralok* and Marwaris: Hindu nationalist, anti-Muslim, and anti-democratic. Nirad Chaudhuri overstates the case when he recalls the *swadeshi* movement as "essentially a movement of Hindu revival."[43] It was more than that—but it was that, too.

Most prominent among the supporters of Bengal's partition in 1905 were members of the nascent Bengali Muslim professional middle class, and most notable among those who were compelled to bear the cost of overpriced *swadeshi* goods were Muslim peasants. The *bhadralok* victory of 1911 gave an unintended impetus to the imagining, inventing, and secularizing of Muslim "communalism" and nationalism in Bengal. A coalition of dominant Bengali Muslim classes came into being that was to impact both on the future of Bengal and on the nondevelopment of parliamentary democracy in Pakistan.

We have already encountered a coalition, or coalitions, of Muslim peasants and artisans and their *ulama.* Centered in Bengal, the Wahhabis and *Faraidis* were hardly coalitions of *dominant* classes, but they contributed significantly to the shaping of this coalition among Bengali Muslims. Their nascent urban middle class found their landed peasant partners in a countryside whose political ground had been prepared by Wahhabis and *Faraidis.* It was they who first coupled "community" and class for Muslim villagers: Islamic anti-imperialism and puritanism on the one hand, with rebellion against the exactions of Hindu landlords supported by the imperial state on the other. The coupling required no elaborate theoretical or theological explanation. It was made of the reality of peasant life in Bengal—there, on the ground. Its landlords were the creatures of the Permanent Settlement or they were British indigo planters. Both were protected in their property rights—which included the right to exploit peasants—by British courts and bureaucrats. Adding insult to injury, Hindu landlords forbade the slaughtering of cows, for food or religious sacrifice, by their Muslim tenants and assessed them for the maintenance of Hindu shrines and temples.

In, but not of, Bengal, at the peak of its social pyramid, was a miniscule Urdu-speaking, well-to-do *ashraf.* At the pyramid's broad base was an impoverished and powerless Muslim peasantry. At points midway between them were Muslims of good family. Many of them were landed peasants, *jotedars,* or of landed-peasant background. Most of them were "backward" in providing their sons with an education appropriate to higher bureaucratic and professional employment in British India. Indeed, it was from this situation peculiar to Bengali Muslim good families that Sir Saiyid Ahmad and his British allies generalized the myth of Muslim "backwardness."

Inspired by Hunter's *Indian Musalmans* and the realpolitik of "balance and rule," the British government encouraged Western education among the sons of these Muslim families and favored their employment. By 1905, there was an emergent and growing Muslim professional middle class in Bengal. It was largely to their advantage that the province was partitioned and a capital city for them, in Dacca, established, separate from Calcutta and its overweening Hindu *bhadralok.* To be sure there were Muslim professionals, mostly of Calcutta, who shared with their Hindu colleagues an interest against partition and in favor of reunification. But to Muslim professionals as a class, the events of 1905 to 1911 left them feeling drubbed and trumped by the *bhadralok* and betrayed by the British. "Balance and rule," in Bengal as elsewhere, but perhaps more so in Bengal, helped to effect a separation of nascent Muslim professional middle classes from their well-established, newly nationalist Hindu counterparts. The Hindu nationalism of the *bhadralok* pushed, "balance and rule" pulled.

The reunification of Bengal in 1911 hastened Muslim political organization in Bengal, in opposition to the Hindu *bhadralok* and in reposition to the Raj that had capitulated to them. Although the political advantages of belonging to a religious "community" favored by the government were theirs to share, the Muslim professional middle and landlord classes were united (or reunited) much less in Bengal than in northern India by reservations and weightage. They shared no past, real or imagined, as service gentry. Many of the Muslim professional men came from *jotedar* backgrounds. The most powerful opponents of the Permanent Settlement's *zamindari* system were Muslim *jotedars.* Muslim *zamindars,* no keener on extinction than their Hindu counterparts, were few: Urdu-speaking *ashraf,* culturally remote from the commonality of Muslim Bengalis, if not contemptuous and fearful of them. For their political allies in the countryside, the Muslim professional middle classes turned to their roots: the *jotedars.* Enemies of the *bhadralok* qua lords of the land were thus joined to the Muslim middle-class enemies of the *bhadralok* qua lords of the city.

In 1906, at the inaugural meeting in Dacca of the All-India Muslim League, one of its first resolutions had been to applaud the partition of Bengal and condemn the Hindu agitation against it.[44] But having hosted the League's formation, its branch in Bengal dissolved into a pastime for the province's *ashraf*.[45] They had "no effective ties or relations" with the Bengali Muslim peasantry and sought none.[46] As elsewhere, the League in Bengal was an agglomeration of notables' factions and was of little political significance until "Pakistan" was re-imagined in the 1940s. The development of a popularly based, Muslim politics in Bengal, a politics that would best the *bhadralok* in the provincial assembly maneuvering that had been their forte, was in no small measure the accomplishment of Abdul Kasem Fazlul Huq: "an outsider in the sophisticated world of the . . . [*ashraf*] who dominated Muslim politics in Calcutta."[47]

The Lucknow Pact of 1916 framed the world of "communal" politics in which Fazlul Huq came to prominence. As the pact, later incorporated in the Government of India Act of 1919, weighted provincial assembly representation in favor of Muslim minorities in Hindu-majority provinces, so it weighted Hindu-minority representation in Bengal. But that weighting was hardly necessary to ensure *bhadralok* dominance over virtually every public institution in the province. It was ensured and perpetuated by a franchise restricted to the educated and well-to-do, by a system of English-medium higher education centered on the University of Calcutta in and over which the *bhadralok* dominated, and by the propensity—demonstrable not only in India—of officeholders and other notables to favor as their subordinates and successors people like themselves.

But by the 1930s, the *bhadralok* hold on things was being attenuated by a rapidly growing Muslim professional class of townsmen and a village Muslim electorate of *jotedars,* grown politically large on relative prosperity and on the Raj's liberalization of the franchise. More than a decade before the abolition of the Permanent Settlement, it was no longer *zamindars* but rather *jotedars* who were the dominant group in the Bengali countryside. Led by professional men and followed by *jotedars,* these classes were joined in the Krishak Praja Party, a disciplined and well-organized coalition of classes. It was largely the work of Fazlul Huq, built on the groundwork of populist Muslim politics. Avowedly, Krishak Praja was based on class rather than "community," and it even garnered some support from lower-caste Hindu peasants, who were no fonder of the *bhadralok* than were their Muslim neighbors. But political courtships and marriages of convenience between lower-caste Hindus with Islam and it with them are recurring dramas in the Indian countryside, and not only Bengal's. Krishak Praja was a Muslim party. Fazlul Huq was a Muslim politician.

The central plank on the party's platform was the abolition of the *bhadralok's* economic base: the Permanent Settlement. We might note here for future reference that the settlement's *zamindari* system penalized particularly the countryside's peasant uppercrust: the *jotedars* who paid rent to landlords. To rural underclasses—subtenants, share-croppers, landless laborers—the Permanent Settlement was of little concern. Their exploiters were the land-holding peasantry. Krishak Praja was their party—a *jotedar* party in the countryside. It was a Muslim populist party, not a proletarian party.

I have no hard evidence to connect directly Fazlul Huq's political mobilization of Muslim peasants with their earlier political–religious mobilization as Wahhabis and *Faraidis*. But I think it fair to assume that their experience of having been mobilized once contributed to their amenability to being mobilized again.[48] The Wahhabi and *Faraidi* Movements existed, after all, in the living memories of the parents and grandparents of the peasants who rallied to Fazlul Huq. At the end of the nineteenth century, when these movements were waning, their Islamic puritanism, Muslim "communalism," and explicit or implied anti-Hinduism were perpetuated in the Bengali countryside in the sermons of itinerant *ulama* and by a flood of inexpensive and easy-to-read "manuals of religious instruction."[49] Fazlul Huq's Muslim peasant contemporaries had memories of being coerced or cajoled into supporting the *swadeshi* movement by their *bhadralok* landlords and creditors. The Krishak Praja Party, while not Islamic, was Muslim, and the enemies of Muslim *jotedars* were landlords and money-lenders, most of whom were Hindus.

Bengal's underlying "communal"-class enmity of Muslim peasant versus Hindu landlord was papered over, but thinly, during the early 1920s by a "communal"-class accord. The Khilafat and Non-Cooperation Movements, which were not particularly active in Bengal, converged with the "Bengal Pact's" agreement of 1921 to reserve a disproportionate share of government jobs for the Muslim professional middle class. The pact was the work of C. R. Das, the leader and organizer of the Bengali Congress as a party in the countryside and "the one Hindu leader who inspired unreserved confidence among Muslims. . . ."[50] But the paper came unglued with the crash of the Khilafat–Non-Cooperation accord in 1922 and Das's death three years later. From then on, "communalism" became the dominating "-ism" of Bengali politics.

Two Muslim parties challenged Congress during the 1937 elections in Bengal and afterwards formed a coalition government. The latter was led by the Krishak Praja Party, which reluctantly took as its junior partner a provincial Muslim League, revived by the Muslim political rhetoric post-1937 elections of a "communal" identity that transcended class differences among the faithful. Together, this Muslim coalition successfully challenged the *bhadraloks'* every interest: rents, debts, markets, cow protection, government jobs, and control of local and district boards, municipal councils, schools, and higher education. Fazlul Huq led, and the Muslim League's *zamindars* followed. They agreed to go along with Krishak Praja's promise to abolish the Permanent Settlement, and they demanded for their acquiescence only compensation for their loss of income. Presumably they expected additional compensation and future gain from their treasury-bench political advantage in the provincial assembly

The Hindu *bhadralok* could have no such expectations. In majoritarian politics, they were a permanent minority. Their Congress Party was factionalized between defenders of Hindu "communal" and class interests, and a smaller group that sponsored a campaign to promote "mass contact" with Muslims. But that failed for want of *bhadralok* support and Muslim attraction—further discouraged by *ulama* and *ashraf* disapproval. Farsighted *bhadralok*, however, and Marwaris, whatever their antidemocratic proclivities, did attempt to broaden their *Hindu* class support. In 1939, Congress committed itself to the abolition of the Permanent Settlement and its *zamindari* system. For a while, *bhadralok* and Marwari defectors from Congress nurtured the unequivocally "communalist" Hindu Mahasabha. Like the League, and the Congress in Bengal, the Mahasabha imagined a Hindu "community" that transcended its divisions into castes and classes. En passant, and paying the devil his due, the abolition of untouchability in contemporary India is, in theory and in part, a spin-off of Hindu *sangathanan* ("communal" unification).

By 1946, the *bhadralok* and the Marwaris had returned to the Bengal Congress. It had been more or less unified and disciplined under the National Congress's direction. Its "leftists" and Muslim sympathizers had been purged, and the "pipe dream" of a "united and sovereign Bengal" which they shared with leaders of the Bengal Provincial Muslim League was shattered by the Congress "high command."[51] The overtures of Congressmen to the Hindu lower-castes were beginning to pay dividends and were as yet costless. Congress was no less representative of the Hindu "community" than the Mahasabha, and far more likely to deliver the goods as the British government's successor in Delhi.

But not in Calcutta! Not unless it was the capital city of a Hindu-majority western Bengal, partitioned from the Muslim-majority districts of the east. For the *bhadralok*, there was no alternative to partition. The dominant right-wing of the Indian National Congress agreed, as did Jawaharlal Nehru. Either as an independent state, or an autonomous part of an Indian confederation, or (on horror's head horrors!) a province of "Pakistan," a unified Bengal would be ruled by a dominant class coalition of Muslim professionals and landed peasants. Its commitment would be to the promotion of Muslim political, commercial, and professional interests. In 1937, Fazlul Huq had turned to the League for his coalition partner only after being spurned by Congress, presumably because it would not collaborate in Krishak Praja's promotion of Muslim interests. A half-century after partition, Joya Chatterji documented Nirad Chaudhuri's wry observation in 1951: "The same class of Hindu Bengalis who opposed Lord Curzon's partition of Bengal . . . brought about a second partition of their country."[52]

They did not, however do it alone. After a brief stint in the Muslim League, Fazlul Huq ditched it in 1941 for an inter-"communal" government, which included the leader of the Hindu Mahasabha. Opportunism was born before 1947 as the guiding "-ism" of subcontinental politics. This marriage of convenience between Muslim populism and Hindu revivalism lasted for two years and was succeeded by a League ministry in 1943. The leaders of this resurgent Bengal Provincial Muslim League were not, however, *ashraf*, whom Jinnah favored, but successful urban middle-class competitors for Fazlul Huq's populist mantle and his coalition leadership.[53] By 1946, the coalition of professional men and *jotedars* that had been put together by Fazlul Huq and dominated Bengali Muslim politics was consolidated in a Bengal Provincial Muslim League that was reorganized by the Calcutta notable H. S. Suhrawardy and revivified on the ether of "Pakistan." It captured virtually every Muslim seat in the crucial provincial elections of that year. The League's *ashraf* only shifted the coalition's politics somewhat to the right. *Zamindars* would be compensated for their loss of income when (*not if*) the Permanent Settlement was annulled.

Congress made a virtually clean sweep of the Hindu seats in the 1946 elections. In the following August, Calcutta erupted, not into its usual and occasional "communal" rioting, but into open warfare between Hindus and Muslims. After this "Great Calcutta Killing," partition was probably inevitable. Neither the Bengal Provincial Muslim League's leaders nor the Quaid, no love lost between them, got their "pipe dreams"—for the one, an "undivided and sovereign" Bengal; for the other, an undivided Bengal province in a sovereign "Pakistan."

What Pakistan got, of course, and, ironically, to the detriment of its democratic development, was an eastern Bengal with a relatively broad-based coalition of professionals and land-holding peasants, relatively well organized as a political party, successful at the polls, and experienced in parliamentary politics. The Bengal Provincial Muslim League, whose organizational center had been in Calcutta, survived partition only in name. But the coalition of politically dominant classes which had produced the only truly popular Muslim provincial government in British India persisted into Pakistan. In 1954, it reappeared as a triumphant United Front that swept what remained of the Quaid-i-Azam's Muslim League from the political map of East Pakistan. The irony here is this: The coalition of Bengali professionals and landed peasants, successful in parliamentary politics, its winning card in British Bengal, was to become a major obstacle to the establishment of parliamentary democracy in Pakistan. Supported by Pakistan's Bengali majority, its coalition of dominant classes—in composition and organization friendly to the development of parliamentary democracy—threatened the hegemony of West Pakistan's dominant coalition of landlords, bureaucrats, generals, and industrialists.

As the partition of the subcontinent which brought eastern Bengal into Pakistan precluded the development of parliamentary democracy there, so the bifurcation of Bengal facilitated the development of parliamentary democracy in its western districts. The fearful Muslim majority that dominated parliamentary politics in the unified Bengal of British India disappeared into Pakistan. Hindu-majority western Bengal became the state of West Bengal in a quasi-federal union ruled at its Centre by the Congress Party. The *bhadralok* had never been enthusiastic supporters of Gandhi's leadership of the Indian National Congress. It was too cautious, too accommodating, too rural-centered, too steeped in religious obscurantism, too lacking in Bengali élan. Two of the most serious challenges to Gandhi's leadership of Congress had come from *bhadralok*: C. R. Das and Subhas Chandra Bose.

Independence brought to the Delhi *gaddi* a Congress that was led not by Gandhi but by other non-Bengalis. Bengalis behaved prudently and appropriately. The *bhadralok* may not have been democrats, but clearly their future was to be determined in a parliamentary democracy dominated by Congress. It swept the polls in independent India's first three general elections in West Bengal. Hindu parties were erased from its electoral map. The Congress Party in West Bengal chose its own leadership, but it led with the patronage and support of Congress's "high command" in Delhi. Dr. B. C. Roy, the choice of his Bengali colleagues, was West Bengal's chief minister for its first thirteen years. But as such, he was coopted into the National Congress's "syndicate" of provincial leaders as West Bengal's representative. Under Roy's leadership, the *bhadralok* expanded their control over every aspect of Calcutta's life, save business. Marwari businessmen were brought under the Congress umbrella and assessed for its protection. Land reform that favored the interests of landed peasants was emplaced in the countryside. In a word, West Bengal became a province in the Congress *raj*. Marcus F. Franda summarizes the process as follows:

[To men who are already influential in their localities, Congress] offers administrative rewards, influence with ministers, seats in Parliament or the Assembly, or perhaps even a ministry. . . . Congress acts to enhance or maintain the prestige which a Congressman already has in his locality. . . . [It] attracts funds from businessmen . . . because it is the party in power, and it uses these funds to run its widespread organization. . . . In periods of famine or flood, or after a riot in Calcutta, the Congress often takes on the character of a relief organization in the localities affected. Finally . . ., Congress personnel have jobs to distribute . . . and they have a great deal of influence in the administration—in schools, and colleges, and in private and public business concerns. . . .[54]

"Ice in the summer, coal in the winter." In New York City of the late nineteenth and early twentieth centuries an instrument of parliamentary democracy was Tammany Hall.[55] In western Bengal, it was Congress. And at its Centre, it held.

NOTES

1. Philip Mason, *A Matter of Honour: An Account of the Indian Army, Its Officers and Men* (London: Jonathan Cape, 1974), p. 350.
2. Ibid.
3. "Proper" Sikhs, with uncut hair and beards.
4. *Durbar Sahab*; literally, *The* Honorable Court.
5. "Punjab" is a contraction of the Hindi/Punjabi words for "five" and "rivers."
6. From Percy Bysshe Shelley's "Ozymandias."
7. Malcolm Darling, *The Punjab Peasant in Prosperity and Debt* (Bombay: Oxford University Press, 1947), p. 33. First published in 1925.
8. The most comprehensive and politically sophisticated work on the subject is Imran Ali's *The Punjab under Imperialism, 1885–1947* (Princeton, NJ: Princeton University Press, 1988).
9. Darling, *Punjab Peasant*, p. 118; emphasis added.
10. Ibid., p. 174.
11. P. H. M. Van den Dungen, *The Punjab Tradition* (London: Allen and Unwin, 1972), p. 169.

12. David Gilmartin, *Empire and Islam* (London: I. B. Tauris, 1988).

13. Ibid., p. 19.

14. Denzil Ibbetson in 1895, quoted in Van den Dungen, *Punjab Tradition*, p. 217.

15. Quoted in Norman Barrier, *The Punjab Alienation of Land Bill of 1900* (Durham, NC: Duke University Commonwealth Studies Center, 1966), p. 83.

16. Darling, *Punjab Peasant*, p. 198.

17. Ibid., pp. 98–99.

18. Gilmartin, *Empire and Islam*, p. 128.

19. Barrier, *Punjab Alienation of Land Bill*, p. 94.

20. Gilmartin, *Empire and Islam*, p. 199.

21. Ibid., pp. 199–200, 221.

22. Ibid., p. 144.

23. He used the term regularly, but never defined what he meant by it. What he really wanted, Ayeshi Jalal argues, was Muslim-majority provinces in a Muslim-majority "state" in an Indian confederation. What he got was not what he wanted. *The Sole Spokesman: Jinnah, the Muslim League and the Demand for Pakistan* (Lahore: Sang-e-Meel Publications, 1992).

24. Van den Dungen, *Punjab Tradition*, p. 282.

25. Clive Dewey, "The Rural Roots of Pakistani Militarism," *The Political Inheritance of Pakistan*, edited by D. A. Low (London: Macmillan, 1991), pp. 255–283.

26. Ibid.

27. Gail Minault, *The Khilafat Movement: Religious Symbolism and Political Mobilization in India* (New York: Columbia University Press, 1982).

28. Gilmartin, *Empire and Islam*, p. 124.

29. Gurdarshan Singh Dhillon, "Punjab Problem: The Historical Perspective," *Punjab: Past, Present and Future*, edited by Gopal Singh (Delhi: Ajanta Publications, 1994), pp. 243–277.

30. W. Ladejinsky, "Extracts from Study of Tenurial Conditions in Package Districts," *Readings in Indian Agricultural Development,* edited by Pramit Chaudhuri (London: Allen and Unwin, 1972), pp. 177–189.

31. *Punjabi Suba* was a ploy: it was a politically unacceptable demand for a "communal" state under the guise of a politically acceptable demand for a "linguistic" state, a state whose majority language was Punjabi (see chapter 4). The southeastern districts of bifurcated Punjab became the Hindi-speaking, Hindu-majority state of Haryana. In the 1951 Census of India, Punjabi was listed as a dialect of Hindi. Political reality subsequently intervened, and that linguistic categorization was, of course, reconsidered and changed.

32. Literally, it means no more than someone who has something to do with agricultural land, *zamin*. In other parts of India, *zamindars* are cultivators.

33. Nirad C. Chaudhuri, *Autobiography of an Unknown Indian* (London: Hogarth Press, 1991), p. 226.

34. J. H. Broomfield, *Elite Conflict in a Plural Society: Twentieth Century Bengal* (Berkeley, CA: University of California Press, 1968), p. 269.

35. Chaudhuri, *Autobiography*, p. 225.

36. Vincent A. Smith, *The Oxford History of India*, 3rd edition, edited and Part 3 rewritten by Percival Spear (London: Oxford University Press, 1961), p. 759.

37. Alexander Pope, "An Essay on Man."

38. Chaudhuri, *Autobiography,* p. 236.

39. In part as a sop to Muslims, the king announced that the imperial capital would move from Calcutta to a former capital city of the Mughals, Delhi.

40. The name derives from Marwar, once the princely state of Jodhpur, now a district in western Rajasthan.

41. Jainism is a religion indigenous to India. Its followers, about three million people, date its founding to the sixth century BCE.

42. Chaudhuri, *Autobiography*, p. 232.

43. Ibid., p. 222.

44. Abdul Hamid, *Muslim Separatism in India: A Brief Survey 1858–1947* (Lahore: Oxford University Press, 1971), p. 79.

45. By virtue of their putative association with the *ashraf* of northern India. Their language was Urdu or Persian rather than Bengali, and they claimed Arab, Mughal, Pathan, or Rajput ancestry.

46. Harun-or-Rashid, *The Foreshadowing of Bangladesh: Bengal Muslim League and Muslim Politics 1936–1947* (Dhaka: Asiatic Society of Bangladesh, 1987), p. 1.

47. Joya Chatterji, *Bengal Divided: Hindu Communalism and Partition 1932–1947* (Cambridge: Cambridge University Press, 1994), p. 69.

48. Lawrence Ziring, a prominent student of politics in Bangladesh, is unequivocal in making the connection and extending it to post-Partition leaders in East Bengal.

49. Pradip Kumar Lahiri, *Bengali Muslim Thought 1818–1947* (Calcutta: K. P Bagchi, 1991), p. 40.

50. Chaudhri Muhammad Ali, prime minister of Pakistan in 1955; quoted in Leonard A. Gordon, *Bengal: The Nationalist Movement 1876–1940* (Delhi: Manohar Book Service, 1974), chap. 7.

51. Chatterji, *Bengal Divided*, p. 260.

52. Chaudhuri, *Autobiography*, p. 218.

53. Particularly H. S. Surawardy and Abul Hashim. Harun-or-Rashid, *Foreshadowing of Bangladesh*.

54. "West Bengal," *State Politics in India*, edited by Myron Weiner (Princeton, NJ: Princeton University Press, 1968), p. 288.

55. The reference is to the city's most powerful and corrupt political "machine."

4

Democracy in India

Nowadays, for anyone who wants the political power of government in India there is no alternative to parliamentary democracy. That is the extent of its development. Through a process of elimination, we can establish this at the outset.

With regard to "revolution from above," its usual executors in South Asia—the military, as in Pakistan—represent no dominant class interests in India and only those institutional interests common to militaries in other parliamentary democracies. As in these, India's generals occasionally chafe against the directions and disbursements of their civilian masters. But replacing them has never been on the military's agenda. In 2000 and into the foreseeable future, a military coup is no more likely in India than it is in, say, Britain or the United States.

Congress's "one-party dominance," about which I have much more to say below, had the potential, at least, of becoming a one-party dictatorship. But that era has passed into India's history and is unlikely to recur. Coupled with no fond public memories, in general, of Indira Gandhi's tyrannical "emergency" of 1975 to 1977, the disappearance of "one-party dominance" makes another such palace party coup increasingly unlikely. Headquartered at the India International Centre, Delhi's much maligned and sent-up "chattering classes," and other politically conscious and articulate urban upper-middle-class assortments elsewhere, lament the growing proletarian corruption, criminalizing, and vulgarizing of India's parliamentary democracy. They hold seminars at which the resurgence of "casteism" and "communalism" in Indian politics is deplored. The urban upper-middle classes are still among the major beneficiaries of parliamentary democracy, but it has become more democratic over time and less theirs, except to deplore. They suggest no alternative to it, however. They are, after all, all democrats.

With regard to "revolution from below," of its archetypical leaders—communist parties—India has two major ones and some fragments. The fragments, although organizationally unrelated or tenuously related, are known generically as "naxalites."[1] They are "revolutionary" communists and operate at various times in various parts of India: Bihar and Andhra Pradesh, most notably of late. They effect some local situations, as armed combatants in rural caste and class warfare, for example. They influence by terror or otherwise the calculations of some local or state politicians. In areas of their operations, they have been a vital force for raising the political consciousness of the Dalits and tribal people whose causes the naxalites usually champion. But, ironically, the battles that they lead are more than likely to be won or lost in the parliamentary democratic arenas that naxalites usually scorn: as a consequence of the intervention of an elected government acting on political calculations appropriate to parliamentary democracy. Naxalites function largely as pressure groups by other means. In spite of themselves, they are largely a force for parliamentary democratic reformism. Their revolution is nowhere on India's horizon, and probably never has been.

The two major communist parties know this. They have traveled the "parliamentary path," certainly from the late 1950s, and have done so with some regional success. In West Bengal, the *bhadralok*-led (*plus ça change . . .*) Communist Party of India-Marxist (CPI-M) won its first legislative assembly elections in 1967 as part of a left front. It has been the government party in West Bengal without interruption since 1977. Its on-and-off estranged parent, the Communist Party of India (CPI), has the distinction of being the world's first communist party voted to power in a free election, in Kerala in 1957. And since 1967, the CPI and/or the CPI-M have belonged to virtually every coalition government in Kerala. More than other Indian parties in general, and Congress certainly, the communists have represented the interests of lower castes and classes. They are more ideologically concerned and well disciplined than other Indian parties, but they are more like than unlike them in political practice—in state government or opposition, or in their calculations at the Centre. Neither communist party has a monopoly on lower-caste or -class support anywhere. Both have mixed-caste and -class constituencies everywhere. At India's Centre, communist leaders have become brokers and shareholders of political power, as it eludes—for the foreseeable future, it would seem—the grasp of any one party and stumbles into and out of the reach of one or another tenuous coalition of parties.

Extraparliamentary violence sponsored by noncommunist, usually ethnic, groups is hardly a rarity in India. In recent years there has been ethnic violence among Sikhs in Punjab, tribal people in northeast and central India, Assamese in Assam, Gorkhas in northern West Bengal, and, most notably, Muslims in Kashmir. But whatever the motives of its perpetrators, this sort of violence has been most effective in serving to state grievances and then negotiating positions to be reconciled with opposing positions through the mechanisms—nonviolent and relatedly violent—of parliamentary democracy.

In sum: Whatever its failings—and they are many—parliamentary democracy in India is something. And as everyone save anarchists acknowledges: you can't beat something with nothing.

Three of the sections below—"Elite Adaptation and One-Party Dominance," "Land Reforms and Parliamentary Democracy," and "The Consolidation of Fragments"—are rather discursive chronologies of the development of parliamentary democracy in India, from the parliamentary politics of an upper-class, high-caste elite to the vibrant, rough-and-tumble parliamentary democracy of today. Collectively, these sections might be subtitled: "The Triumph of the Landed Farmer." The final section, "Old and Unfinished Business," deals with five issues of Indian parliamentary democracy which are unresolved but, in my opinion, are resolvable—insofar as complex human problems are ever resolvable. Four of these issues are corruption; caste, untouchability, and compensatory discrimination; gender inequality; and *Hindutva*. This latter—literally, Hinduness—refers to the apparent revival of Hindu nationalism and its apprehended threat to the constitutional secularity of the Indian state. The fifth issue is the instability of coalition governments at the Centre.

Much of what I describe in this chapter as parliamentary democracy will appear to many readers as distinctly, even grossly, undemocratic. Mr. Dooley's wry description of the American game of democratic politics at the end of the nineteenth century, "it ain't beanbag,"[2] aptly characterizes Indian politics at the end of the twentieth. In describing the game in India, I have tried to look behind its sordidness and brutality, its bias toward serving the interests of the well served, to search for two related things in particular: first, a competitive dynamic in parliamentary politics that gradually brings ordinary people into its arenas and their "creamy layers," at least, into parliamentary democracy's coalitions of dominant classes; second, here and in chapter 6, some indication that the expectations of social justice that are embodied in the general ideology of parliamentary democracy are being approached, if not realized, in its Indian variant.

ELITE ADAPTATION AND "ONE-PARTY DOMINANCE"

Parliamentary democracy—or more exactly its prototype, parliamentary politics—was first established in India as an Indian elite, high-caste and upper-class, adaptation to an imported structure of elite representation. It came during the nineteenth century in a package of desirable or unavoidable Western goods wrapped in Britain. To make the best of these while retaining access to the customary goods that they valued, Indian elites and ordinary Indians adapted one to the other and/or compartmentalized them. These were gradual processes.

New skills were developed, for example: in the English language, for remunerative bureaucratic or professional employment; in clock time, for factory work or railroad travel; in the use of money, for purchasing manufactured goods and servicing debt. Adjustments in values coincided. The Brahmo Samaj was the church of *bhadralok* who wanted to retain their Hinduism but make it more compatible with the values of modernity and more respectable to those who held to these values and to the European foreigners who ruled India. Upwardly mobile castes tried to use the decennial censuses of India as a blue book. Indians in contact with modernity compartmentalized it by removing it, or some of it, from the strictures, or some of them, of customary values. A great tolerance of ambiguity is the legacy to Indians from living simultaneously in their indigenous old and imported new worlds.

Adaptation to the Values of Modernity and Their Compartmentalization

The practice of allopathic medicine in India provides an instructive, apparently nonpolitical, though politically relevant example of Indian elite adaptation to European modernity. Allopathic medicine came in the British package as a prestigious and remunerative profession. The career of medical doctor was taken up largely by the sons (and later daughters) of families that could bear the opportunity and out-of-pocket costs of medical college and were of those "twice-born" castes that valued and cultivated the skills of literacy and numeracy. Now, as we know, allopathic medical practitioners deal professionally and on a day-to-day basis with death and human excreta. In Indian villages, the people who deal, or even whose ancestors dealt, professionally and on a day-to-day basis with death and human excreta belong to Dalit castes, regarded by their neighbors as the lowest of the low: cremation ground attendants, collectors of night soil, leather workers, laundrymen, barbers, for example. And any village Brahmin who took up a Dalit caste's profession would be, at the very least, outcasted. But nowadays Brahmin pathologists and urologists are certainly not outcastes. Quite the contrary! Brahmin medical specialists earn infinitely more money than *pujaris* (temple priests), do far better in the marriage market, and, in general, are more highly regarded by their caste-fellows as contributors to their castes' social status.

Of interest to us in this hypothetical but assuredly commonplace instance are the following. First, and to reaffirm the known, in India as elsewhere respectability is defined by the respectable. Second, our doctors' adaptation to modernity is within closed contexts. Occupationally, Brahmin doctors' professional dealings with death and human excreta in their medical practice neither defile them nor mitigate the defilement of Dalits who deal (or dealt) professionally with death and human excreta in their villages. Socially, a Brahmin doctor is still a Brahmin and a Hindu, and, in the context of his or her Brahminhood and Hinduism, his or her marriage, for example, may have been no less arranged and caste endogamous than those of village *mochis* (cobblers). Third, and contrary to the example above, there are adaptations to modernity which have taken place within more porous contexts than that in which our hypothetical Brahmin adapted to doctorhood. So, members of all castes travel by rail, attend colleges and universities, hold jobs in urban industries, settle in towns, vote in elections, and are affiliated with political parties. As a result, the commensal restrictions that are basic to Hindu rules of purity and pollution and customarily separate and hierarchically position castes are more and more confined to village life and observed less and less strictly in the public life of India's modern, urban social compartments. There is increasing evidence nowadays that this urban-centered relaxation of commensal taboos has fed-back into similar though less extensive relaxation in the countryside. Politics has been a significant feedback mechanism. In return for their votes, villagers of all castes expect, at the very least, to be treated respectfully by their politicians. Finally, and of particular concern to us here, at least until recently modernity altered the hierarchical order of the old society more in form than in substance, and in some cases reinforced it.

Caste, Class, and Parliamentary Politics under the Raj

There was (and is) in Indian society a rough correlation between caste and class. Although now partially overtaken by new forms of social climbing, "sanskritization"—unfortunately named but brilliantly articulated by the anthropologist M. N. Srinivas—even provides a correlating process. Thus, the claims of particular castes to higher status than they are generally accorded in village hierarchies are frequently preceded and fortified by changes for the better in the fortunes of those castes.[3] In towns and cities, caste relationships of higher to lower are less evident or different in form than they are in villages. But they are manifest in substance, though not identically, in class relationships of higher to lower. Near enough is good enough: The secular hierarchies of modern society tended (and still tend) to replicate the sacred hierarchies of caste.

And so it was as parliamentary politics developed under the Raj. Shortly after the Mutiny, the imperial government began to see some value in establishing municipal and provincial fora to provide it with political information and support from the wise, the wealthy, and the wellborn and to shift to them some of the burden and onus of public housekeeping and routine administration. They, in turn, as they had in the past, hastened to accept imperial confirmation of their *izzat* and related material benefits—contacts and contracts, for example—in return for adapting themselves to British-sponsored schemes of elite representation.

In this process of adaptation, the Indian National Congress played a crucial role. Congress, *as an organized party,* mobilized pan-Indian, English-educated, upper-caste, professional middle classes to press for the grant of legislative power to these quasi- or proto-parliamentary fora in which the professional middle classes provided most of the Indian representation. The interests that they wanted to serve by legislation were primarily those of their class. But in representing them, they identified themselves and their party as representative of an Indian *nation*—a phenomenon whose existence the British government denied!

In its Government of India Act of 1919, the Raj sought at once to placate and divide the professional middle classes and to dissipate Indian nationalism by consigning Indian political participation to the provinces of an empire whose only bond was properly the imperial "steel frame." The act endowed provincial assemblies with limited legislative power, transferred some of their governments' housekeeping portfolios to Indian ministers (albeit under the watchful eyes of British civil servants), and allowed some of the assemblies' members to be chosen by restricted and "communally" separate electorates.

Congress, from 1920, led by Mohandas Karamachand Gandhi, barrister-at-law and *mahatma*,[4] responded by recruiting the largely Hindu component of the newly enfranchised landed peasantry and even reorganizing itself into ethnolinguistic *pradesh* (provincial) committees to do so. Gandhi, ever the lateral thinker, mobilized Indian provincialism in support of Indian nationalism. He was organizing Congress's and India's coalition of dominant classes: professional men and landed peasants. *Satyagraha*—Gandhi's strategy of nonviolent conflict and conflict resolution through negotiated settlement—was acceptable to those with something to lose as well as something to gain. It could never have forced the British government to "Quit India,"[5] but it encouraged it to negotiate. It was appropriate to the horse-trading inherent in parliamentary politics and doubtlessly encouraged its development, although the Mahatma was not himself among parliamentary politics' greatest enthusiasts.

In the Government of India Act of 1935, the British government, over the objections of some notable nay-sayers—Winston Churchill, for example—realized that in law it could most economically and efficiently retain its Indian empire as follows: first, by continuing to parcel out provincial political power in "communal" or corporate packets to Indians while, second, retaining a viceregal veto on the exercise of provincial power and organizing the princes at the empire's center as a bulwark of empire. About one-quarter of the adult population of British India was enfranchised to vote in the 1937 provincial elections. As a result of these, Congress or Congress-dominated ministries were brought to fully responsible government in seven of British India's eleven provinces. The business and industrial classes, as I noted above, began to drift toward Congress in the late 1930s, particularly in response to the conservatism of Congress provincial governments.

In the elections of 1946, Congress was again triumphant in the "general"—that is, Hindu—constituencies across India. Thus, as the parliamentary politics of elites, parliamentary democracy had an incubation period of three decades before the British quit India. To be sure, during that time there were agitational politics as well, Congress's and others', and they are well researched in the history and well remembered in the mythology of Indian nationalism. But, then as now, conflicts raised in agitation were frequently resolved by negotiation. Congress, representing a coalition of professional middle classes, landed peasants, and businessmen, became the "one dominant party" in opposition to the imperial government. When the British negotiated their final settlement with the Indian National Congress, and the Muslim League took its Pakistan and evaporated, the Congress Party—representing India's coalition of politically dominant classes— became India's government.

The "One-Party Dominance" of Congress

In the 1950s and 1960s, much was written, most notably by Rajni Kothari and by W. H. Morris-Jones, about Congress's "one-party dominance."[6] Congress ruled, virtually without exception or interruption, in all India's states until 1967, and at India's center until 1977 and again from 1980 to 1989. During these periods of dominance, there was no dearth of opposition parties in India and they were free to oppose. But singly none could effectively challenge Congress at the polls. Collectively they were an agglomeration of mutually contentious parties unable or unwilling to form oppositional coalitions that were capable of bidding for power. They were communists, democratic socialists, Hindu revivalists, secular conservatives, regional or caste parties, the entourages of great men. Democratic socialist parties at India's center annihilated themselves in a perpetual process of fission and fusion. In the 1960s, groups of landlords, led by a few princely families and industrialists, were briefly united in the right-wing Swatantra Party, but it was short-lived. In a politically regulated economy, industrialists who failed to support the dominant Congress Party did so at their peril. The demonstrable power of government ministers gradually overshadowed princely charisma.

But while in India's "first-past-the-post" electoral system Congress always won a majority of parliamentary seats, it never in parliamentary elections and hardly ever in state legislative assembly elections secured a majority of the votes polled. In opposition to the British, Congress's India-wide coalition of professionals, landed peasants, and businessmen had been a mosaic of local and provincial factions of professionals, landed peasants, and businessmen. In the post-Independence Congress, it became even more mosaiclike. Congress's electoral pluralities were put together by congeries of local factions and fragments of factions all over India. Many of these shared with one another only the desire to win office and enjoy its spoils. So Congress was at once undefeatable and vulnerable to defeat. It could be overbearing, unmindful of opposition only at its peril, particularly on social issues like the reorganization of Indian states on linguistic lines (see below). If it gave opposition parties a cause or a pretext for an "electoral alliance," Congress was in trouble. Moreover, if and when an "electoral alliance" of opposition parties began to look like a winning coalition, however transient and opportunistic, it began to look like a bandwagon for disaffected Congressmen.

Congress's coalition of dominant classes placed the party in the middle of the road, and its hierarchs' overriding ambition to maintain its "one-party dominance" kept it there. Again, I am sympathetic to the conviction of Jawaharlal Nehru and his Congress colleagues that in the early years of India's parliamentary democracy the alternatives were Congress or chaos. Albeit in factions, Congress's coalition was doubtlessly consolidated by its "one-party dominance." But, more than likely, "one-party dominance" was also a necessary post-Independence continuation of parliamentary politics' transition to parliamentary democracy—a learning experience. Opposition parties learned to organize, to mobilize their constituencies, and to compete. Tens of millions of people who had never voted before, to whom voting was an exotic exercise, learned to vote. Elections were always won by Congress, but its winning was predicated on its sensitivity to opposition. It learned how to be opposed.

During its first decades, parliamentary democracy could not, I think, have borne much more than this. A threat to Congress hegemony might well have led to one-party dictatorship or authoritarian rule in the fashion of Indira Gandhi's "emergency." Sixteen years earlier, in 1959, her father, a great champion of parliamentary democracy, had used the Centre's power to negate the Communist Party's successful challenge to Congress's hegemony in the 1957 elections in Kerala. Alternatively, the absence of "one-party dominance," before India was consolidated as a nation and parliamentary democracy established as its system of government, might well have produced in the 1950s the provincial parties and coalition instabilities of today—tolerable now but probably not half a century ago.

The costs of "one-party dominance" have been greater to Congress itself than to Indian parliamentary democracy. Jawaharlal Nehru understood that Congress's dominance at the center was predicated on its political dominance at the provincial level. In turn, its provincial dominance was dependent on the constituencies of well-entrenched, powerful, and relatively autonomous Congress political bosses in the states—"Sons of the Soil," grown large! His daughter and grandson apparently lacked this understanding; so, most recently, did his grandson's widow. As prime ministers, Indira Gandhi, followed by her son, Rajiv, were consistent in their attempts to consolidate Congress's "dominance" under their direct command. This seriously undermined the party's organization at the Centre and, with disastrous effect, in the states.

In the states, Indira, in particular, replaced locally based politicians with her own placemen and state governors[7] with her apparatchiks. She meddled in the internal politics of opposition parties, and if they came to state government, she tried to topple them. Apart from costing her her life,[8] these tactics drove political talent out of Congress and into a host of provincially based parties. Rajiv did nothing during his prime ministership to reverse the process, and it continued unabated. Provincial parties proliferated. They contributed to, if they did not cause, the end from 1967 of Congress's dominance in the states. And this provincial-centering of India's politics presaged an end to Congress dominance at India's Centre. Until it was too late in the campaign that led up to the 1999 parliamentary elections, the Congress leader, Sonia Gandhi, apparently imagined not the unimaginable—that Congress's "one-party dominance" could be resurrected in one election—but that Congress could be elected to rule without carefully constructed alliances with provincial parties. It was a fantasy that produced the worst electoral results for Congress in all its years of contesting parliamentary elections.[9] Today, Congress is a shadow of the organization that was led by Jawaharlal Nehru—riven by corruption, driven by opportunism, incompetence, nepotism, and sycophancy—except in its attachment to past glory, probably no worse than any other Indian political party, but certainly no better.

LAND REFORMS AND PARLIAMENTARY DEMOCRACY

Even before Independence, Congress had officially committed itself to moderate land reforms. The landed peasantry, whose interests would further moderate the party's post-Independence land reforms, were being drawn to the Congress banner, certainly from the advent of Mahatma Gandhi as Congress's strategist and supremo. In practice, these reforms paid little more than lip service to social justice: to the interests of subtenants, sharecroppers, and the landless. Coincidentally, the Indian constitution of 1950 established adult suffrage for elections to state legislative assembles: the post-Independence transformations of the provincial assemblies of British India. But given the social milieu in which adult suffrage was exercised—a rural ambience of landed patrons and landless clients—elections for state legislative assemblies tended to reinforce the service of land reforms to the interests of the landed.

Land Reforms

Land reforms of the 1950s, sponsored by Congress, which was dominant at India's Centre and in all its states, was a necessary (though insufficient) first step toward parliamentary democracy. The schema of these reforms, in general, was to confirm peasant proprietors in their landownership and to transfer landownership from noncultivating landlords to their tenants-in-chief—that is, tenants who had paid rent to the landowner. The reforms transferred some landownership; they transferred very little land. Thus, these tenants-in-chief, too, became peasant proprietors, and peasant proprietors became most of the countryside's landowners.

For the future of parliamentary democracy, this transfer had the initial effect of freeing a critical mass of peasants from the economic, political, and ideological direction of their landlords. In a word, approximately half of India's peasant population were thus relieved of the compulsion to vote for their landlords or for their landlords' candidates. They were freed to use in their own interests their new legal right to adult suffrage. Their mass in its number and socioeconomic variety was critical to setting in motion a delayed effect of parliamentary democracy: its competitive dynamic—its potential for the realization of social justice.

But in the 1950s, this was not the consideration of those who profited from land reforms or the governments that presided over them. Former landlords were generously compensated for their losses of rental income and were permitted to keep for their "personal cultivation" holdings up to the generous legal ceilings on the ownership of agricultural land. More often than not, their "personal cultivation" was in fact the labor of tenants and sharecroppers. India's greatest landlords, the princes, were bought out of their *gaddis* with particular generosity. Among both landlords and peasant proprietors, *benami*[10] evasions of the land-ceiling provisions in reform legislation were commonplace and winked at by politicians and bureaucrats.

Almost coincidentally with becoming the major beneficiaries of land reform, peasant proprietors became the major force in most of the state legislative assemblies. In its quasi-federal division of powers between the Centre and the states, the control of agriculture, of the rural economy, and of rural society in general— education, small business, and law and order, most importantly—went to the states. In effect, it went to their peasant proprietors.

It did not go to the other half, more or less, of village India: to the clients of peasant proprietors, their dependents and underlings—subtenants, sharecroppers, artisans, laborers. Adult suffrage was of little benefit to them. They remained, as they had been before land reform, subject to the economic and political direction of landed peasants. To village underclasses, land reform legislation and parliamentary democracy at the state level were of less benefit than harm. The effects of land-ceiling laws were often dispossession from lands that they held on customary but not legal tenure, or a denigration of their customary tenure by legal subterfuge. Under threat of dispossession, for example, subtenants were coerced into signing legal documents in which they accepted the status of laborers, thus forfeiting any future claim to the land that they tilled. Provisions of land reform laws that were meant to benefit rural underclasses—minimum wages for agricultural laborers, maximum shares from sharecroppers, safeguards on the holdings of subtenants, special protection for the holdings of "scheduled tribes and castes"—were openly flouted by peasant proprietors and soon became dead letters.

Great friends of parliamentary democracy in India are often severe critics of its land reform legislation, particularly its implementation and nonimplementation in favor of the land-owning classes of the countryside rather than its non-land-owning underclasses. As I have suggested above, a reasonable response to this criticism is that while it is morally and democratically sound, it is politically naïve. Parliamentary democratic politics, to particularize Harold Lasswell's classic dictum, are about who gets what, when, and how.[11]

These are what land reforms in India are about. The land reforms that it got were directly consequent on the establishment in the countryside of parliamentary democracy: by a coalition of dominant classes whose partners most interested in land reforms were land-holding peasants and who, through their control of the institutions of parliamentary democracy, could serve their interests. We might note in passing that radical land reforms after the Second World War—in Japan, China, Korea, and Taiwan, for example—have been the work of regimes unrestrained by parliamentary democracy.

It may be that a prerequisite to the establishment of parliamentary democracy is the acquiescence of the wealthy and powerful and of those who can aspire to wealth and power. Unfavored and abused, fearful of losing their wealth and power to the "masses," in Pakistan, for example, these classes can be formidable opponents of parliamentary democracy, particularly where it is newly established. In India, their acquiescence was obtained by a coalition of dominant classes whose central political organization was the Congress Party. Its coalition had interests in the persistence of some social and economic inequalities and the emergence of some others. That these would be reduced over time by the competitive dynamic of parliamentary democracy was the expectation and hope of at least some in the Congress Party. There is no doubt, however, that their party sacrificed social and economic justice to the establishment of parliamentary democracy.

Provincial Parliamentary Politics

Their control of state legislative assemblies enabled peasant proprietors to tighten their grip on the countryside and reach out for new, nonagricultural opportunities. Again, the Indian constitution allots responsibility for the maintenance of law and order and the provision of education to the states. Thus, the police became the peasant proprietors' stick for the settlement of disputes with their underlings. State legislatures by 2000 had created more than 200 universities whose optional or principal medium of instruction, other than in science and professional courses, is the particular state's official language: Hindi, Gujarati, Marathi, Telegu, Tamil, and so forth.[12]

There was certainly a step toward social justice in this. The monopolistic hold that the tiny self-perpetuating classes of upper- and middle-class anglophones had had on higher education and professional employment in British India was broken by their peasant proprietor allies. Their children were provided by state universities with employment credentials for expanded state bureaucracies that worked in the state's official language. Some minority of the brightest and most ambitious of these "sons of the soil" attained the certification and English-language competence to enable them to compete professionally and join socially with the anglophone, upper-caste, and upper-middle-class children of urban India. State financial institutions were created to lend money to small businessmen, thus bringing them into state Congresses' provincial coalitions of dominant classes. The investment and business opportunities for peasant proprietors in farming and nonfarming activities were also increased by loans from state financial institutions. Perhaps nothing testifies more unequivocally to the political power of peasant proprietors than the unwillingness of state authorities to press for repayment of these loans. Nor do they press for the collection of arrears on unpaid bills for irrigation water and electricity. Nor do state legislative assemblies levy taxes on agricultural income.

As peasant proprietors tightened their control over provincial politics, they became more and more a significant force in Congress politics at the Centre. Again, Congress's "one-party dominance" was the consequence of a patchwork of local alliances and arrangements, many of them unrelated to one another, except that their key participants in the countryside were in the main landed peasants.

According to Eric R. Wolf's classic definition, "only when a cultivator . . . becomes subject to the demands and sanctions of power-holders outside his social stratum . . . can [we] appropriately speak of peasantry."[13] If this is true—if peasants are by definition subject cultivators—then as a result of parliamentary democracy at the state level and, relatedly, the implementation of land reform legislation, Indian peasants have ceased to be peasants. Land-holding peasants have become farmers, cultivating proprietors. Across the divide of class, landless peasants have become, or are rapidly becoming, farm laborers and rural workers. In the considerable overlap between the poorest of the owners and the best-off of the rest are millions of "middle peasant" families. Certainly, they have concerns and interests of their own, different from those of their more prosperous neighbors. In general, however, India's villagers can be thought of as belonging to either of two economic classes, separated according to ownership or nonownership of land.

The first class, cultivating proprietors, farmers, are no more subject to the political and economic direction of noncultivating "power-holders" than farmers in Iowa. Like these, Indian farmers vary considerably in their holdings and in their ability to exercise political influence. Often at the top, former landlords who have become cultivating proprietors have, in general, become economically integrated into the class of farmers. Usually at the bottom, "middle peasants"— more accurately, small farm families—also associate themselves with this class of cultivating proprietors and have been in the forefront of various "farmers' movements," most notably in Uttar Pradesh and Maharashtra. However much they are dependent on income supplementation from their labor on other families' fields or on remittance income from factory-working sons, however much they are indebted to cooperative societies and moneylenders, however impoverished their household economy, small farm families are landowners— and in village India, land-owning is *the* distinction. Without it and subject to the political and economic direction of cultivating powerholders—the farmers on whose fields they labor—the second class is landless: a generally unorganized and unprotected proletariat of subtenants, sharecroppers, laborers, and artisans.

By virtue of their control over state Congress organizations, the major beneficiaries of Congress's dominance in the countryside until the past decade or so were those groups that anthropologists call "dominant castes." If we roughly translate caste into class, then within the class of landed farmers, dominant castes are generally at the top. As groups, they generally hold more land than do other castes in their villages, and large farmers are likely, though not exclusively, to be from dominant castes. They are usually village patrons rather than clients. In profile, they are relatively numerous, areally concentrated, and productive of their own leadership. In comparison to other groups of farmers, dominant castes tend to be of unquestionably touchable status and relatively advanced in literacy and education. The Jats in Punjab and much of the Hindi-speaking north, the Patidars in Gujarat, the Kammas and Reddis in what used to be Hyderabad and is now Andhra Pradesh, the Nairs in Kerala—these are some dominant castes.

Congress's "one-party dominance" began to wane at the provincial level from 1967. It coincided with the waning of the political dominance of dominant castes and/or their turning to other political parties. There are twenty-five states in the Indian Union. As of this writing, there are Congress or Congress coalition governments in only three small "tribal" states and five "linguistic" states, of which one—Goa—is the smallest in India. Indira Gandhi's authoritarianism, her apparent unwillingness or inability to share power outside her family circle, contributed to Congress's demise in the states. But, its impetus, I think, was in the competitive dynamic of parliamentary democracy, a dynamic that began its course before Indira came to the Dehli *gaddi.* The first general election in which Congress was led by Indira was in 1967, and she did not begin to dismantle the Congress organization until a few years later.

Over the past two decades, parliamentary democracy's competitive dynamic has brought to successful competition for provincial political power the vast congeries of castes, mostly Hindu, known collectively as "other backward classes" (OBC). By and large, their vehicles are parties that are in name or reality provincial. Two prominent ones are the Samajwadi (socialist) Party in Uttar Pradesh and what is now the Rashtriya Janata Dal (national peoples' party) in Bihar. Both have recently been or are now governing parties, and both are dominated by Yadavs: a populous OBC caste of Hindi-speaking northern India. In every part of India, OBC castes have challenged with considerable success the political predominance of dominant castes at the state legislative assembly and *panchayati raj* (councillor government) levels.

Many OBC castes have a "creamy layer" of large farmers. Otherwise, they are typically the owners of farms smaller than those owned and operated by families of dominant castes, and they lag behind these castes in the usual social indicators. They are the countryside's lower middle classes. OBC is a legal and constitutional category, whose constituent castes have demanded some of the benefits of "compensatory discrimination" (see below) and now generally receive them. But the OBC, with the possible exception of Tamilnadu's "non-Brahmins," are nowhere even imagined as a "community," much less have they been invented as such. The political success of the Yadavs, for example, has produced a competitive reaction against it from other OBC castes in Bihar and Uttar Pradesh.

Coincidentally, however, the common interests all over India of OBC communities, primarily in the extension to them of "compensatory discrimination," facilitated the formation of a tenuous coalition of provincially based, OBC-dominated parties to do battle at the Centre. Its breakthrough was the 1989 elections. Their winner, the electoral alliance first led by V. P. Singh, later renamed the United Front, was just such a coalition. And for one and a half years it formed ministries dominated by OBC. The front collapsed in 1991, returned to power briefly in 1996, collapsed again in 1997, and, as such, may never again be brought together. The OBC now swim in the mainstream of Indian politics. The United Front was succeeded first, in 1991, by Congress and then, as a result of the 1998 parliamentary elections, by a coalition led by the Bharatiya Janata Party (BJP). The BJP's national leaders are by and large from upper castes, but in its coalition there were OBC-dominated parties, and its ministry reflected this. Apart from the BJP, which leads it, the National Democratic Alliance—victorious in the 1999 parliamentary elections—is a coalition of eighteen parties, any number of which are dominated by OBC. No less than any other party leaders, the BJP's recognize that the new men of India are from the OBC.

In sum: dominant cultivating castes came, via land reforms and parliamentary democracy, to political prominence in Congress's coalition of dominant classes. Nowadays, the competitive dynamic of parliamentary democracy is bringing into more diffuse, multiparty coalitions of dominant classes those lesser beneficiaries of land reforms, the OBC.

Panchayati Raj and the Green Revolution

Of a piece with land reforms, two other initiatives of the Indian government in the 1950s and 1960s redounded to the benefit of the countryside's cultivating farmers: *panchayati raj* and the Green Revolution.

With democratic intentions, I think, Congress introduced *panchayati raj* in 1959 to accelerate rural development by devolving some measure of its direction from state legislative assemblies to newly created bodies of local self-government. Legislated at the state level, *panchayati raj* was meant to suggest, if only in name, some continuity and resemblance between it and the old, familiar customary village councils, *panchayats*. In substance, however, there were meant to be significant differences between the new and the old.

Under the regime of customary *panchayats,* villagers were ruled through informal processes of consultation and decision-making by village factions of—usually and predominantly—well-to-do landed peasants, often of locally dominant and/or "twice-born" castes. It was government of, by, and for the wealthy and well-born: self-selected and with no, or only tenuous, connection to the state. Its ideological commitment was to maintaining the *dharma*—the customary order of *jatis*, genders, families, and things in general. In contrast, the scheme of *panchayati raj* was of tiered institutions, at whose village base, *panchas* (councillors) and their *sarpancha* or *pradhan* (chair) would be chosen by adult suffrage and representative of ordinary villagers. *Panchayati raj* was meant not only to stimulate rural development, but to do so by introducing social and economic democracy into the countryside. It did not work out that way. The new regime replicated the old, but not entirely. The class base of the customary *panchayat* survived the change, but the caste base has been gradually eroded.

Initially, elected *pradhans,* like their self-selected predecessors, were largely from the upper-caste, patron class of farm families with large holdings. Their electoral successes were largely the cumulations of the mobilized votes of their clients. In most states, these *pradhans* constituted the "nonofficial" memberships and chairs of the upper tier or tiers of the *panchayati raj* structure at the "block development" and district levels. Government funding for development projects was allocated and dispensed at these levels. Here were the game's prizes, and they were hard fought for. Ranbir Singh, a keen observer of *panchayati raj,* describes politics at its middle tier in 1970s Haryana:

The rival groups which cut across party lines, caste identities and religious affiliations are based on personal networks or coalitions of factions formed after hard bargaining. [These groups] try to gain the majority by . . . appeals to parochial sentiments and primordial loyalties, official pressure, threats of reprisal, promises of patronage, bargaining for offices, kidnapping and physical reprisal.[14]

The contestants were diverse in every way but class. Whoever got what, when, and how, his family almost certainly will have belonged to the upper crust of farmers, and the lion's share of government largesse will have gone to patron families like his. With their access to public funds, elected *pradhans* could expand their client bases and humble rival patrons. The new system effectively swallowed up the old. At the upper tiers of *panchayati raj,* there were patrons of patrons whose range of power and influence extended beyond the confines of their villages and into state politics. In effect, *panchayati raj* incorporated and networked into state politics patron–client relationships that had previously been contained, by and large, within villages.

Accelerating the social changes begun by land reform before, and further accelerated afterward by political party competition for *panchayati raj* office and by the Green Revolution, *panchayati raj* has helped to carry landed OBC families to political power and relative affluence. In turn, these OBC "creamy layers" effected the encouragement of political awareness and efficacy among their lesser caste-fellows and, consequently, precipitated the beginning of the end of Congress's "one-party dominance." In Uttar Pradesh, for example—once a bastion of upper-caste Congressmen and now with only ten Congress members of parliament[15]—by 1982 more than one-third of *pradhans* were from OBC castes.[16]

The Green Revolution was a "package" put together by scientists of the American Rockefeller Foundation in the 1960s. It was meant to deliver substantial increases in the agricultural productivity of poor and "overpopulated" countries. The crucial contents in these packages were seeds of new, high-yielding varieties (HYV) of wheat and rice. For high outputs, however, the appropriate infrastructure had to be in place. There had to be access to high inputs of chemical fertilizers and irrigation water. High outputs of grain needed the protection of storage facilities and high inputs of chemical pesticides. To enable farmers to pay for the package, and to encourage them to do so, credit and marketing facilities had to be available.

It worked in India. While India's population has doubled since the early years of the Green Revolution, its food grain production has increased threefold. With about 90 percent of its wheat crop and 75 percent of its rice crop in HYV, these two major food grains have become largely the products of commercial agriculture. The Green Revolution has been a major force in the commercializing of Indian agriculture. Indian agricultural scientists have developed new HYV strains not only in wheat and rice, but in other crops as well.

It worked, not surprisingly, to the advantage at least initially of already relatively prosperous and productive agricultural areas, like Punjab, where the infrastructure for commercial agriculture was already in place. And it worked for relatively large farmers who could afford to experiment with Green Revolution technology and purchase the credit to buy its requisite inputs. The Green Revolution made it more profitable for landed cultivators to farm their lands than to exploit their subtenants and sharecroppers, and many of these were dispossessed. To work the enlarged farms now directly cultivated by them, farmers bought tractors and sacked laborers. In using the Green Revolution to serve their interests, cultivating farmers were supported by state legislative assemblies, which they controlled, and less directly by the Congress government in Delhi, which depended for its dominance on the cumulation of Congress dominance in the states.

In its history of three decades, the Green Revolution—again, in conjunction with land reforms and *panchayati raj*—has had a number of socially significant effects. First, and particularly in areas where a Green Revolution infrastructure was in place, smaller farmers increasingly turned to HYV agriculture and profited from it.[17] It works without regard to farm size, and smaller farmers make up in family labor for what they lack in capital. Many of these smaller farmers are from OBC castes, and I have already alluded to the Green Revolution's effect on their politics. It was a turning point for them. Relatedly, the Green Revolution has had some effect on the nature of sharecropping. The usual unproductive rack-renting of land to sharecroppers by proprietors has in some Green Revolution areas given way to a more productive and equitable relationship to which sharecroppers supply their families' labor and proprietors provide the capital.

In areas under Green Revolution cultivation, wages are probably highest for agricultural labor. But it has not been a revolution for them. Demand for their services has decreased in some Green Revolution areas, and in most the social distance of class between landed and landless families has probably increased. Second, barring an improbable red revolution, the Green Revolution has more than likely put paid to any further redistributive land reforms in India. It has increased the constituency opposed to further land reforms. Even in West Bengal, the CPI-M's "radical" land reforms are most notable not for redistributing land but for protecting the tenure of sharecroppers. Finally, we note the importance attached by Barrington Moore Jr. to the positive relationship between the commercialization of agriculture and the development of parliamentary democracy. To this relationship he attaches two caveats: "1) . . . the form of commercial agriculture [is] just as important as commercialization itself and 2) . . . the failure of appropriate forms of commercial agriculture to take hold at an early point in time still [leaves] open another route to modern democratic institutions."[18]

Moore continues: "the transformation of the peasantry into some other kind of social formation appears to augur best for democracy."[19] In India, the Green Revolution has been a form of agricultural commercialization sponsored by parliamentary democratic governments and effected by landed peasants. In addition, it has probably served the cause of parliamentary democracy by undermining the patron–client relationship that was pervasive in Indian villages. Former clients can no longer count on being served from the crumbs on their masters' tables. They must serve themselves: organize and use the instrumentalities of parliamentary democracy. Commercial agriculture was late in coming to India— later than the publication of Moore's great work—but there is no doubt that it has come and that it has been a major force in transforming the landed peasantry of India into "some other kind of social formation": farmers.

THE CONSOLIDATION OF FRAGMENTS

The consolidation and expansion of the political power of landed farmers occurred within the parameters of parliamentary democracy, primarily at the provincial level. It also occurred within the parameters of the integration of these provinces and their societies into an Indian state. This latter occurrence is one of the subjects of this section. Another is the integration of British India's princely states into the Indian Union, as its states or parts of states. These territorial integrations in the first decade or so of Indian independence, and the realignment of most state borders so as to create a union of "unilingual"[20] states, contributed both to the establishment of parliamentary democracy in the Indian countryside and the triumph of the landed farmer.

The Integration of Princely States and the Creation of "Unilingual" States

Begun by the Indian government in 1947, the integration into the new republic of the British Indian empire's 554 princely states was completed by the time the

Indian constitution came into force in 1950—a truly remarkable political achievement! India gained a larger area and population from the integration of the princely states than it lost to Partition.[21] Some of the princely states were amalgamated into states of the Indian Union: the principalities of Rajputana into Rajasthan, for example. Others were integrated with parts of British India into a state: Travancore into Kerala, for example. Others, like Hyderabad, were divided among states. Thus, the land reforms that benefited the land-holding peasants of the former British provinces of India were extended to the land-holding peasants of its erstwhile princely states. They, too, became farmers.

Ties of caste as well as class within peasant groups and conflicts among them—between the Jats and Rajputs of northern India, for example—crossed and crisscrossed the borders of British and princely India. The integration of the princely states into the Indian Union, coupled with the establishment of parliamentary democracy in its new states, frequently tipped the balance of power in the countryside in favor of dominant peasant castes. Thus, Jats became the dominant political caste in Rajasthan almost coincidentally with its creation in 1948–49. In most of the twenty-one princely states from which Rajasthan was created, the Jats had been a collection of peasant groups, restive and rebellious under the social domination of Rajputs—less numerous, but connected by ties of caste and clan to the courts of Rajput princes and their noblemen. The power of the Muslim aristocracy in the subcontinent's largest principality, Hyderabad, was destroyed when it was parceled out into three states of the Indian Union—all with Hindu majorities.

A national coalition of dominant classes, one of whose partners were land-holding peasants, would not have suffered the continued existence of "feudalism" in the princely states. Its other partner, the professional middle classes, were unwilling to sacrifice their employment and political ambitions to princely state absolutism. From the 1937 elections, certainly, Congress in general and Congress provincial hierarchs in particular began to look covetously at the princely states. In any case, they would have been an unlikely fit into an Indian Union at whose Centre and provinces there were parliamentary democratic governments. They would have been a perennial source of popular and political discord for a Congress government in Delhi. It never seriously considered allowing them to survive.

The redrawing of India's provincial borders to produce "unilingual" states was begun in 1953 and, but for Punjab, completed in 1960.[22] It was of a political piece with the integration of the princely states. Both concentrated in the same states the same dominant castes of landed peasants. Like castes in general, dominant castes are almost always "unilingual." So the creation of "unilingual" states concentrated dominant caste numbers and their powers of patronage in a particular state legislative assembly or, in the case of Hindi-speaking castes, assemblies—and in these, dominant castes were politically dominant.

The promise of a reorganization of Indian provinces/states on linguistic lines, first made by Congress in 1920 and reiterated as late as 1946, was reneged on two years later by the Nehru government. It was a frightened response to the "communal" frenzy and inter-"communal" savagery that accompanied the subcontinent's partition. "Nationalism and sub-nationalism are two emotional experiences which grow at the expense of each other."[23] That was the government's first rethinking on the matter. Its second rethinking, however, was in response to creditable threats to Congress hegemony from "linguistic" movements in various parts of India. Prominent in most of these movements were cultivating proprietor groups, frequently of dominant caste. "States' reorganization"—the re-division of India into "unilingual" states—was largely the work of Congress hierarchs negotiating among themselves. One of the earliest masterworks of "one-party dominance," "states' reorganization" has been of enduring value both for India's integrity and its integrity as a parliamentary democracy.

Parliamentary Democracy and the Consolidation of Fragments

The subcontinent's society is one of fragments. It fragments into clusters of language speakers. The Indian constitution now lists the great majority of Indians as speakers of one or another "principal language." Except for Sindhi, a language of Hindu migrants from Pakistan, these are the sixteen official languages of India's "unilingual" states.[24] They are literate languages: like "proper English," they have written and colloquial standards. For millions of those who are calculated as speakers of these "principal languages," however, they are, at best, second languages: official, media, and school languages. First languages are "mother tongues"—that is, dialects. Some dialects grouped under a particular "principal language" are mutually intelligible, and some are not. When there is a question of whether a particular mother tongue is a dialect of one or another "principle language," in border areas between them, for example, the official determination has invariably been on political criteria.

Almost invariably, there are minorities who use languages other than the official language of the states in which they live. Other millions speak "mother tongues" or use languages that are not included in the constitution's schedule of "principal languages." Many of these are "tribal" languages. Largely in attempts, only partially successful, to blunt various tribal insurgencies by means complementary to armed suppression, the Indian parliament has since 1963 created six "tribal" states in India's northeastern wing. The total population of these states is less than ten million, of which about one-half are tribal people.

Language and mother-tongue speakers fragment into castes. Not only dominant-caste borders but caste borders in general are coterminous with the borders of "mother tongues" and languages. Caste hierarchies are local and locally determined, and but for twice-born castes at the top and untouchable castes at the bottom, contention for upper-middle positions, particularly among cultivating castes, is constant. The more successful the cultivating caste, the more likely it is to be riven into factions—based on locality, lineage, continuing feuds, competition among its leading families, the ambitions of its very important men. Lesser castes have their factions and are, in addition, factionalized as the client support groups of competitive patrons. India's tribal population, about eighty million people, is divided into some hundreds of tribal groups, which have their own fragments, sometimes their own languages, and are sometimes integrated or partially integrated into the fragments of caste societies.

The reorganization of India into "unilingual" states helped to preserve Congress's "one-party dominance." I have already speculated on its contribution to the establishment of parliamentary democracy. In general, "unilingual" (and, to a lesser extent, "tribal") states have helped in the development of parliamentary democracy by bringing the fragments of Indian society into some political order—and not merely *some* order, but an order that corresponds to the concerns of its constituents. The lines of politics in general, and conflict and competition in particular, are from their village roots, between classes of people within the same ethnolinguistic group. The reorganization of Indian states on linguistic lines enabled material and nonmaterial provincial demands, particularly those of dominant castes, to be met within an Indian Union that was, at the same time, creating national interests for these same groups. An engineer, for example, son of a farm family, ineligible for admission to an elite English-medium university, trained at the engineering college of a state university, has a potential employment market many times larger than his state's because he is an Indian. Many of the goods sold on the Indian market nowadays are the products of provincial entrepreneurs, sons of the "unilingual" soil, who were nurtured by provincial capital.

But while these fragments were brought into political order, none was made a political majority. India has no political majorities, only transient majority coalitions of minorities and transient minority coalitions of minorities. Nationally, there is no ethnolinguistic group to fear, as there was in Pakistan before 1971. There is no ethnolinguistic group capable of dominating, as there has been in Pakistan since 1971. Other than in the tribal states, there are no states and no more than a handful of districts in which any one community is a majority. For dominant and OBC castes alike, only half-loaves are on offer in Indian state politics, and only to be bargained for or shared. No attempt to mobilize a political majority from the disparate and contentious parts that constitute the majority Hindu "community" has succeeded recently or in the past, or is likely to succeed in the foreseeable future. Parliamentary democracy, it seems to me, is particularly suitable to societies in which there is no dominant majority, and the wealthy and powerful must, in order to protect their wealth and power, come to terms with others like them, at least.

OLD AND UNFINISHED BUSINESS

From its inception, parliamentary democracy at the state level changed the distribution of agrarian power and economic resources in favor of land-holding farmers of dominant castes, then landed families of OBC castes. But until recently it had little positive distributional effect for the countryside's underclasses. Since the collapse in 1967 of Congress's "one-party dominance" at the state level, subordinate groups have been more and more empowered through their participation in the processes of parliamentary democracy.

To be sure, there have been changes for the worse as well. There has probably been more distribution of wealth upward than downward. But there have certainly been downward changes in the apportionment of political power and influence, social honor, and respect. Concurrently, there has been a broadening of the coalitions of dominant classes on which parliamentary democracy in India is based. The competitive dynamic of parliamentary democracy has been a major vehicle for such changes. Their pace, in absolute terms, has been slow. But relative to the longevity and ideological entrenchment of inequality in India, change in the direction of general human welfare has probably been more rapid and profound in the past half-century than in the millennia that preceded it. Below I address some issues in the old and unfinished business of parliamentary democracy in India: corruption, social inequality, the secularity of the state, and the instability of coalition governments in New Delhi.

Corruption

Perhaps the most rigorous, systematic, inclusive, and ongoing statistical study of worldwide corruption today is being pursued by Transparency International, a nongovernmental organization located in Berlin.[25] In its 1999 Corruption Perceptions Index, its league table of countries according to how corruption-ridden they are perceived to be in sample surveys of "business people, risk analysts and the general public," India ties with Colombia as the seventy-second most corrupt of the ninety-nine countries surveyed. Anecdotal evidence gives witness to these perceptions. Corruption in India is widespread at every level of government: from *panchayats* to state legislative assemblies and the national parliament, from *sarpanchas* (*panchayat* heads) to government ministers, from village functionaries to the upper reaches of the bureaucracy. Even more widespread than corruption itself is what Gunnar Myrdal calls the "folklore of corruption": the abiding belief among ordinary people that even their citizens' entitlements under the law are unlikely to be realized without someone being bribed.[26]

Some of the stock explanations for corruption in India are "cultural." Thus, there is the age-old custom of doing business through middlemen, who, of course, take their cuts. Between government and government contractors, artisans and merchants, sellers and buyers, peasants and rent-collectors there has always been, is now, and ever shall be the *gumashta*—agent, intermediary, go-between, middleman. Alternatively, corruption is sheeted to the deeply rooted Indian variant of what Edward Banfield calls "amoral familyism." Thus, the individual Indian's moral universe is bound by the ties of blood and limited to those so bound;[27] outside of those bounds, Rafferty's Rules apply.[28] I am unconvinced by these "cultural" explanations.

Much of the business in the industrialized countries of the world that rank as least corruption-ridden in Transparency International's tables is routinely done through middlemen: agents and brokers, lawyers and accountants, for example. "Amoral familyism" is, in my experience, by no means a characteristic peculiar to Indians and members of other "traditional" societies. The incidence of "universalist" values in "modern" societies is, I think, exaggerated. And, ironically, civil servants—the group of Indians most schooled in these values and apparently committed to them—are, in the general opinion of their countrymen, among corruption's major fonts and sumps. Indian corruption flourishes less in Indian "culture" than in the "modern" nexus between businessmen, bureaucrats, and politicians in an economy dominated by government and regulated by government servants who are, at once, endowed with considerable discretionary power and poorly paid in comparison with their counterparts in the private sector.

A conventional rationalization for corruption is that it greases wheels of progress that might otherwise be mired in "third-world" slough. I am also unconvinced by that. Briefly, the wheels greased by corruption are not necessarily those that are likely to take India, or any other country, to higher levels of economic development and certainly not to higher levels of human development. Corruption, by its very nature, discriminates against the poor and powerless. One of the promises of economic reform in India is that by reducing the role of government in business and business in government corruption will be reduced. Whether or not this path to "privatization" is the one to take remains to be seen. What is clear, however, is the striking negative correlation between the ranking of countries on the UN Development Programme's Human Development Index[29] and Transparency International's Corruption Perceptions Index. In a word, the more human development, the less corruption; the less human development, the more corruption. The work of a handful of resolute corruption-fighters who make (and then fade from) India's media headlines is certainly to be encouraged and applauded,[30] but they are likely to do less major and lasting damage to corruption in India than governments committed to human development—to primary education and to the supply to villages of clean drinking water, for example.

Finally, there is a symbiotic relationship between corruption and the political regimes in which it takes place, a topic that I explore in my discussion of Pakistan (in comparison with India) in chapter 5.

Caste, Untouchability, and Compensatory Discrimination

In the fifteenth century, Portuguese traders and missionaries established the first modern European colonies on the subcontinent's Arabian Sea coast. It was here that they encountered a social system that seemed to them based on sacred Hindu notions of ritual purity and contagious pollution. From that encounter, the term "caste" derived. It is cognate to the Portuguese "casta" and the English "chaste."

In an earlier work, I abandoned the use of "caste" in favor of the Sanskrit-derived terms, commonly used by anthropologists and north Indian villagers, alike: *jati* and *varna*. In brief, *jatis* are local endogamous social groups, ritually separate from one another and hierarchically ranked. "*Jati*"—literally, "breed"—is, at once, a tie of blood among those who belong to the same *jati*, and an indication, both sacred and natural, of the breed's inherent and irradicable capabilities: Tigers do not and will not eat grass; goats cannot and cannot be taught to hunt. So it is with the breeds of mankind. *Varna*—or, more properly, *varnadharma*, the order of human categories—is the sacred ideological referent used by *jatis* to legitimate or contest their hierarchical ranking. The different capabilities of *jatis* are differently valued. *Jati* and *varnadharma*, the social group and its ideological referent, were conflated and thereby confused by "caste," and it was largely for that reason that I abandoned that term. It was a good reason for a bad decision, particularly for someone who writes about politics.

Nowadays, "caste" is a commonplace term that describes an increasingly important social and political reality. As *jatis* are the largest inclusive units of families, so castes are the largest inclusive units of *jatis*. Castes identify their included *jatis* by name: Chitpavan, Oswal, Chamar, Mahar, Kamma, and so forth influence (rather than determine) their status in local *jati* hierarchies and define the furthest limits of endogamy. By ideological extension from *jatis*, castes too are "communities" of blood. Otherwise, they are communities in an associational sense, not unlike Baptists or Tasmanians. They are not like *jatis*: face-to-face communities, more or less, whose members know or know of one another and/or are demonstrably related, albeit in varying degrees. In thousands of villages across northern India, for example, there are millions of people, most of them unknown to one another, who belong to the same castes of cultivators: Rajput, Bhumihar, Yadavs, Jats. Between India and Pakistan, among Hindus, Muslims, and Sikhs, for example, there are certainly more Jats than there are Swedes, Danes, Norwegians, and Finns in Scandinavia. Castes are of particular political significance for the following reasons.

First, castes have become active associations in response to the challenges and opportunities of competitive parliamentary politics. In this context, castes are manifest as benevolent societies, interest groups, political parties, blocs and "vote banks" within political parties, the constituencies of ministers. In a word, like "we Hindus" or "Muslims like us," politics provides arenas for "our castes" to become "communities."

Second, *varnadharma* posits a sacred social order, at once divinely ordained and natural, whose groups are properly both separate, one from the other, and descendent from the most to the least ritually pure. However imperfectly, impermanently, and distorted by secular inputs, *varnadharma* is reflected in local *jati* hierarchies. Caste in politics makes use of the sacred separation of *jatis*, enlarges and politicizes it, but secularizes its hierarchy. Castes in politics are groups of people who share the same "blood"—a compelling bond in any society![31] But in competitive parliamentary politics, while caste hierarchies may be influenced by notions of ritual purity, or claims to it, or fears of contagious pollution, they are not determined by such "sacred" concerns. They are determined by political muscle. The *varnadharma's* hierarchical ordering of *jatis* served from time immemorial as the countryside's social order. It is gradually being supplanted by the social order of parliamentary democracy.

Finally, the competitive dynamic of parliamentary democracy set in train by cultivating proprietors has helped to convert, however partially, the caste and communal societies of the Indian countryside into civil societies. Dominant alliances have been fragmented in the politics of who gets what, when, and how, and their fragments have recruited subordinate groups as allies or they have set themselves up as competitors. Castes and religious communities have been organized for defensive and offensive participation in provincial parliamentary democracy. The threat of universal suffrage, for example, to the power of dominant groups has been mitigated for them by their organized social and economic power. The rise of subordinate groups to positions of political power has been facilitated for them by their caste and communal organization. Relationships of political competition and collaboration between caste and communal groups has probably been a factor in reducing social distances between them. As institutions of civil society, castes and religious communities have served parliamentary democracy by imposing limits on state power.

Varnadharma has had its secular consequences. Even today, the political power of castes is not unrelated to the secular benefits or disabilities that have accompanied for centuries the sacred status of their *jatis*. Which families own land and which labor on it, which cultivate the values and skills of literacy and numeracy, which expect to be deferred to and which expect to defer to them, which accumulated capital and which accepted indebtedness as an unavoidable incident of life, which did what work—these have been some of the secular consequences of sacred status. They have produced, even within a single village, a society of vast inequalities. And these had to be confronted by Indian professional, middle-class constitution-makers in order to construct a constitution whose cornerstone was parliamentary democracy. The document they produced reflects the influences on them of nineteenth- and twentieth-century European liberalism qualified by modern Hindu reformism and humanitarianism.

Parliamentary democracy itself has grown on the subcontinent as an exotic transplant: a shoot of British imperialism and Indian reactions to it. Every public institution, directly or indirectly related to parliamentary democracy—adult suffrage and a free press, for example—has its origins here. None are indigenously Indian. Indigenously Indian is a social order reflective of the *varnadharma*, which embodies perhaps the world's most ancient, well-articulated, pervasive, and extant system of social inequality— not merely undemocratic, but articulately antidemocratic. The political relevance of this *jati* system is that it envelops Indian society and positively denies, in its theory and customary practice, any notion of democracy's sine qua non: the belief in an essential human equality.

"One person one vote, one vote one value" are preposterous propositions—contrary to nature and to the divine scheme of things.[32] Supportive of the *varna-dharma* and at the core of *jati* rankings, a belief in what Louis Dumont calls *Homo hierarchicus* pervades Indian society.[33] Relationships, in general, are properly (if not actually) unequal, hierarchical: twice-born *jatis* and others, touchable *jati* and untouchable others, upper and nether untouchables, upper and nether clans within the same caste, husbands and wives, fathers and sons, elder and younger brothers, mothers- and daughters-in-law, elder and younger daughters-in-law, senior teachers and teachers, teachers and students, employers and employees—and certainly, rulers and ruled.

Confronted by this, the framers of India's constitution of 1950 addressed themselves directly to its reform by incorporating into their work, first, a list of fundamental rights to be enjoyed equally by all Indian citizens; second, and of lesser legal standing, a list of "directive principles" or constitutionally mandated directions to future parliaments—for example, to provide a uniform civil code for all Indians and free and compulsory education for all Indian children to the age of fourteen.[34] In comparison to the brief and loosely worded American Bill of Rights, which was one of its inspirations, the fundamental rights of the Indian constitution are laid out in twenty-four legal documents. Of these, Articles 15 and 17 are related and are particularly, though not exclusively, relevant to a discussion of the capacity of the competitive dynamic of parliamentary democracy to deliver social and economic change. These articles conveniently serve as a framework for our inquiry in this subsection.

Article 15 prohibits discrimination *against* Indian citizens on the grounds of religion, race, caste, sex, and place of birth by all public authorities and by private owners of public facilities—shops and wells, for example. It (and Article 16), however, permits discrimination *in favor of* Indian citizens who are regarded as socially and economically disadvantaged: "scheduled tribes and castes," "other backward classes," women (and children). Specifically proscribed by Article 17 is untouchability, and its practice by anyone in any way, shape, or form is deemed to be a criminal offence.

Beginning in the 1950s, the Indian government pioneered what is usually called in India compensatory or protective discrimination, better known in the West by its American euphemism, "affirmative action." Its rationale in India and the United States has been the same: only by allowing a period of unequal favor to those sections of society that have been most socially disfavored can they ever be brought to a level of equality with the generality of their fellow citizens. The framers of India's constitution had no doubt but that the majority of their most socially disfavored fellow citizens, the most suppressed and brutalized of their countrymen, were those who belong to groups that the British government termed "scheduled castes," Mahatma Gandhi called "*Harijans*" (God's people), and who have now renamed themselves "Dalits."

"Scheduled castes" was one of several British designations for castes whose *jatis* were treated as untouchable: the lowest of the Hindu low, condemned by birth to do society's dirty and demeaning work, stigmatized and quarantined as carriers of the most virulent and contagious pollution. "Scheduled tribes" were also made eligible for compensatory discrimination. They are much less numerous than Dalits, nowhere as well dispersed throughout India, and less ideologically and functionally related to the life and work of ordinary Hindu village society. Tribal people are, with some notable exceptions,[35] poor and illiterate and frequently treated as untouchable in Hindu village society. They have been the proverbial and particular objects of the venality of forest officials, the greed of *baniyas*, and the solicitude of the Raj's paternalism. So, for these two groups, building on precedents established by the Raj, Indian lawmakers constructed an elaborate network of compensatory measures shortly after the constitution's adoption.

Dalits and tribal people are the recipients of special school and university scholarships and reduced university-admission criteria. With reduced application criteria, positions in university colleges and at all levels of government employment, whether bureaucratic or industrial, are reserved for them.[36] Parliamentary and legislative assembly seats in proportion to the population of "scheduled tribes and castes" are reserved for the competition of candidates who must belong to untouchable castes or tribes. Their representation in *panchayati raj* institutions is legally mandated.

The discussion here is limited to Dalits. Dalits make up about 16.5 percent of India's population, approximately 165 million people; more or less equally spread throughout the country, they are members of thousands of different *jatis* and hundreds of separate castes, and, as their mudsill, they are integral parts of Hindu and village society.[37]

Until recently, the most notable effect of compensatory discrimination for Dalits had been a dramatic increase in the opportunities for embourgeoisement open to their "creamy layers," particularly in the higher levels of government employment. In effect, the best-off and brightest members of these underprivileged, disproportionately rural castes were coopted into urban professional and bureaucratic employment.

In the countryside, dominated by touchable Hindu farmers, in situations where state authorities took any notice of Article 17—other than to assist in its evasion—they were more inclined to skirt the problem than to take it head on. States were more likely to facilitate the construction of separate sources of household water for untouchable *jatis*, for example, rather than to enforce their constitutional right to use village wells or tanks on terms of equality with other villagers. The anonymity of cities and the presence there of government agencies facilitated the access of urban untouchables to Hindu temples, secular public facilities, and employment opportunities alongside urban touchables. For the vast majority of village untouchables, however, the poverty, illiteracy, and fear of touchable-caste violence in which they lived and had always lived was little affected by Article 17 and by laws passed in pursuance of it.

What was almost immediately effected by Indian independence was, however, the gradual disappearance of some of the most degrading manifestations of untouchability. And that has been an important change to people for whom their enforced acceptance of sumptuary degradation was symbolic of their social status as Hinduism's *untermenschen*. As late as 1930, for example, the Kallars, a touchable cultivating caste of south India, published a list of "eight prohibitions" for local untouchables:

(i) . . . [they] shall not wear ornaments of gold and silver;

(ii) . . . [their] males should not be allowed to wear their clothes below their knees or above the hips;

(iii) . . . [their]. . . males should not wear coats or shirts or [vests];

(iv) . . . [none of their men]. . . shall be allowed to have his hair cropped;

(v) . . . [they] should not use other than earthenware vessels in their homes;

(vi) . . . their women shall not be allowed to cover the upper portion of their bodies by clothes or [blouses];

(vii) their women shall not be allowed to use flowers or saffron paste; and

(viii) the men shall not use umbrellas for protection against sun and rain nor should they wear sandals.[38]

Nowadays, no touchable caste would dare to publish such a list, and no untouchable caste would submit to its prohibitions. In 1931, however, the Kallars extended and amended their list to include the following: "children [of untouchables] should not read and get themselves literate or educated."[39] Indeed, it was commonplace all over India for untouchable children to be excluded from village schools or, at best, seated at some disadvantageous and humiliating distance from touchable pupils and their touchable teacher, lest they be polluted by untouchability's contagion.

In post-Independence India, education for their children—second only to land for their families—has been the ambition of touchable farmers. For his family, an educated son can be the provider of a daughter-in-law accompanied by a substantial dowry, prestige, remittance income, and, if he is well placed in government, political influence. More recently, an educated daughter can bring her upwardly mobile family into a promising marriage alliance. Education, in a word, is a good investment, and because it usually begins for their own children in government primary schools, farmers are loath to put them at risk by unlawfully denying admission to Dalit children. It has been a minor concession *to* Dalits, scaled according to the conventional touchable measurements of pollution's contagion—compared, for example, to allowing Dalits access to village wells or temples. But, paradoxically, access to education has been a major concession *for* Dalits.

At a basic level, education is some barrier to exploitation and cheating. A secular consequence of their lowly sacred status is that Dalits are readily exploited and cheated. They cannot read the print, much less the fine print. But that is changing. The literacy rate among Dalits, close to zero before Independence, is still lower than the general literacy rate, but the gap between them has been slowly but surely closing over the past half-century.[40] Although the great majority of Dalit families are villagers, the sine qua non of village influence and respectability, landownership, has probably been declining among them, and there is little chance anywhere in India of substantial, further redistributive land reforms. Education and educated employment have become the routes to Dalit advancement in India, and even to power.

Other things are changing too. The agencies of change—particularly though not exclusively nor, certainly, exclusive of one another—have been, first, a fast-growing assertiveness, organized and unorganized, among village Dalits. In localized caste warfare, it is not infrequently Dalit push for touchable push or even shove for push. The touchable castes' *senas* (armies), which terrorize and brutalize Dalit villagers in central Bihar, pay a perverse tribute to the social changes wrought by parliamentary democracy and compensatory discrimination. In the past, Dalits were kept in their place by the mere presence of touchable villagers. Now, they need squads of armed thugs to do the job—and Dalits fight back. The second agency, related to the first, is the politics of parliamentary democracy. Educated Dalits, beneficiaries of compensatory discrimination, are making their careers in the countryside—not as landowners, but as politicians whose bases are in their Dalit castes, and as civilian and police officers.

I have already referred to naxalite activity on behalf of Dalits and tribal people in violent confrontation with their local enemies. Battles are won, battles are lost. The war goes on. But its major effects, apart from those felt directly by their local combatants, are those that influence the politics of parliamentary democracy. Intercaste warfare serves to deliver messages that are read, translated, and processed by elected politicians and bureaucrats. One message, at least, is clear and unambiguous: after centuries of being abused or patronized by others, Dalits are acting in their own interests.

Their icon and inspiration is Bhimrao Ramji Ambedkar [1892–1956]. "*Jai Bhim* [Hooray for Ambedkar]," Dalit students at a Haryana university campus greet one another—and not with the usual Hindu salutation, "*Jai Ram* [Hooray for God]." Ambedkar's is the inspiration of Dalit determination to work parliamentary democratic politics to Dalit advantage. Ram is an epithet for God and symbolic of the Brahminic Hinduism that turns human beings into untouchables. These Dalit students do not want to be Gandhi's "*Harijans*"—people of the Mahatma's Ram.

Ambedkar was from a good, educated army family of Mahars, a very large and, for Dalits, an educationally advanced caste in what is now the state of Maharashtra. Driven by his own intellect and ambition and fuelled by the benevolence of sympathetic Hindu princes, Ambedkar studied abroad during the second and third decades of the last century, earning a Ph.D. from Columbia University in New York and, in London, a D.Sc. and admittance to the Bar. On his return to India, he established his reputation as a leading academic lawyer— he was to become one of the Indian constitution's chief draftsmen—and a militant and outspoken champion of India's Dalits. Here, he clashed with that other inveterate foe of untouchability, Mahatma Gandhi. Gandhi, a high-caste, self-professed *varnashradharma* (observant) Hindu, wanted the "sin" of untouchability absolved in Hinduism. Ambedkar increasingly saw Hinduism itself as the "sin." The two men came into direct political conflict in 1932.

Ambedkar wanted the India Act of 1935 to specify a reservation policy for untouchables in provincial elections on the model of the policy for Muslims, in place since 1909. Specifically, he wanted specified *separate* constituencies of "scheduled caste" voters to be contested exclusively by "scheduled caste" candidates. Whatever else it had done, reservations and weightage had made Muslim politicians a force independent of the upper-caste Hindu Congress in provincial politics. Ambedkar wanted that independence for Dalits. That was acceptable to the British government—"balance and rule," after all. It was absolutely unacceptable to Gandhi, *mahatma* and Congress supremo, and he embarked on a "fast unto death" to oppose it. Ambedkar relented. Gandhi agreed to a scheme of compensatory discrimination that remains in place today for state legislative assembly and parliamentary elections: specified *general* constituencies to be contested exclusively by "scheduled caste" candidates.

Educated Dalits have never forgiven Gandhi for his victory, nor forgotten Ambedkar for his defeat. After a few largely unsuccessful attempts to organize his caste-fellows as a political party, Ambedkar in the last years of his life began to lead millions of Mahars and Chamars, a "scheduled caste" of leather-workers from northern India, on a journey toward self-respect. They converted en masse to Buddhism. Two decades before, Ambedkar had publicly denied the Hindu belief that caste in general, and untouchability in particular, were inevitable and immutable consequences of birth. Ambedkar would choose not to be an untouchable. Although he was born a Hindu, he promised that he would not die one. The name "Dalit" is derived from Ambedkar's conviction; its translates as "oppressed." Untouchability is not a condition derived from birth, but from oppression.

"Dalit" is a product of that exercise in self-imagining and re-naming followed by degraded and despised groups elsewhere. Not surprisingly, it and much articulate Dalit militancy originated in the political and literary activities of Maharashtra's educated Mahars. In recent years, the center of Dalit assertiveness has shifted from Maharashtra to the Hindi-speaking north, particularly Uttar Pradesh. The Bhujan Samaj (common people's) Party (BSP), was founded in the 1980s and is led by its founder, Kanshi Ram. He is a Dalit from Punjab and a former bureaucrat. The BSP is the most apparent manifestation of Dalit assertiveness in parliamentary politics today and its most successful party. In the 1999 parliamentary elections in Uttar Pradesh, the BSP won more seats than Congress did, and it more than trebled the BSP's representation in parliament.[41] Its growing success as a political party makes the BSP an attractive coalition partner in the politics of India's most populous state. But no more than that—it can never be more than a minority party. In no reserved constituency in Uttar Pradesh is a majority of the voters Dalit, nor do all Dalit castes support the BSP, nor do all Dalits vote for its candidates.

The BSP notwithstanding, Dalits are as yet an imagined rather than an invented "community." There are hundreds of Dalit castes in India, and in any state there may be scores. In general, they separate themselves one from the other in conventional *jati* or caste terms, neither intermarrying nor interdining, for example, nor following the leader of another Dalit caste. Nowadays battles among the *jatis* of these most impure castes to establish which among them is least impure are often more intense than are such contests over sacred hierarchical status among touchables. Dalit disunity is compounded as a problem for their politicians by the relative political weakness on the ground of their Dalit caste constituencies: still unequally poor, illiterate and uneducated, clients to touchable patrons, susceptible to intimidation by others.

In 1999, the BSP chose to contest the parliamentary elections from Uttar Pradesh unallied to any other party. It worked. But the BSP cannot have an eye to power in Uttar Pradesh without some postelection arrangement with another party or other parties. Apparently, for the BSP any arrangement will do: with parties of touchable farmers or the parties of *Manuvad*—"twice-born" caste Hinduism.[42] Any arrangement will do so long as it yields some real share of political power for the BSP. "We have a one point program—" said Kanshi Ram, "take power."[43] The BSP's most conspicuous candidate for power is Kanshi Ram's protégée, the firebrand Mayawati, a Delhi University graduate and a former schoolteacher.

In 1995 and 1997, for two very brief and tempestuous terms, both under an arrangement with the "A-team of *Manuvad*"—the BJP—Mayawati served as Uttar Pradesh's chief minister. As such, she openly and defiantly used her power to serve the interests of the state's Dalits. First, she funneled a considerable flow of the state's scarce resources to building memorials to Ambedkar and to undoing in his name and by public works the "historical injustice" suffered by Dalits.[44] Second, with no ordinary Indian politicians' lip-service to parliamentary democracy's norm of an apolitical civil service, Mayawati hastened to bring the state's bureaucracy under her political control and, particularly, to place Dalit officers to serve Dalit interests.

Ram Vilas Paswan of Bihar, no friend of Kanshi Ram or Mayawati, is the third major Dalit politician in India today. The center is his arena. Most notably, he served from 1996 to 1998 in the eighteen-month United Front government in Delhi. As railways minister, he paid particular and unapologetic attention to converting the subcontinent's largest employer and particularly its many Dalit employees into his very own "vote bank." Paswan would like to be India's first Dalit prime minister. Unlike Kanshi Ram and Mayawati, Ram Vilas does not target the upper castes for his abuse. After the 1999 elections, Paswan's party, in effect a Bihar-centered grouping of OBC and Dalits, became one of the major constituents in the coalition led by the BJP's prime minister, Atal Bihari Vajpayee. Paswan is a minister in Vajpayee's government.

Ironically, in view of their various "arrangements" with *Manuvadi's* "A-team," the BSP's leaders and Paswan agree—in theory, at least—that the Dalits' best allies are OBC parties. This politicians' understanding of an OBC–Dalit affinity is probably based on a combination of ideology and a perception of complementary interests. OBC are, after all, also *bhujan* (common people) and no great friends of *Manuvad*. Ideology, however, is thin on the ground. Dalit oppression is less likely to come from families of "twice-born" castes than from OBC farm families who employ and exploit farm labor—much of it supplied by Dalits. Nonetheless, there is a complementarity of interests between the two groups. That is an insight of the master-builder of the OBC–Dalit alliance in Bihar: its former chief minister and current chief minister de facto via his wife, the controversial, populist, allegedly corrupt, but nonetheless remarkable OBC politician, Laloo Prasad Yadav.

Both OBC and Dalit villagers aspire to upward mobility. But their levels of aspiration are not the same:[45] OBC politicians want state power and power's rewards; Dalits aspire, for the time being at least, only to a share of political power, or access to it, sufficient for the protection of their lives and property and their legal rights to social honor. So, for example, OBC want a state government that will tend to their material interests. Dalits want a state government that obliges its police officers to pay serious attention to complaints by Dalit women of molestation by touchable men. State politics in India are now reaching the point—and in northern India have reached it—where any state government must address itself to keeping these aspirations in their separate trajectories, minimizing—if not avoiding—collisions. And it may be possible for other states to do so with less than Laloo's tolerance for violence and criminality and a greater commitment than his to the material welfare of the people.

Over the years, the Indian government has emplaced various antipoverty programs, and however laced with inefficiency and corruption in their administration, they have not been without some marginal effect. But the vast majority of the poor are still poor, and Dalits are still the poorest of the poor. What in theory may (or may not) be the most effective antipoverty program for Dalits—redistributive land reforms—is unlikely to be realized in practice any more than it already has been. Simply, the farmers who own the land dominate state politics, and increasingly this dominant class of farmers includes OBC. Whatever their castes, farmers are unequivocally opposed to any further land reform. And, again, not only in the states, but at the Centre landed farmers have become a major political force.

As education and educated employment is the key to the Dalit future, parliamentary politics is the door. There is none other. Compensatory discrimination is best understood as it was meant to be understood: a complement to parliamentary democracy. Together, they will not efface untouchability, but they are likely to chip away at it. It is certainly true that Indian governments, largely of touchable Hindus with touchable Hindu constituencies, have tilted half-heartedly at untouchability. It is equally true that even if there had been a whole-hearted government assault, including an expansion of compensatory discrimination (to the private business sector, for example), it would have been unlikely to efface in half a century so harsh and enduring a system of social inequality, both sanctioned by religious ideology and woven into the fabric of village life throughout India and into the psyches of villagers—and not only villagers. Parliamentary democracy may be a vehicle for reform, but it is rarely, if ever, for revolutionary social change.

Again, Dalits' best use of parliamentary democracy nowadays is probably in coalition state governments, with Dalit ministers well-enough placed to ensure that district-level officers in government service—civil and police (and preferably themselves Dalits)—serve Dalit interests on the ground, by protecting, for example, Dalit families from being cheated, Dalit women from being molested, Dalit laborers from being enserfed or beaten, Dalit voters from being barred from polling stations. Fifty years of compensatory discrimination has prepared and positioned tens of thousands of Dalits for the task. In 1953, less than 1 percent (133) of the upper two of four categories of central government employees were Dalits. In 1995, more than 11 percent (20,434) of the upper two categories of central government employees were Dalits.[46] They have not yet reached the quota reserved for them in these employment classes—about 15 percent—but there is no doubt that they will, and sooner rather than later.

Moreover, about five times the number of people employed by the Centre work for state and local governments and public sector enterprises. On the fair assumption that Dalits serve these employers in their upper echelons in much the same proportion as they do in central employment, there are now about six million Dalits—workers and their family members—who enjoy income and position that would have been unimaginable to their parents and grandparents. More and more, this Dalit bourgeoisie have become the servants of Dalit social welfare and political militancy. Like the elite fragments of other despised groups, Dalits who have made it come more and more to appreciate the inseparability of their and their "communities'" fates.

It may be a source of self-esteem or consolation to Dalits to have one of them, K. R. Narayanan, as India's president. I cannot imagine that their virtual non-representation on high-court benches or in Indian embassies abroad makes much difference to the lives of most Dalits.[47] The places where Dalit officers and politicians can best serve Dalit interests are in the Indian countryside. In this service, they will doubtlessly be aided by the increasing literacy, assertiveness, and unwillingness to grin and bear it of ordinary village Dalits. As state governments, of whatever parties and caste compositions, factor Dalit assertiveness into their political calculations, their civilian and police officers are likely to alter their behavior accordingly. More problematically, untouchability may be devalued by the general secular devaluation by touchable castes of the sacred concerns of their *jatis.*

An appropriate footnote to this discussion of the importance of compensatory discrimination relates to "mandalization." This inelegant Indian–English neology refers directly to the Second Backward Classes Commission, appointed in 1979 and chaired by B. P. Mandal. Its recommendation that 27 percent of the jobs in central government service be reserved for OBC was accepted in 1990 by the short-lived, non-Congress United Front coalition government headed by V. P. Singh. Turmoil followed. The government fell. The upper castes—which dominate government service—were outraged, and a handful of their children, aspirants for government service and the professions, committed suicide. The list of OBC castes compounded by the Mandal Commission was taken from the last complete census of Indian castes—in 1931. Academics and journalists wrote in scores of articles and editorials what everyone knows: over sixty years, there have been castes upwardly mobile from "backward" and others downwardly mobile to "backward." Politicians of all parties read the writing on the wall. Altogether, Mandal's OBC make up more than half of India's population.

With some legislated and judicially imposed attempts to keep all its benefits from accruing to the "creamy layers" of OBC castes, compensatory discrimination in their favor—mandalization—has become general throughout India, for state and central government services and in university colleges, particularly of engineering and medicine. For Dalits, compensatory discrimination has been a stepping-stone to professional employment and political influence. For OBC, mandalization has been a consequence of political power. Again, their power base is on the land. But they have fallen behind Dalits in the upper levels of government service and, perhaps, in the prestigious, remittance-income producing professions. Mandalization represents their acknowledgment of the importance of compensatory discrimination to who gets what, when, and how in India's parliamentary democracy.

Gender Inequality

First, there is the rule: Indian women and girls live in a society that disfavors them with omnibus gender inequality. Second, there are the rule's notable exceptions and subverters: for the most part, the female members of the society's thin layer of urban, wealthy, and upper-middle class families.

Unlike most countries of the world, India has the uneasy distinction of having in its population a higher and increasingly higher proportion of males to females: 1,000 to 941 in 1961, to 927 in 1991. To what extent this is the cumulative result of outright female infanticide and the infanticidal neglect of female children is unknown. What is generally acknowledged is that scarce family resources are more readily spent on the nourishment, medical care, and education of boys rather than of girls. Although its use to determine gender is prohibited by law, amniocentesis has become a weapon in female feticide.

The giving and taking of dowries is also prohibited by law. But that law is generally and openly flouted. Both the practice of giving dowries and the size of dowries given and demanded have increased over the years. The burden imposed by daughters on family exchequers has increased accordingly. Dowry, which probably had its origin in *stridan*, a daughter's marriage gift of movable goods from her natal family, has evolved into her disinheritance and the price paid to his family for a son-in-law. Following the usual Indian custom of patrilocalism, daughters-in-law at marriage move into their husbands' family homes or circles. There, any number of these young women have been seriously abused, murdered, or driven to suicide by allegations that their natal families have failed to deliver on their dowry promises. The extent of this particularly Indian form of domestic violence is unknown, but it is certainly not rare. It is extensive enough to have chastened police departments for looking the other way and provided a *cause célèbre* for the Indian women's movement. Girls are given in marriage in their early teens and bear the mortal risk of frequent childbirth under frequently unhygienic conditions. As mothers, their capacity to care for themselves and their children is severely limited by their illiteracy and lack of education. Compared to more than half of their men, less than one-third of India's village women are literate.

Most of India's agricultural workforce are women. In ordinary farm families, women do the backbreaking work of agriculture along with men and, in addition, bear the responsibility for housekeeping and child-rearing. Even more than when they were daughters, their nutritional, medical, and educational welfare as daughters-in-law is usually of secondary family consideration to that of its sons. The primary duty of young daughters-in-law is to produce sons for their husbands' families, and those who produce either no children or, worse, daughters are likely to suffer for it at the hands of their in-laws. Purdah—the practice by "respectable" Hindu and, particularly, Muslim families of confining women to their homes—is doubtlessly detrimental to the intellectual growth and mental health of these incarcerated females. The incidence of widows becoming *sati*—immolating themselves on their husbands' funeral pyres—was never general in India and nowadays is prohibited by law and occurs only rarely. But the customary ban on the remarriage of widows remains (there is no such ban on widowers), and the child bride who becomes a child widow has before her a life-long career of drudgery in her in-laws household. Women inherit no land as daughters-in-law, and few of them are willing to outrage their brothers by exercising their legal right as daughters to claim their portion of land from their fathers' estates.

Though insignificant as a proportion of Indian women, those who inhabit the thin layer of urban, wealthy, and upper-middle-class families are neither in themselves insignificant nor insignificant as pacesetters for Indian women in general. They are prominent in life and in art—as prototypes of the new woman in popular magazines, on television, and on the great, ubiquitous Indian silver screen. Our focus here, as in the pages above and below, is on the political; but it is neither a narrow focus nor one unblurred about its edges.

Indira Gandhi, Benazir Bhutto, Hasina Wajed, Khaleda Zia—all the states of South Asia have had women prime ministers; Bangladesh has had two.[48] What, in a civilization and societies characterized by gender inequality, can explain this apparent political anomaly—the exercise by women of great political power. And moving from this explanation, can we garner from it any insights into the possibility of change in the political status of women in Indian society—of women, in general, in a changing India?

Shakti, the concept of power in Hinduism, is female, and the Hindu pantheon has many female incarnations of the One to which men offer their obeisance. But I am inclined to the belief that the sacred in Hinduism is applied by its worshipers to the mundane no more nor less selectively or self-interestedly than it is by worshipers of any other faith. Mahatma Gandhi's empathy with women, sympathy for their condition in India, and belief in the equal value of men and women is well known. He is rightly credited with bringing large numbers of women into active participation in the public sphere by recruiting them for his campaigns of nonviolent noncooperation. But that was a moment a long time ago, and, as most of the Gandhian agenda today, it resonates largely in the empty rhetoric of politicians. In any case, the leading women in Gandhi's campaigns came largely from the thin layer of the privileged.

More significantly related, I think, than *shakti* or Gandhi to the possibility of change in the female future in India is the aristocratic nature of Indian society and its interface with modernity. Paradoxically, Western democratic societies' ideological assertions of the equality of Man have tended to generalize the inequality of Woman. If Jack is as good as his master, and his master—head of his household—is better than his wife, then so is Jack. In aristocratic societies such as India, on the other hand, where birth is an important determinant of status, upper-status women and lower-status men are the ideological norm and the social commonplace. Interaction between these superordinate females and subordinate males gives routine witness to their status differences, and generalizes these from birth to class. One may see this daily, for example, in the interactions between matrons traveling on first-class coaches and the coolies who carry their baggage, or between the ladies of the house in upper-middle-class suburbia and their sweepers and laundrymen or between business and professional women and the *chaprasis* (office menials) who tote their files.

These women are unlikely to be "aristocrats." They may not even be of very elevated caste standing. What distinguishes them from their male subordinates is not birth but class. Only their model is aristocratic: upper-status women and lower-status men. They are models of gender equality only indirectly. Equality is a new idea in India—whether between genders, castes, classes, or people in general—and it sits uneasily in a society whose norm and reality is *Homo hierarchicus.* Whatever their positions at home, superordinate women in the modern world are the equals only of men who are equally superordinate. I think that in the first instance, the gender issue in India is less equality for women than exemplary access for women to superordinate positions in public spheres.

Greater gender equality may follow—slowly, in social compartments, from the urban top to the rural bottom.

The number of women in superordinate public positions is growing. Their arena is the city. The percentage of the population listed as "urban" by the decennial Census of India has increased since Independence from 17 to 26. Of these urbanites, more than 65 percent live in cities whose population is greater than one hundred thousand—proper cities! While politics in parliamentary democratic India has become increasingly centered in the countryside—74 percent of the votes are there, after all—modernity in all its ideational, media, and material aspects radiates from the city. And while the city is no longer the background of most politicians nor the primary focus of political activity, its national leaders, bankrollers, ideologues, Bollywood celebrity campaigners, criminal connections, advertising agencies, and official spin-doctors and word-spinners belong to the city. Modernity, in politics as in general, radiates from the city's well-educated and well-employed population.

In these categories, women do not lag far behind men. According to the 1991 census, 12.3 percent of the urban population of men and 8.7 percent of the urban population of women are university graduates. It is certainly true that many of these women do not use their tertiary education, usually in arts or science, for work outside their homes. They were never meant to. Their university education was meant by their families to make these women more attractive items on the marriage market: modern wives for well-connected and well-employed modern men—mistresses of urban nuclear families, adepts in ways of the city, partners in the oversight of their children's education, companions for their husbands, hostesses for his colleagues. It is equally true, however, that many of these women seep into the urban, white-collar workforce. It is as difficult in Indian cities as elsewhere to maintain an appropriate level of middle-class consumption on one ordinary middle-class income. And the more middle-class matrons work outside their homes, the more socially acceptable it becomes for them to do so. And not only outside, but within their families, these women are multipliers. Educated mothers who have working careers are probably more likely than mothers who have neither to educate and motivate their daughters for middle-class working careers.[49]

For whatever these statistics are worth (and they are probably at least indicative), in the census category "professional, technical and related workers," the percentages of male and female workers are equal. In the category "administrative, executive and managerial workers," men outnumber women by six to one—more or less as they seem to do in the United States.[50] So while there has been since Independence a marked decline in the percentage of women workers in factories and mines, there has been an increase—far less substantial in numbers, but more substantial perhaps in social effect—in women's employment in prestigious, role-model professions—not in all, and not in engineering, but certainly in medicine, for example, a very well regarded career in India as elsewhere. In medical colleges, from 1950–51 to 1980–81 the number of women students quadrupled. The All-India Institute of Medical Sciences, perhaps the most esteemed medical facility in India, has had a women director.

With regard to politics as such, and reflective of its rural centeredness, women's participation as political candidates is marginal. In recent years, there has been a rise to prominence of a handful of women politicians who, unlike many of their predecessors and contemporaries, are neither consanguineously nor conjugally related to some "great man." A handful of women have made it to the upper echelons of the bureaucracy. But after the 1999 elections, only about 12 percent of the members of parliament are women. That is the best that they have ever done. In state legislative assemblies, the number of women members is also negligible. A proposed constitutional amendment that would have reserved one-third of the seats in parliament for women has been opposed by caste-based OBC politicians who argue, quite rightly, that such a change would likely increase upper-caste representation in the Lok Sabha. The thin layer is disproportionately upper caste.

Under the Seventy-Third Constitution Amendment Act of 1992, one-third of the total seats in all *panchayati raj* tiers must be reserved by state governments for women; of seats reserved for "scheduled castes and tribes" or OBC, one-third must go to women; and one-third of chairs must be reserved for women at every *panchayati raj* level.[51] It is perhaps too early to say, but for a number of reasons this constitutional change may hold less promise for ordinary village women than it appears. First, from the time that it was instituted, *panchayati raj* has been viewed with suspicion by many state governments. Simply, politicians in state legislative assemblies tend to fear the elected heads of *panchayati raj* institutions. They are, after all, the state-subsidized patrons of client networks, and as such they have the power of political spoilers or rivals. In consequence, state governments have generally allowed their *panchayati raj* institutions to languish. It was, in part, to correct this that *panchayati raj* was given the constitutional status of local government by the Seventy-Third Amendment. But the amendment still allows state legislative assemblies considerable control over *panchayati raj* institutions, and they remain, as ever, and perhaps more than ever, worrisome to provincial politicians. Second, before the amendment women were both elected and/or coopted members of *panchayati raj* institutions throughout India. Doubtlessly, some of these women effectively promoted village women's interests: in restricting the sale and consumption of whisky, for example, in Andhra Pradesh and Haryana. But in village India, the interests of their families are no less, and perhaps more, compelling to the women who marry into them than to their husbands. Anecdotal evidence is strong in suggesting that many if not most women *panchayati raj* members were either the puppets of their husbands and brothers-in-law or deputies representing their families' rather than women's interests. Most of the family interests represented by *panchayati raj* members and chairs, either men or women, of OBC or dominant caste, were the interests of landed families. Whatever it may do for the situation of village women, the Seventy-Third Amendment is unlikely to change the coalition of politically dominant classes in India.

So, whether the situation of women in village India will be substantially changed under the Seventy-Third Amendment or not remains to be seen. It may be well to recall that the rural female literacy rate of 31 percent is about half the rural male literacy rate. There is a smaller proportion of girls to boys at every level of education, and the higher the level the smaller the proportion. The lower the status group to which women belong, the less likely they are to be literate— 24 percent of Dalit women, most of whom live in villages, are literate. Finally, there is the matter of rural propriety—and it is no small matter. Far less than urban women do rural women regard public space as an arena in which respectable women voice their opinions.

In sum, my guess is that the path to gender equality in India will wind slowly from the urban top to the rural bottom. Although the women's movement in India is omnibus in its concerns and notable for its energy and intelligence, its direction is in the hands of women who inhabit the thin layer of urban, wealthy, and upper-middle-class families. They are part—perhaps a leading part—of the urban drift into the countryside: the drift of modernity into "traditional" villages, the ethos drift of parliamentary democracy's egalitarianism into the "sacred" hierarchy of villages. We have already noted the changes that these drifts have brought to the hierarchy of castes in the rural-centered arena of politics. They may bring, are perhaps bringing, changes into the hierarchy of gender. But the pace will inevitably be slow. As untouchability is built into the social ideology and structure of village life, so are some crucial aspects of gender inequality. Not wife-beating, certainly, but the noninheritance of land by females, for example, is probably basic to the maintenance of the patrilineal family. There are changes in Indian society that run counter to gender equality. As the practice of dowry marriages, for example, becomes increasingly respectable, widespread, and expensive, the financial burden of daughters on their families increases accordingly. The slow march to gender equality in India is likely to proceed as elsewhere, with steps forward and backward.

Hindutva and the Secular State

Of late, the apparent resurfacing of Hindu nationalism as a major force in Indian politics has become of increasing concern to friends of parliamentary democracy in a secular Indian nation-state. The focus of their concern is the spectacular rise to political power and prominence of the Bharatiya Janata Party—from 2 seats in parliament in 1984, to 119 after the 1991 elections, to 160 after the 1996 elections, to 178 after the 1998 elections. In 1998, the BJP was either the governing party or a major partner in the governing coalition in seven of the most populous of India's twenty-five states and in its national capital. Until it collapsed in May 1999, the coalition government that ruled at India's center for thirteen months was led by the BJP. The parliamentary elections of 1999 returned the BJP to power in Delhi as the leading party in a National Democratic Alliance of eighteen parties. The BJP had 182 candidates elected, and the alliance holds 300 of the Lok Sabha's 545 seats. The elections confirmed the prime ministership of the BJP stalwart, Atal Bihari Vajpayee.

The BJP is the latest and most successful party to emerge from the movement, at least as old as the Arya Samaj, for what has come to be called *Hindutva* (Hinduness)—for Hindu, as apparently opposed to secular Indian, nationalism. Various *sabhas* (organizations) have come and gone, waxed and waned, been repressed and gone underground, but the popular urge toward Hindu nationalism has never disappeared from independent India. As a political party, the BJP made its first, unpromising appearance as the Jan Sangh (people's party), with its roots in the urban petty bourgeoisie of northern India. The BJP now has rural and small-town constituencies in most parts of India, although it is thin on the ground in the east and south. In its alliance, however, there are provincial parties from every part of India. Their primary interests are in the rewards of political power. They are not much concerned with *Hindutva*, if not outright hostile to it.

The BJP first came to international notoriety in 1992 as a participant in the wrecking of the Babri Masjid (Babur's mosque) in the Uttar Pradesh temple town of Ayodhya. It was the culmination of a long campaign by *Hindutva's* votaries. Their propaganda, which brought thousands of Hindu pilgrims to Ayodhya, was that the mosque had been built as a particular insult to Hinduism by Mughals in the sixteenth century, on the site of a temple wrecked by them because it marked nothing less than the birthplace of the Lord Ram—among Hindus, the most widely celebrated incarnation of God. The vindication of Lord Ram at Ayodhya in 1992 was the most terrifying single event post-Independence in the dark history of Indian "communal" violence. There is no doubt but that the BJP government of Uttar Pradesh and some of its prominent national politicians were complicit in the mosque's destruction. It was followed by murderous "communal" riots in various parts of India, most notably in Mumbai (Bombay). In these riots, members of the BJP were also participants. The party makes no secret of its inclusion in a *pariwar* (family) of organizations—cadre, religious, cultural, labor, youth—which were heavily involved in this lawless Babri Masjid-Ram Janmabhumi (the temple at the Lord Ram's birthplace) affair and can be fairly described as Hindu revivalist and supremacist, anti-Muslim, or, at best, unfriendly to Islam.

Indian Muslim politicians are long reconciled to the permanence of their minority. Theirs is a "community" of the ruled and not of the rulers. They are neither the "nation" of Sir Saiyid Ahmad's imagining, nor the objects of self-interested imperial reservations and weightage. Nowadays, their shelter and reassurance lies in a paradoxically incongruous political arrangement: on the one hand, India's constitutional commitment to secularity; on the other, its Hindu politicians' unwillingness to displace with a uniform civil code the *shariah* as the basis of personal law for Indian Muslims. Many Muslims are fearful that this arrangement will be annulled or curtailed by the BJP: if not now, at some time to come. Their fear is shared by many thoughtful, well-educated, liberal Hindus. Certainly, as I have indicated above, Hindu nationalism is no new thing in India and was, arguably, the antecedent of secular Indian nationalism. Nonetheless, its resurgence is a cause for concern. But there is also a need for understanding—and that is properly the subject of this subsection.

Constitutionally, India is a secular state. But it is a Hindu nation. About 85 percent of India's population belongs to communities that identify themselves as Hindu. Hinduism's homeland is India. India's modern landscape is saturated by ancient Hinduism. Ayodhya is about 120 kilometers west of Lucknow, the capital city of Uttar Pradesh. Southwest of Ayodhya, 200 kilometers distant, on the banks of that great life-giving, sacred river, *Gangamata,* Mother Ganges, is Varanasi, known to Hindus as Kashi and sacred to the Lord Siva. It is from his hair that the river flows. Allahabad, 125 kilometers east of Varanasi, is known to Hindus as Prayag, a great pilgrimage site at the confluence of the Ganges, Yamuna, and fabled Saraswati rivers. The great battle described in the Hindu epic *Mahabharata* and in its included scripture, one of Hinduism's holiest, *Bhagavad Gita,* was fought in the vicinity of Kurukshetra, a small city 150 kilometers north of Delhi. Vrindavan, on the train line between Delhi and Agra, is where the Lord Krishna, perhaps the most worshipped incarnation of God, was born and dallied with the *gopis* (milkmaids) and, among them, with Radha, his divine companion. Three hundred fifty kilometers west of Agra, in the footprint of Brahma, another of God's incarnations, lies Pushkar Lake. All this within a radius of 700 kilometers from the capital of secular India! Elsewhere and everywhere in India, rivers, lakes, hills, trees, towns and cities, village festivals and rural fairs, urban concerts and dance recitals, movies, the dashboards of cars, the decorations of trucks, the talismans of shopkeepers, the brand names of their merchandise, their names — all tell Hindu stories. The television events of recent decades, literally bringing ordinary life to a halt during their viewing times, were productions of the Hindu epics *Mahabharata* and *Ramayana*, both of a hundred or so episodes, done in popular Bollywood fashion and viewed as religious observances by many in their audiences. Certainly, there are Muslim as well as Hindu ingredients in the "composite culture" of modern Indian society. But no less certainly, most of the major and defining ingredients of the *masala* are Hindu.

Although its influence in Asia has been great—directly, and indirectly, through its off-shoot, Buddhism—Hinduism never really or successfully, substantially, or permanently left home, unlike the world's other great religions. Hinduism is particularly Indian. The vast majority of Hindus outside India are of Indian descent. When Islam came to India, Hinduism was already an ancient faith. Islam filtered into Hinduism without changing it. Hindus, for example, brought their worship to the *dargahs* (tombs) of Sufi saints. Indian Muslims are overwhelmingly the progeny of converts from Hinduism, and well into the twentieth century, as noted above, most ordinary Indian Muslims professed and practiced an Islam that was barely different from the Hinduism professed and practiced by their neighbours.[52]

Earlier, I discussed the processes by which these like Hindus and like Muslims became to each "the other"—different and separate "communities"—and how Indian nationalism was first conceived as an alliance between these "communities" before it was put forward in secular terms. Again, only after the failure of the Khilafat–Non-Cooperation Movement in the 1920s did secular nationalism—nationalism officially indifferent to religious "communalism"—gain currency in Congress. But many in the Congress Party continued (and continue) to define Indian nationalism, implicitly or explicitly, as Hindu. That definition was never exclusive to the BJP or to its predecessors or to their *pariwar*.

Secularism came to the Indian constitution via a terse injunction in the American Bill of Rights against the making of any law in the United States "respecting an establishment of religion, or prohibiting the free exercise thereof." But, in the real politics of both countries, I suggest that secularism is best understood as a restraining ordinance imposed by the majority religious "community" on itself. It is a self-restraining ordinance whose interpretations and amendments, legal and extralegal, as to what constitutes "an establishment of religion" and/or the "free exercise thereof" is reserved by the majority "community" to itself.

In the United States, Prohibition was the culmination in 1919 of a successful Protestant Christian campaign to legislate contemporary Protestant Christian morality by banning through constitutional amendment "the manufacture, sale and transportation of intoxicating liquors. . . ." To this day, only Christian religious festivals are celebrated as national holidays in the United States. The births, deaths, marriages in civil ceremonies, naturalizations, degrees from state universities, and military commissions of non-Christians in the United States have regularly been certified in their particular "year of our Lord." The "moral majority" of "fundamentalist" Christians, who campaign to ban or severely restrict medical terminations of pregnancy and to reinstitutionalize the saying of prayers in public schools, exercise a virtual veto on the Republican Party's choice of its presidential candidates. At the end of the twentieth century, Christian groups in some states in the American Bible Belt have succeeded in banning or substantially curtailing on religious grounds the teaching of natural evolution in public schools. Replete with salacious details, the videotapes of President Bill Clinton's testimony to a Congressional committee regarding his adulterous affair with a young woman in his office was broadcast in September 1998, on the first of the solemn high holy days in the Jewish calendar. It was not meant as an insult. It was only an oversight. But neither the oversight nor the broadcast would have occurred on Good Friday.

In India, to ensure their auspiciousness, the openings of public buildings, the inaugurations of official functions, the beginnings of the day in government offices are routinely preceded by Hindu benedictions. For India's "national language," Hindi—the official script designated in India's constitution, Devan-agari—was regarded by both major religious "communities" of British India as the Hindu script. It is virtually identical with the Sanskrit script of sacred Hindu texts. The tune, though not the words, of India's national anthem originates in the Hindu nationalism of the Bengali *bhadralok*. Of late and in response to the challenge of *Hindutva*, more than a few secular politicians, including Congress prime ministers, have "saffronized"—taken on a chameleon's Hindu coloration. Others, strident secularists who decry "communalism," have built their base on caste—Hinduism's fundamental social institution, Hinduism by other means. Complicit in the Ayodhya tragedy was a Brahmin Congress Party prime minister who thought he could do business with the Brahmin leadership of the BJP.

Thus, secularism is qualified. In the United States it is Christian secularism; in India, Hindu secularism. It is to this political reality that the BJP has attached itself. Its ideological framework was, of course, supplied by the nineteenth- and twentieth-century imaginers and inventors of religious "communalism," Muslim and Hindu. The BJP has immediately tapped in to popular disaffection with a Congress Party that has surrendered itself to slavish dependence on the resurrection of the Nehru–Gandhi dynasty and is otherwise distant, directionless, and riddled with corruption. The BJP has successfully connected this disaffection to the widespread belief among Hindus that Congress governments "pampered" Muslims in return for their "community's" services as a reliable "vote bank." That belief is not entirely fanciful. More broadly, however, the BJP has sensed an increased political self-consciousness in the Hindu "community" that India belongs to it: an awareness bred of a half-century of having its votes bidden for, of voting governments in and out of power, of being Hindus in *Hindu Rashtra*—the Hindi nation.

Like *Hindutva, Hindu Rashtra* is a term of various and no definite meanings: from "Hindu state"—as, for example, Israel is a "Jewish state"—to a secular parliamentary democracy whose underlying culture is undeniably Hindu, just as the United States' is Christian. At least in their public statements, the BJP's parliamentary leaders incline toward the latter meaning: *Hindutva* defined in cultural terms. To be sure, the *pariwar* has its ideologues to whom *Hindutva* means Hinduism, and the BJP has in its ranks a fair share of Hindu fanatics and bigots, anti-Muslim hooligans, and rabble-rousers. But the party's leaders and policymakers have nowhere on their known agenda the reduction of Muslims to second-class citizenship, or the imposition on them of any civil or political disabilities. There is no indication of Muslim mistreatment in any state that is or has been governed by the BJP. It has no blueprint for a Hindu theocracy, whatever that might be, nor even for a decisive shift in Hindu secularism toward *Hindutva*. In national office, the BJP has even backed away from its preelection promise to fulfil the constitution's unfulfilled "directive principle" to have in India a uniform civil code equally applicable to its citizens of all religions. Ironically, in recent election campaigns, though not in 1999, the only major

Indian party to support this sine qua non of the modal secular state was the party of *Hindutva*.

Ideology, much less ideological consistency, fares poorly in Indian politics. In its march to political power, the BJP has become more and more an ordinary Indian party. Not unlike the Congress Party of old, it builds its strength piecemeal from a deal here and another there, with local communities and their factions, opposing factions, and factions of factions. But unlike the Congress Party of old, the BJP came to power in Delhi and remained in government, however briefly, in 1998–99 and now, again, on the sufferance of its coalition partners—all of which are provincial parties.

In recent years, the growth of political parties in India has been provincial and abundant. Almost forty officially recognized parties contested the 1998 and 1999 parliamentary elections. Of these, all but Congress and the BJP are, by design, designation, or default provincial. The BJP came to power in 1998 as the leader in a coalition of twelve parties, one of whose defection toppled the government in 1999. At issue was the aim of the defecting party's supremo to escape prosecution on charges of corruption. *Hindutva* had nothing to do with it. The BJP is now the leader of an even larger and more diverse coalition of provincial parties, but no single party in this coalition has the numbers to bring the BJP government down. Ironically, what would be most likely to precipitate the toppling of this government by the defection of more than one of its coalition partners would be any attempt by the BJP to legislate the items on its *pariwar's* agenda: the "rebuilding" of the Ram temple in Ayodhya, the "reclaiming" for Hinduism of Muslim sacred sites in the cities of Mathura and Varanasi, the revocation of a constitutional provision applicable only to Jammu and Kashmir, the adoption of a uniform civil code.

In response to dire warnings from its coalition partners at the center, the BJP early in 2000 ordered its government in Gujarat to rescind the permission it had given to state bureaucrats to join the *pariwar's* cadre organization, the RSS.[53] A few months later, and belatedly, the BJP publicly condemned the recent spate of violent attacks on Christians by Hindu zealots and dissociated itself from the anti-Christian propaganda of the *pariwar*. The defence minister of the National Democratic Alliance (NDA) and the leader of one of its largest constituent parties is a Christian.[54] Neither the NDA nor any other imaginable coalition supports the *Hindutva* of *pariwar* ideologues. The BJP, as the leader of India's ruling coalition, has become the leading member of its *pariwar*. As has been the case in other successful parliamentary parties elsewhere, within the BJP itself power has shifted from its organizational wing and its ideologues to its parliamentary party. Some months after the BJP coalition came to power in 1998, the leader of the RSS noted publicly that, "though the party which prides [itself] in *Hindutva* is for the first time ruling the nation, it has not been able to work as expected."[55] The BJP is no more likely to fulfil RSS expectations in the Vajpayee government's second time around.

In sum, I do not think that either the BJP or *Hindutva* threaten India as a secular parliamentary democratic state. And not only because there is no coalition to support it in an era, into the foreseeable future, of coalition governments in Delhi. The manifestation of castes as major political actors serves parliamentary democracy by adjusting it to the social realities of its adoptive Indian state. So it may be with *Hindutva*. In parliamentary democracies, people decide what is important to them, and politicians act accordingly. Hinduism is important to the majority "community" of Hindus. It would be excessively naive to imagine that the Indian constitution could do more than moderate Hindu secularism, could serve as more than a porous barrier between *Hindutva* and the politics of parliamentary democracy in India.

But it would be no less naive to envision a Hindu theocracy. In the late-nineteenth century, Hindus began to be imagined as a political "community," but they have not yet been—nor are they ever likely to be—successfully invented as a political bloc. They are too diverse and contentious a population of 850 million people, divided into thousands of castes and sects, hundreds of thousands of *jatis* and villages, riven by old and new hatred and contempt, separated from one another by distance, religious practices, language, and "mother tongue," differentiated by class, education, dress, diet, whether they are townspeople or villagers, from one part of the subcontinent or another. The luxuriant and inexorable growth of provincial parties and the dependence of national parties on local circumstances gives us some insight into the political reality of this great diversity.

As for Indian Muslims, they are no less diverse a population. They are the minority "community," but they are a huge minority: 120 million people, 20 percent of the population in Kerala and West Bengal, 15 percent in the Hindu heartland of northern India, and no less than 5 percent virtually anywhere in India. There are any number of parliamentary and state legislative constituencies in which the votes of Muslims are decisive. On the reasonable assumption that Indian politics is more about sandwiches than candles, the BJP has courted Muslim politicians and constituencies, and they have allowed themselves to be courted. Muslims can be trifled with only at a cost that no Hindu partner in India's coalition of dominant classes is willing to pay. Most Indian Muslims are poor and uneducated, but they are not without resources apart from their numbers. They have among their coreligionists an elite that is well placed, secure, and well integrated with their Hindu counterparts. The head of India's Defence Research and Development Organization, A. P. J. Abdul Kalam, for example, is one of the science bureaucrats most responsible for the success of India's nuclear weapons tests in May 1998. Thereafter, he was prominent in his share of photo opportunities with Atal Bihari Vajpayee. With good reason, to be sure, the ruling party in Jammu and Kashmir—the (Muslim) National Conference—is part of the BJP's coalition.

In response to the BJP's rise and the post-Ayodhya desertion of Muslims as Congress-voters, there is, at least in embryo, a modernist Muslim political and social leadership that wants not merely to shelter behind Hindu secularism, but to take advantage of its commitment to equal educational and employment opportunities for all India's citizens. They want to play minority politics more imaginatively and productively than by putting Muslims once again into a political ghetto—some party's "vote bank." They do not like the BJP, but they think they can do business with it.

Coalition Instability

Coalition instability at India's Centre is its most immediate political problem. In the era of the provincial party, an era that shows no sign of ending, no party—neither the BJP nor Congress—is capable of forming a national government on its own or even with like-minded allies. Opportunism reigns supreme. Party and coalition policy statements are cover stories. In the expectation that their coalition's electoral success will end the pursuit of corruption charges against them or presage the destruction of their provincial enemies, political leaders take their parties from one coalition to another. In the decade from 1989, there were five parliamentary elections, and no government served its term. In the three years through 1999, four coalition governments fell and there were three parliamentary elections.

The results of the 1999 elections increase the likelihood of the second BJP government completing its term. If so, it would be the first such event in the history of Delhi's coalition governments. Unlike its predecessor, the NDA cannot be toppled by the defection of any one of its parties, although two or three of them could do the job nicely. As Congress gradually disintegrates and a "third force" fails to emerge, except in the deliberations of a handful of yesterday's politicians, the BJP's hold on its coalition leadership has probably tightened.

There is a possible institutional solution to coalition instability, variants of which have been legislated elsewhere: the constructive vote of confidence. Voters of no-confidence would have to accompany their motion with the nomination of an alternative government appropriately supported by a parliamentary majority. But that would limit the bargaining and wrecking power of small parties, and they are unlikely to support it. So, politics continues to turn in on itself. It becomes less and less about affecting the society in which it operates, and more and more about itself. Politics about politics!

To end where we began: parliamentary democracy at India's Centre is protected by the lack of any alternative to it, now and in the foreseeable future. It is also sheltered by a reasonably competent bureaucracy at the Centre and reasonably stable, competitive parliamentary democratic systems in most of its states. Still, we need not argue too long or hard that political stability at India's Centre is at least desirable, if not immediately essential. A nationwide policy of industrial development and appropriate fiscal, monetary, and educational policies can only be determined and managed from the Centre. A communications infrastructure to serve the real possibility of India becoming one of the world's centers of information technology can only be built from New Delhi.[56] In India's unsettled Asian environment, foreign and national defense policies—including the management of one of the world's largest military establishments and its nuclear arsenal—can only be determined by national government. Including the running of one of the world's largest railroad systems, the superintendence of India's interstate transport and commerce can only be done from the Centre. There are social issues national in their scope that require some Central input, at least: the persistence of inequality, poverty, and illiteracy. Crucial to India's integrity as a parliamentary democratic multination state of nation-provinces[57] is the maintenance of the dynamic balance between the centrifugal forces of provincialism and the centripetal forces of nationalism—and that balance can only be maintained from New Delhi.

NOTES

1. So named after the Naxalbari area of West Bengal, in which the revolutionary communist party (CPI-ML) made its debut.

2. Mr. Dooley was the pen name of Finley Peter Dunne, an Irish-American political satirist who wrote at the turn of this century.

3. M. R. Srinivas, *Social Change in Modern India* (Berkeley, CA: University of California Press, 1966).

4. A title of great respect, for a specifically Hindu holy man.

5. The slogan raised by Gandhi and Congress in 1942.

6. Rajni Kothari, *Politics in India* (New Delhi: Orient Longmans, 1970), and W. H. Morris-Jones, *The Government and Politics of India* (London: Hutchinson University Library, 1964).

7. Officially a ceremonial position, analogous to the president's position at India's center.

8. By encouraging the radical religious wing of the Akali Dal against its ruling government of moderates, she incidentally brought to political prominence one Jarnail Singh Bindranwale, a murderous Sikh fanatic who took over the Golden Temple in Amritsar as his headquarters, arms-stash, and safe-house for assassins. The army's storming of the temple complex in 1984 and Mrs. Gandhi's assassination by her Sikh bodyguards followed.

9. "India Votes," http://elections99.indiavotes.com/states_party99.html.

10. Literally, false name; listing property owned or transferred under a false name, usually of a relative or client.

11. Harold Lasswell, *Politics: Who Gets What, When and How* (New York: Meridian Books, 1958).

12. In 1970, there were 62 Indian universities with about 2.5 million student. In 1999, 6 million students attended 232 Indian universities and affiliated colleges.

13. Eric R. Wolf, *Peasants* (Englewood Cliffs, NJ: Prentice-Hall, 1966), p. 11.

14. Ranbir Singh, "Haryana," *Patterns of Panchayati Raj in India*, edited by G. Ram Reddy (Delhi: Macmillan, 1977), p. 115.

15. Out of eighty-five; and this was an improvement—after the 1998 parliamentary elections it had none.

16. Ali Ashraf, "Uttar Pradesh," *Status of Panchayati Raj in the States of India 1994*, edited by George Mathew (New Delhi: Institute of Social Sciences, 1995), p. 211.

17. D. P. Chaudhri and Ajit K. Das Gupta, *Agriculture and the Development Process: A Study of Punjab* (London: Croon Helm, 1985), and Peter B. R. Hazell and C. Ramaswamy,

"Conclusions and Policy Implications," *The Green Revolution Reconsidered: The Impact of High-Yielding Rice Varieties in South India,* edited by Peter B. R. Hazell and C. Ramaswamy (Delhi: Oxford University Press, 1991), pp. 238–253.

18. Barrington Moore Jr., *Social Origins of Dictatorship and Democracy* (Boston: Beacon Press, 1966), p. 420.

19. Ibid., p. 422.

20. The states are unilingual in principle and to some extent in literate practice. But virtually every state has a minority whose "mother tongue" is not the state's official language, and some of the "mother tongues" that are categorized under the state's official languages are dialects unintelligible to one another.

21. V. P. Menon, *The Story of the Integration of the Indian States* (Bombay: Orient Longmans, 1961), p. 468.

22. The insistent demand by Sikhs for *Punjabi Suba*, a Punjabi-language state, was understood and opposed by Jawaharlal Nehru as a demand for a Sikh-majority state. It was acceded to by his daughter.

23. Quoted in Robert W. Stern, *The Process of Opposition in India* (Chicago, IL: University of Chicago Press, 1970), p. 12.

24. For Hindu cultural reasons, Sanskrit is also listed—as the language of 0.01% of the population, probably an exaggeration.

25. www.transparency.de.

26. Gunnar Myrdal, *Asian Drama,* abridged edition, edited by Seth R. King (New York: Vintage Books, 1972).

27. Edward Banfield, *The Moral Basis of a Backward Society* (New York: The Free Press, 1958).

28. That is, no rules at all.

29. The index combines "indicators of income, life expectancy and educational attainment into a composite. . . ." In 1999, India ranked 132 of the 174 countries surveyed. www.undp.org/hdro.

30. The most recent is the Central Vigilance Commissioner, N. Vittal, who posted on the commission's website the names of about 200 leading bureaucrats against whom the commission has sought criminal or departmental proceedings for major penalties. In the past, when the CVC presented such a list of names to parliament, "nobody noticed," but "now that it is on the internet, everybody has woken up to it," and parliament has acted accordingly by apparently increasing the power and independence of the CVC. *India Today,* 6 March 2000, pp. 16–21.

31. In Rajasthan, a synonym for *jati* is *khun,* blood.

32. The Hindu devotionalist *bhakti* movements of about the eighth to the sixteenth centuries had an essentialist egalitarian strain, but it has not survived them.

33. Louis Dumont, *Homo hierarchicus* (London: Weidenfeld and Nicolson, 1970).

34. As of 2000, neither have been provided.

35. Second to Kerala, the small "tribal" state of Mizoram in the northeast has the second highest literacy rate among Indian states.

36. Public sector (i.e., government-owned) industry employs more than twice the number of people employed in the nonagricultural, medium- to large-scale industrial private sector.

37. The population of "scheduled castes" is about twice that of "scheduled tribes"; spatially, socially, economically, and ideologically they are less central to Hinduism than Dalit castes.

38. J. H. Hutton, *Caste in India,* 3rd edition (London: Oxford University Press, 1961), p. 205.

39. Ibid., p. 206.

40. Oliver Mendelsohn and Marika Vicziany, *The Untouchables: Subordination, Poverty and the State in Modern India* (Cambridge: Cambridge University Press,1998), p. 141, and "Panel Dissatisfied with SC, ST Progress," *Times of India*, internet edition, 27 April 1998.

41. Congress won ten seats in the 1999 elections. The BSP won fourteen, up from four Uttar Pradesh seats and one seat from Bihar in the 1998 parliamentary elections.

42. Reference is to the *Manu Smriti,* the Code of Manu, a handbook of Hindu jurisprudence collected between c. 600 BCE and c. 300 CE. "The chief design of the code seems to have been to give divine sanction to the institution of caste, to make caste supreme in India and the brahmins supreme among the castes. . . ." Benjamin Walker, *The Hindu World,* Vol. 2 (New York: Praeger, 1968), p. 28.

43. Quoted in Zoya Hasan, *Quest for Power: Oppositional Movements and Post-Congress Politics in Uttar Pradesh* (Delhi: Oxford University Press, 1998), p. 160.

44. "Doublespeak Duo," *India Today International*, 22 September 1997, pp. 12–17.

45. "Panel Dissatisfied."

46. National Commission for Scheduled Castes and Scheduled Tribes, Report 1998.

47. "Panel Dissatisfied."

48. Because it was not part of the British Indian Empire, Sri Lanka is not part of this study. But it is certainly part of the subcontinent's great civilization. Its current prime minister, Chandrika Kumaratunga, is the daughter of one of its previous prime minister, Sirimavo Bandaranike, who is the widow of her predecessor.

49. Susan Verghese and Savita Pagnis, "Women in Engineering Education," *Changing Status and Role of Women in Indian Society*, edited by C. Chakrapani and S. Vijaya Kumar (New Delhi: M. D. Publications, 1994), p. 145.

50. "Misleading Statistics—'Women Rising in Management'—Sort Of," *DataLine, I:*9, March 1992, internet edition.

51. B. S. Khanna, *Panchayati Raj in India* (New Delhi: Deep & Deep, 1994).

52. M. Mujeeb, *The Indian Muslims* (New Delhi: Munshiram Manoharlal, 1985), chap 1.

53. *Times of India*, internet edition, 9 March 2000.

54. Ibid., 14 July 2000.

55. "RSS Unhappy with Vajpayee Government," *Times of India*, internet edition, 2 October 1998.

56. "At Your Service," *Far Eastern Economic Review*, 2 September 1999, pp. 8–12.

57. An unfortunate neology, perhaps. But I cannot think of any term in general use that describes the combination of political authority at a provincial level and ethnicity that characterizes Indian states. The analogy, of course, is to "nation-state," itself a neology of the twentieth century.

5

Pakistan and Bangladesh

The failure of parliamentary democracy to develop in Pakistan and in Bangladesh stems, for much of their histories, from parts of the same story. Albeit of different legacies, both are political legatees of the same British empire—one, of the "Punjab tradition" of bureaucratic authoritarianism; the other, of representative institutions. Both emerged, though differently, from British Indian histories of Muslim opposition to imperialism and collaboration with it, "communalism" and nationalism, adherence to the "Pakistan" movement, and inclusion in Pakistan. Uncomfortably, Pakistan and Bangladesh were the western and eastern parts of the same Pakistan until 1971.

Since then, the development of parliamentary democracy in Pakistan has been impeded by the undiminished power of those antidemocratic dominant classes that originally coalesced, in part, to protect their interests against the threat of an elected government dominated by Bengalis. The development of parliamentary democracy in Bangladesh has been impeded to a degree by its legacies of twenty-four years as Pakistan's subordinate and disaffected province, its "colony," and by the dislocation of a year's war of liberation to secede and its chaotic aftermath.

In a comparative study of the subcontinent's experiences of parliamentary democracy, juxtapositions of its nondevelopment in Pakistan and Bangladesh with its development in India are both appropriate and useful to our understanding. In this chapter's interstices, the third party is India.

PAKISTAN AND THE "PUNJAB TRADITION"

"Political parties emerged," from Rueschemeyer, Stephens, and Stephens's notable survey, *Capitalist Development and Democracy*, "in a crucial role as mediators in both the installation and consolidation of [parliamentary] democracy." Congress did the job in post-Independence India. At once, it, "mobilize[d] pressures from subordinate classes for democratization" and "effectively protected dominant class interests."[1] As India's "one dominant party," Congress served India's democratic future by limiting political competition to what its newborn parliamentary democracy could likely bear, and, coincidentally, it energized the competitive dynamic that inheres in parliamentary democracy and was latent in Congress's hegemony.

No such institution was more critically lacking in Pakistan than one dominant *nationwide* political party. Mohammad Ali Jinnah—Pakistan's Quaid-i-Azam, its great leader—together with his colleague, Allama Mohammad Iqbal, the poet–philosopher of Indian Muslim nationalism, and many of the lesser political lights who met in Pakistan's constituent assembly, all aspired to unite Pakistan's two wings into one parliamentary democratic state. But without a nationwide party or parties capable of mediating between conflicting provincial interests, inducting subordinate classes into the political system, reassuring dominant classes, and governing, that aspiration was doomed to almost certain failure.

Compared to other British provinces, parliamentary politics was a relatively new arrival in what was to become Pakistan's political center, Punjab. And on arrival, such politics came largely into the domain of great landlords. Again, Punjab's National Unionist Party was not really a political party, but a great-landlord-dominated "agriculturalists'" interest group. Its primary concern was with implementing the Alienation of Land Act of 1900 in collaboration with the British provincial government. Great landlords, of course, had their individual "constituencies" of lesser landlords, *biradari*-fellows,[2] local allies, tenants, dependents, debtors, and clients of one sort or another. But the Unionist Party, as such, had virtually no popular constituency of its own. When the "Pakistan" slogan became irresistible to ordinary Muslims of northwestern India and to some of their most influential divines, Unionist landlords acceded to the inevitable or hedged their bets. They changed their party colors or had family members change theirs to become Muslim League landlords. Most of them would probably have preferred a continuation of British rule to the establishment of "Pakistan," much less of a Pakistan that bifurcated their Punjab. Partition had its consolation, however. It did not disturb landlord domination of the countryside and may even have increased it. Nor did it transform the Unionists into a party.

As for the Muslim League, until the 1940s it existed as an organization only among a handful of townsmen in an overwhelmingly rural western Punjab and Sindh. As a coherent organization, the League was most present and active in those districts of the northern subcontinent that remained in India to become the state of Uttar Pradesh—with the vast majority of its Muslim population included.

By virtue of his charisma and his political stature and skill, Jinnah might have established the emigrant Muslim League as a party in western Pakistan. But Jinnah died in 1948, as did Gandhi. Unlike the Mahatma, however, the Quaid bequeathed to his countrymen a spent movement rather than a governing party.

Of Pakistan's population, about 55 percent were Bengalis—by far and away its largest ethnolinguistic group and the legatees of a political inheritance from the Raj that was quite different from Punjab's. Politics was party politics among Bengali Muslims. In British Bengal, more than anywhere else in the empire, and among Bengali Muslims, more than among their coreligionists anywhere else in the empire, representative institutions and popular parliamentary politics were the best developed and the most long lived and successful. Only in Bengal, among British India's Muslims, and then in East Pakistan, was there a popularly based political party—an organized coalition, similar to Congress's, of urban professionals and landed peasants.

In the 1940s, the Krishak Praja Party was deserted by the ever-mercurial Fazlul Huq and his friends and enemies in favor of a vigorously reorganized and rejuvenated Bengal Provincial Muslim League. But, the latter was virtually independent and politically at odds with its All-India parent, the Quaid's Muslim League. To be sure, "Pakistan" rejuvenated both—but not the same "Pakistan." To the understanding of Bengali Muslims, "Pakistan's" provinces were to be, at the least, autonomous, if not independent.[3] From the Krishak Praja Party's program, the League in "Pakistan's" prospective eastern province had taken its commitment to implement a policy of land reforms favorable to the landed peasantry. What Jinnah meant by "Pakistan" was (and is) unclear, but it was not this. Organized as the Bengal Provincial Muslim League, the coalition of politically dominant classes in Bengal threatened every interest of its counterpart in the west. Ominously, as it turned out, for the future of parliamentary democracy in Pakistan, the 1946 election in Bengal produced the one and only popularly based and supported Muslim League government in British India.[4]

Thus, both in composition and organization the coalitions of dominant classes in Pakistan's two wings were different. They differed in their vital interests, and there was no nationwide parliamentary democratic organization—a party or parties—that might have mediated between them, bridged the gap. There were, however, in the west other-than-parliamentary democratic political organizations: legacies of the Raj. Most notably, there was an elite bureaucracy, an army, and a relabeled landlords' "party." These were centered almost entirely in Punjab, as was the model that their coalition represented: a capable and functioning nondemocratic administration. This was British India's "Punjab tradition" of an authoritarian bureaucracy: buttressed on the sword-arm side of "law and order" by the army, and on the cudgel-arm, by great landlords who maintained the political quiescence of the peasantry and encouraged its sons to serve in the Indian army. In collaboration with the great landlords of Punjab and Sindh, later with Muhajir industrialists, and, indirectly, with the aid of the United States and

China, elite bureaucrats and generals attempted to construct a domesticated variant of the "Punjab tradition" and to govern both wings of Pakistan in accordance with it. It was a political disaster.

In part, but only in part, this revival, domestication, and extension of the "Punjab tradition" was a dictate of necessity. Pakistan was not, as India was, well begun. The Republic of India was from its inception a going concern, heir to most of the infrastructural and human resources—and largely, in their integrity—that had sustained the Raj. Over the decades, Congress had evolved into an opposition party de facto, ready with its shadow programs and policies, its shadow ministry and premier, to replace the government in power. And this it did. The official British description of what occurred on the subcontinent in August 1947—a "transfer of power"—is apt. But only as it applied to India.

For Pakistan, it was a different story: torn from the edges of a map that was otherwise intact, one ethnolinguistic shred in the east and—separated by 2,000 kilometres of hostile India—shreds of ethnolinguistic differences in the west. East and west spoke different languages and wrote them in different scripts. Their self-perceptions and their perceptions of the other were stereotyped and contemptuous: Bengalis were untrustworthy, Punjabis were landlords and cannon-fodder. Sindhis and Baluch were wary of Punjabis. The doyens of Muslim society in the west, and its politicians, were landed aristocrats. Politics in the east was the occupation of Muslim *vakils*. Western Punjab was a granary; Eastern Bengal, a "rural slum." The only pocket of the subcontinent's modern commerce and industry that went to Pakistan, Karachi, was in the west; the east had no modern industry. Calcutta, the empire's "second city" and the great hole in Jinnah's "moth-eaten" Pakistan,[5] remained in India.

Pakistan's parting from India was hostile and almost ruinous. With far fewer resources than India, Pakistan had to resettle a roughly equal number of refugees: in total, for both, about thirteen million. The "communal" bloodshed that preceded and accompanied Partition was followed in 1948 by a shooting war in Kashmir. India became the enemy, an enemy with which Pakistan had to negotiate—and from a position of weakness—for its survival. New Delhi controlled the headwaters of the rivers that irrigated Pakistan's fields, west and east. It withheld Pakistan's fair share of the Indian empire's cash assets and government and military supplies. Mahatma Gandhi began a penitential fast, his last, to coerce his India into keeping its promise to treat Pakistan fairly.[6] The Congress government of India was suspected by Pakistanis, and not without reason, of regarding their new republic as "nothing but a temporary secession of certain territories from India that were soon to be reabsorbed"[7]—by Indian design, and the sooner the better. Only, let the British quit.

No less than India's contiguity, industrialization, and resources, in general—and more crucial to the moment—what its unfriendly neighbor had and Pakistan lacked was an emplaced system of government capable of governing. Nothing was more immediately threatening to Pakistan's survival than that deficiency. Government had to be invented or reinvented in Pakistan, and without delay. It could not be party government, not only because there were no national parties, but because there was no national social base on which a national party could be built, no coalition of politically dominant classes that was national. Chaudhri Muhammad Ali, an elite diplomat at Jinnah's side, leaves us with this diplomatic portrait of the League in West Pakistan:

The pillars of society, the landlords, the well-to-do lawyers, the rich businessmen and the titled gentry were [the League's] main support. . . . They were, by and large, estimable men who served their country and their community *within the limits dictated by discretion.*[8]

In East Pakistan, a different coalition of dominant classes threatened to shake all these pillars. From the dawn of Pakistan, the Bengali coalition felt betrayed by these "estimable men" of the west; in reprisal, the League in the east was gradually deserted and finally demolished by a United Front of Bengali parties in the provincial elections of 1954. The United Front's largest constituent party, the Awami League, was led then by Maulana Abdul Hamid Khan Bhashani, a left-wing firebrand and a politician whose ambitions extended westward.

The United Front's "21-point" election manifesto, particularly as it was articulated by Bhashani, threatened every interest of every partner in West Pakistan's coalition of dominant classes: "complete autonomy" for East Pakistan, reduction in the "fat salaries of . . . higher officials," official scrutiny of " the income and expenditure of government officials and private businessmen," nationalization of the jute industry, introduction of cooperative farming, the total and gratuitous replacement of landlords by peasant proprietors, and arming an East Pakistan militia.[9] In addition, Bhashani, in particular, campaigned against Pakistan's emerging Cold War alliance with the United States.[10] It was an alliance calculated by the new masters of the "Punjab tradition" as their makeweight not only against India but in Pakistan's domestic politics. The results of the 1954 elections in East Pakistan left no doubt as to the political sentiments of the great majority of Pakistan's Bengali majority. In 237 contests for "Muslim seats" in the provincial assembly, the United Front won 215 and the League 9.[11] The West's oligarches responded by nullifying the election's results, abandoning any thought of parliamentary democracy, and extending their domesticated "Punjab tradition" eastward.

So, the domestication of the "Punjab tradition" by West Pakistan's coalition of dominant classes was, in part, a reversion in crisis to what was at hand in the absence of what was not. But it was hardly a disinterested reversion. And the tradition that was reverted to differs considerably from its original. Nonetheless, as a matter of economy, I propose to continue my discussion of the "Punjab tradition" for the remainder of this section, building on comparisons of its pre- and post-Partition manifestations and constructing a framework, an organizational device, and a metaphor for an inquiry into the nondevelopment of parliamentary democracy in Pakistan.

Autonomy and Responsibility

The British imperial bureaucracy that ruled Punjab was, of course, autonomous of Punjabi society. The "Punjab tradition" was originated by foreign conquerors and transpired into a regime headed by foreign bureaucrats and back-stopped by an army commanded by foreign officers. Their government owned land in Punjab. But these officers did not; nor did they marry into Punjabi families or have Punjabi heirs. They were subjects of a foreign monarch and servants of a foreign empire's interests. They were in Punjab for a while a while ago, but never of it.

Their post-Partition successors in West Pakistan, on the other hand, were of it. They had chosen to be Pakistanis, rulers of a new state, 60 percent of whose citizens in the west were Punjabis. The bureaucratic elite were overwhelmingly Punjabi and Muhajir. The structure of Punjabi society, with the addition of some "martial race" Pathans, was replicated in khaki by the army. Its officers were the scions of landlord families, and its soldiers were recruited from the homes of peasants. The countryside in Sindh and Punjab was ruled by landlords, and in Baluchistan and the North West Frontier Province, by tribal chiefs. One percent of Pakistan's landholders owned more than 30 percent of its land. The richest one-tenth of 1 percent of Pakistan's landlords owned more land than the poorest 64 percent of its peasants, most of whom owned no land at all.[12] Even before Partition, but mostly afterwards, Muslim industrialists, largely Muhajir and aspiring, joined this coalition of established landlords, elite bureaucrats, and generals in their "marriage of iron and rye."

In coalition, these groups—politically, economically, and socially dominant—formed an indigenous, homogenizing ruling class. It was factionalized, to be sure, like other such classes elsewhere, largely across the lines of family and personal ambitions and quarrels. "Marriage," however, as applied to alliances within the families of this class, was not merely a metaphor. With some preference for remaining within their ethnolinguistic groups, generals' sons married the daughters of industrialists, industrialists' daughters married the sons of great landlords, great landlords' sons married the daughters of elite bureaucrats, and so forth. There were "marriages" in metaphorical, rather than connubial, form: industrialists invested in land; landlords invested in industry; generals and elite bureaucrats rewarded themselves and each other with land grants. Industrialists and public-sector enterprises managed by bureaucrats awarded contracts to one another, and both endowed retired generals and elite bureaucrats with jobs and sinecures.

The British government of Punjab was responsible not, of course, to its Punjabi subjects, but, in a chain of responsibility, or rather networks, to the Government of India and through it to the "home" government in London and to the parliament at Westminster. To whom or what are the Pakistani inheritors of the "Punjab tradition," its coalition of dominant classes, responsible?

For the first eleven years of its history, government in Pakistan was an ongoing battle for supremacy between the politicians of a disintegrating Muslim League and an increasingly self-confident elite bureaucracy. In 1958, the matter was settled. The republic's senior military officer, General (later Field Marshal) Mohammad Ayub Khan, led an army coup which abrogated a constitution that had taken politicians nine years to draft. Ayub installed himself as Pakistan's president, banned political parties, emplaced a government of elite bureaucrats, and began the industrialization of Pakistan—under government aegis but through private enterprise.

In 1969, Ayub's "decade of development" was brought to a violent end. Pakistan, East and West, was rocked by widespread demonstrations of students and urban workers in protest against the costs of "development": widespread shortages of wage goods, inflation, and the escalation of inequalities of wealth. In East Pakistan, the protesters called once again for provincial autonomy. Ayub's army colleagues eased him from power and replaced him with another general, Agha Muhammad Yahya Khan. After a year-long war of liberation, East Bengal seceded in 1971 to become Bangladesh. In what was left of Pakistan, its western provinces, there followed seven years of political party government. In 1977, there was an army coup again. This was followed by eleven years of more transparent military dictatorship, albeit in collaboration with the elite bureaucracy, until the "accidental" death of the dictator and the army's commanding officer, General Zia ul-Haq.

In 1970, and again from 1988 to 1997, five Pakistani governments were voted into power. *But no Pakistani government has ever been voted out of power.* Save for Zia's regime, which ended with his death, every Pakistani government removed from power has been removed by the army, directly or indirectly through presidential decree. Moreover, under army management, the prime ministership in Pakistan has become a hazardous occupation. Of Pakistan's three duly elected prime ministers, the army ensured the hanging of the first, confirmed the exile of the second and the jailing of her husband, and set the scene for the third to be imprisoned for life. The army, which under the Raj had been the power behind the civilian throne and subordinate to it, bureaucratic authoritarianism's *ultima ratio*, became in Pakistan from 1958 the enthroning and deposing power.

From 1985, the army's preeminent position in Pakistani politics was regulated by the "Eighth Amendment" to Pakistan's constitution, a legacy from General Zia. It provided for a ruling "troika" in Islamabad. Its members were: (1) First among equals, the commanding officer of the army staff. (2) A president "whose appointment [was] tacitly subject to army approval" and who was empowered to appoint military commanders, provincial governors, and superior court judges. It was also his prerogative to prorogue Pakistan's National Assembly or any of its provincial assemblies, and to dismiss their governments.[13] In effect, the president, who had no constituency or organization of his own, was the army's point man in an apparently civilian government. (3) Last, and least among equals, a prime minister who, in Westminster fashion, was leader of the majority party in the National Assembly.

Flushed with victory in the 1997 elections, and sustained by large majorities for his Pakistan Muslim League in the National Assembly and the Punjab Provincial Assembly, Prime Minister Nawaz Sharif had the "Eighth Amendment" nullified by an overwhelming vote of virtually all parties in parliament. It was a mistake, predicated on the fantastic assumption that a political reality could be negated by a show of hands. The army's acquiescence was equally meaningless. Speaking through the president, the army had earlier suggested, as an alternative to the "Eighth Amendment," a Council for Defence and National Security (CDNS). This council would have given the military a formal role in the day-to-day operations of the parliamentary government—a place from which to deliver words to the wise, more effective, subtle, presentable, and less disruptive and troublesome than having the president bring down one government after another. The suggestion was rejected by Nawaz Sharif—another mistake.

In October 1998, an extraordinary series of events took place in Islamabad. In a "stunning" public address, the army chief, General Jehangir Karamat, criticized the performance of the Nawaz government and suggested that it might be improved by the incorporation in it of a National Security Council, a variation, largely in name, of the discarded CDNS. General Karamat was then summoned to an unfriendly interview with the prime minister, and immediately afterward *the general resigned*. Based on the outcomes of similar encounters in the past, it should have been the prime minister who resigned or was dismissed. What happened?

There are various explanations given by the usual "informed sources" for this apparent victory of civilian government. But none of them, so far as I know, doubt but that his army colleagues agreed to General Karamat's resignation not out of some latter-day conversion or compulsion to the democratic belief in military subordination to elected civilian government, but rather out of prudence. A prudent response, perhaps, to a bluff called by Nawaz! It was yet another mistake. No longer able to shelter behind the president and his power under the "Eighth Amendment," the army could only have replaced Nawaz with a coup had he refused to resign or do the army's bidding.

A coup would have been imprudent. It would have burdened the army with the responsibility of digging Pakistan out of the financial morass into which it has sunk, heavily weighted by military expenditure and foreign debt for, among other things, military expenditure. A coup would have further displeased the army's American friends and patrons, who were already displeased by Pakistan's efforts to develop nuclear weapons and mightily displeased by the testing of them in 1998. Better to allow the Nawaz government to continue foundering in office and to collaborate with it: in selective "law and order" campaigns, for example, most notably in the war between ethnolinguistic groups in Karachi, and against rampant corruption and theft in the national electricity supplier. No one doubted, however, but that the army's retreat was a tactical one and dictated by circumstances of the time. No one doubted but that the army, if it were so moved, could and would unseat the Nawaz government as it had its predecessors. And no one doubted but that there would be little popular opposition to such a move.

In the summer of 1999, what has come to be called the "Kargil War" raged between India and Pakistan. It was the bloodiest military encounter between the two countries since the Bangladesh War of 1971. Kargil is a mountainous sector on the "Line of Control," the de facto border between India's state of Jammu and Kashmir and Pakistan's Azad (free) Kashmir. Whatever the government in Islamabad, the army and its intelligence agency have always called the tune in the formation and implementation of Pakistan's foreign policies, overt and covert, particularly with regard to Afghanistan and India via Kashmir. With regard to the Kargil War, it would appear that the decision to send troops and *mujahidin* over the border was made by the army, and assented to by Nawaz. In the face of a determined offensive by Indian troops and the displeasure of the United States, the decision to pull the troops and *mujahidin* back to Pakistan, it would seem, was made, in consultation with the American president, by Nawaz—his final mistake—and reluctantly assented to by the army. What seemed for a moment to be evolving in Pakistan was a duumvirate of its prime minister and its military commander—in place of the "troika," a carriage pulled by two horses. The moment ended with the army coup of October 1999. It ended badly for Nawaz Sharif. His retreat from Kashmir—an attempt to encroach on the army's prerogative to make the decisions about Kashmir—was the last straw. Arrested by the army and convicted in a court of law of attempting to sabotage a Pakistan International Airline's flight and thereby murder—among others—the army chief of staff, Nawaz is presently serving two life sentences in prison. The army chief, General Pervaiz Musharraf, Nawaz's appointee to replace Jehangir Karamat, led the coup to replace Nawaz and is now Pakistan's self-appointed Chief Executive.

Are Pakistani governments, then, responsible to its army? Is it to the generals that their partners in Pakistan's coalition of dominant classes are responsible? No! Or more exactly, in no parliamentary democratic sense of the word "responsible." The army has institutional interests of its own, which it serves by regularly taking *on its own authority* the highest known proportion of GDP—about 6 percent—of any country in Asia and about a quarter of Pakistan's budget. This apart, the interests of the military elite are, as indicated above, enmeshed with the interests of its coalition partners. Their resentment against the generals for having usurped and exploited the place of first among equals in Pakistani politics explains the widespread support among civilian politicians for the annulment of the "Eighth Amendment." It was not their demand for the restoration of parliamentary democracy. What has never been cannot be restored. General Musharraf's[14] coup has nothing to do with parliamentary democracy, neither as its negation nor its purge. It is a reassertion by the army of its primacy in Pakistan's coalition of dominant classes. The 1999 coup is best thought of as an intra-coalition affair. General Musharraf's promise of "'good governance' is essentially a pledge to manage the existing inequities of society more efficiently."[15] While the "troika" arrangement was certainly undemocratic, it did assign to the army a measure of constitutional responsibility for competent civilian government. With the annulment of the "Eighth Amendment" and Nawaz's rejection of a CDNS, the army could only protect its primacy in Pakistan's politics, *its independence from direction by an elected civilian government,* with a coup. Now, postcoup, General Musharraf has installed the National Security Council that Nawaz rejected. And my guess is that it will remain installed when civilian government (I do not say "parliamentary democracy") returns to Islamabad.

Pakistani governments are not responsible to their electorate. That, I think, is clear. In effect, the army has exercised a veto on the electorate's choices and has done so with apparent nonpartisanship. There are currently two major parties in Pakistan: the Pakistan Peoples' Party (PPP), which is led from exile by Benazir Bhutto, the daughter of its founder and former head of one of the great landlord families of Sindh, Zulfikar Bhutto; and the Pakistan Muslim League (PML), which is still led from jail by Nawaz Sharif, the scion of one of Pakistan's largest family conglomerates of commercial and industrial enterprises. Acting through presidential use of the "Eighth Amendment," the army dismissed elected PPP governments in 1990 and 1996. After the first PPP government was dismissed, Pakistan's military intelligence agency, the ISI, cobbled together a coalition, the Islamic Democratic Alliance (IDA), to serve as Nawaz's electoral vehicle. In 1993, with Pakistan in more than the its usual state of turmoil, the army chief arranged the resignation of an elected government headed by Nawaz Sharif.

In 1999, it was no longer possible for the army to use presidential power to unseat a government. Hence the coup. It should be noted that after every election in Pakistan, the losing faction in the coalition of dominant classes has attempted by nonparliamentary "direct action" to entice the army into bringing down the elected government. The army's positive responses to these enticements, its repeated and routine interventions into parliamentary politics, needless to say, have been a major factor in stunting the development of parliamentary democracy in Pakistan.

As the army has the power to veto the electorate's choices, so landlords have the power to determine them in much of the countryside. For want of redistributive land reforms, great landlords continue to dominate Pakistan's countryside. Any number of them enhanced their holdings by seizing valuable, irrigated lands abandoned by Sikh farmers at the time of the subcontinent's partition. At that time, Ayub tried to leaven the weight of landlords in rural Pakistan by bringing landed peasants, as "basic democrats,"[16] into the margins of his regime and by a program of moderate land reforms. Both attempts failed. Zulfikar Bhutto's attempted land reforms of 1972 and 1977 were no less moderate and no more successful.

In truth, neither Ayub nor Bhutto tried very hard. Their reforms were clearly cosmetic and easily evaded. Many landlords actually profited from land reforms—by making waste lands available for government "resumption" at inflated prices, for example. Writing in 1994, one of Pakistan's most esteemed social scientists, Akmal Hussain, estimated that the "0.5 percent of landowners [whose holdings exceed 150 acres] own 30 percent of [the] total cultivated area" in Pakistan.[17] So, Pakistan's largest "vote banks" are controlled by landlords. In his reelection bid of 1977, Bhutto, founder and leader of what might have become Pakistan's first and only popularly based political party, looked to Punjab's landlords to turn out the vote.

The growth of capitalist farming in Pakistan has tightened the grip of landlords on the Pakistani countryside and secured their political future. As in India, capitalist agriculture in Pakistan received its impetus from the Green Revolution of the late 1960s. In Pakistan, however, land reform had neither antedated nor accompanied the Green Revolution. Not surprisingly, Islamabad pursued it through an "elite farmer strategy." Green Revolution inputs—high-yielding varieties of seeds, fertilizers and pesticides, irrigation facilities, credit—were channeled to and through landlords. They bought large tractors and resumed much of their tenanted land for mechanized cultivation with hired labor. Capitalist farming in Pakistan increased the dependence of its rural population on great landlords. The number of landless laborers increased, small tenanted farms increased in number and decreased in size, and smallholders were brought under the sway of landlords who controlled the state-sponsored Green Revolution mechanisms of credit and input distribution.

Cabals of landlords, no more inclined than their National Unionist predecessors to disciplined party organization, "dominate the major political parties, parliament [and] local governments. . . ."[18] The party-less elections held under General Zia's aegis in 1985 produced a National Assembly of whose 200 members 117 were landlords. In the party elections that have followed, nothing much has changed in this regard. According to a recent estimate:

a list of Pakistan's parliamentarians reads like a Who's Who of landed families. In a National Assembly of 207 members, feudal landlords and tribal leaders hold 126 seats, almost three times the number won by businessmen and urban professionals.[19]

In provincial assemblies, it is much the same story. Unaccompanied by land reforms, parliamentary democracy in Pakistan is largely an instrument for the protection and promotion of landlords' interests. Their strength on the ground "forces the rural voter . . . to repeatedly elect the feudal lord" or his candidate.[20] To make assurances doubly sure, the electorate is gerrymandered. It is, of course, largely rural, in fact, but made more so by the government's persistent unwillingness to conduct and/or publish a census. The last one was held in 1981, and there has been considerable village-to-city migration since then.

As for industrialists—the second power in Pakistan's parliamentary politics—they have their differences with landlords, to be sure, over the price of cotton, for example, but they are no more inclined than landlords to settle quarrels by rocking the boat of dominant classes' contentment. Quite the contrary: Not only do they fear "labor unrest," but their "marriages," of one sort or another, with "feudals" have "muted the demands for an egalitarian distribution of land."[21] More insidious, impossible to document, but nonetheless real is the adoption by industrialists and successful professionals of what its Pakistani observers call "feudal culture"—courteous and conspiratorial, fond of conspicuous consumption and waste, chronically and cavalierly in debt, inordinately concerned with *izzat*, lawless, illiberal, inegalitarian, and—in a word—antidemocratic.

In sum, Pakistan's coalition of dominant classes has, at best, held itself—or been held—responsible only to itself. Varying in its authority from time to time, and circumstance to circumstance, the government in Pakistan's National Assembly, has never been more than a part of Pakistan's national government, and it has never been "responsible" in the ordinary parliamentary democratic sense of that word. Had Nawaz not been toppled by a coup, would he have allowed himself to be removed from office at the polls? I doubt it. No precedent bound him. In office, he continued to erode the independence of the judiciary, ordered the police to intimidate his critics in the press, persecuted his political enemies through an Accountability Commission which had been established to prosecute the corrupt, succeeded in exiling the leader of the opposition party, and proposed to make himself the final arbiter of Islamic law.

It is perhaps for lack of responsibility in the ordinary parliamentary democratic sense of the word that partners in Pakistan's coalition of dominant classes are responsible in another sense: as collaborators in the squandering and misuse of their country's resources and as colleagues in the enjoyment of favored and corrupt access to these resources. Shahid Javed Burki, a Pakistani official of the World Bank, who served as finance minister in the caretaker government emplaced indirectly by the army in 1996–97, estimates that during Benazir Bhutto's second term as prime minister, from 1993 to 1996, "the cost to the [Pakistan] economy by way of corruption and wastage was of the order of 20 to 25 percent of GDP."[22] There is no reason to believe that this cost was substantially less during the regimes that preceded Benazir's second term or during the Nawaz regime that succeeded it. One of General Musharraf's first orders of business has been to highlight corruption as Pakistan's problem and to move against it. The arrest of Nawaz Sharif and his father and brothers followed. That their family's industrial empire has flourished on corruption is an open secret in Pakistan. But corruption among the families of Pakistan's coalition of dominant classes is widespread, nonpartisan, and pandemic. Suppose that the paterfamilias is blameless: what about his sons, or his wife's father and brothers, or his daughters' and sisters' husbands, or his cousins, or his indispensable business partners, advisers, right-hand men, courtiers?

Not surprisingly, on Transparency International's Corruption Perceptions Index, Pakistan ranks among the fifteen most corruption-ridden countries of the ninety-nine surveyed.[23] India, among the thirty most corrupt, does somewhat better (as it does in the UNDP's Human Development Index). But the differences in the political effects of corruption in India and Pakistan are less in their scale than in their symbiotic relationship to different regimes. Corruption on the subcontinent exists in a sort of symbiosis with the political status quo: a parliamentary democracy in India, an oligarchy of dominant classes in Pakistan. Thus, for example, by virtue of being democratically elected, politicians in India who become major benefactors and beneficiaries of corruption have a vested interest in the preservation of parliamentary democracy. Certainly, corruption distorts both the inputs and outputs of parliamentary democracy, but it does not now threaten parliamentary democracy in India. Again, there is no alternative to it. It is widely supported, and not only among the corrupt—the "folklore of corruption" notwithstanding. In Pakistan, the symbiotic relationship is between a corruption-enriched and empowered coalition of dominant classes on the one hand, and, on the other, the status quo of a military–bureaucratic authoritarianism. Corruption is indifferent to parliamentary democracy in Pakistan because the latter appears only as an occasional charade. Military intervention, direct or indirect, into Pakistan's politics serves only to reposition the components and factions of the coalition of dominant classes. Corruption among them is general, and they *as classes* would be threatened by parliamentary democracy. Thus, given the best will in the world to root corruption out, it is probably impossible for General Musharraf or any successive "chief executive" to do so except with political selectively—and with economic selectivity, no less. As well as the business of politics, so much of the business of business—the hope of economic (and even human) development in Pakistan, is directly or indirectly tied up in corruption. Some months after Musharraf's coup, this undiplomatic assessment of the situation was attributed to "a western Diplomat": "Everybody expected this government to come in, kick butt and take names. . . . Instead it took them months to get fully staffed, and since then it hasn't done diddly squat."[24] It was a misinformed expectation. And, alas, there are just too many butts to kick and names to take, and many of them belong to Very Very Important People.[25] Who will run the office or mind the shop if everyone is in jail?

A matter for conjecture is the extent to which the incompetence and venality of Pakistan's rulers have contributed to the idealization and increasing popularity of Islam as a moral basis for politics.

Secularity, Provincialism, and Kashmir

Under British administration, the "Punjab tradition" was secular. To be sure, the British thought less of urban Hindus—moneylenders, *vakils*[26] (lawyers), Congressmen—than of landlords, the countryside's "natural leaders," and of the manly Muslim and Sikh yeoman whom they led. The Punjab administration discriminated accordingly: the Alienation of Land Act, for example. But the discrimination was secular: in favor of political friends, and against those who would undermine the existing social order and advocate "sedition." The *sarkar—*government—discriminated against no religious group, as such, and neither established nor favored any "church." Nor did the National Unionist Party. From the party's foundation in 1923 to its collapse in 1947, the three great, knighted landlords who led the Unionists were all members of the Muslim League. But in Punjabi politics they were Unionists first and Muslim Leaguers second: leaders of an inter-"communal" party of "agriculturalists." All tried to keep the League, the Quaid, "communalism," and "Pakistan" out of Punjab, most famously in the Sikander–Jinnah Pact of 1937.

Writers so inclined make much of Jinnah's secularism. His first address, in August 1947, to Pakistan's ill-fated constituent assembly is frequently quoted:

You may belong to any religion or caste or creed—that has nothing to do with the business of the State. . . . [W]e are all citizens and equal citizens of one State. . . . Now, I think, we should keep that in front of us as our ideal, and you will find that in the course of time Hindus would cease to be Hindus and Muslims would cease to be Muslims, not in the religious sense . . ., but in the political sense as citizens of the State.[27]

Noted most tellingly by orthodox *ulama*, the difficulty with this "ideal" is that it does not square with the "ideal" of "Pakistan." "The haunting question will. . . inevitably arise: Why did the Muslims create a separate state of their own if it was to be no different than any other?"[28]

If Muslims had wanted to be equal citizens with Hindus in a state indifferent "in the political sense" to religion, then what was the point of the "Pakistan" movement? Its ideal, articulated by Jinnah pre-Partition, was of a Muslim "nation" that aspired to have a "state" of its own. Resonant in this aspiration, of course, and to Jinnah's advantage though not in his presentation of it, was the older Islamic ideal of such a state being governed according to the religious–political precepts of the *shariah*—or under its shadow, at least. In a Muslim nation-state, the "religious sense" and the "political sense" *should be* one and the same. It is this Islamic ideal rather than Jinnah's ideal of a secular state that has taken root in Pakistan, grown, and spread its branches.

Ironically, it was the *ulama,* or many of the most prominent among them, who, for ostensibly Islamic reasons, opposed "Pakistan." They argued, for example, that the division of the *ummah* into separate nation-states is contrary to the religious–political ideal of Islam. It recognizes no national borders between the faithful. "Pakistan" was conceived and led to fruition by well-to-do laymen. Mohammad Ali Jinnah, a barrister-at-law, was their prototype. They were Muslim by birth and observant—or nonobservant—according to their lights, anglophone if not anglophile, and holding to Westminster rather than Medina as their political model. As W. W. Hunter found them in the 1870s, so they were in the 1940s.[29] But when they sat as a constituent assembly to draft a constitution for Pakistan, Islam came banging at their door.

In the early 1950s, popular hostility to the heterodoxy of a well-established Muslim group, the Ahmadiyya, sparked sectarian rioting. It was fanned for their own reasons by some of the assembly's members and for ostensibly religious reasons by *ulama*. The constituent assembly was pressed to relegate the Ahmadiyya, one of whom was Pakistan's highly regarded foreign minister, to the status of "non-Muslims." But the assembly resisted. Then, largely from *ulama* and their sympathizers, there was pressure on the assembly to draft a constitution that established Pakistan as a Muslim state. The ill-fated constitution of 1956 reflected that pressure, but largely in symbolic fashion. Attached to a variant of the Westminster model were a title, "The Islamic Republic of Pakistan," and a clause making it mandatory for the republic's "Head of State" (a ceremonial position, like the British monarch's) to be a Muslim. The constitution's "directive principles" instructed an unspecified government at an unspecified time in the future to prohibit such irreligious practices as the charging of interest and the drinking of alcohol. Finally, the constitution banned any Pakistani legislature from enacting any law "repugnant" to the basic tenets of Islam. But responsibility for determining repugnance was assigned to a supreme court of judges trained in Anglo-Indian law rather than a bench of *ulama*.[30] Nevertheless, symbols can portend that which they symbolize. The door to Islamization was opened.

Ayub Khan tried to shut it. Pakistan's first constitution, nine years in the drafting, was nullified after only two years in existence by his army coup of 1958. A decade after their detachment from the British Indian army, Pakistan's military officer corps was still secular in its élan. The cornerstone of the constitution that was enacted under Ayub's direction in 1962 was "basic democracy": a relatively benign but subsequently discarded and discredited subcontinental variant of those post–Second World War dictatorships diaphanously cloaked, on the Right, as "guided" and, on the Left, as "people's" democracies.[31] Though little of its substance, "basic democracy" had some of Westminster's form. Of Medina's, it had virtually nothing: a few soothing references to Islam and an Advisory Council on Islamic Ideology. It was simply the "Republic of Pakistan" in Ayub's constitution. His contempt for politicians was excelled only by his distrust of the *ulama*: those *mullahs*[32] who shamelessly sought refuge from India in the Pakistan whose creation they had "bitterly opposed" and then, no less shamelessly, launched their campaign for the "Muslimization" of Pakistan's "hapless people." Islamization was "really a façade" behind which the *ulama* schemed to rule Pakistan. Ayub would have none of it.[33]

Of all the *ulama* whom he despised, Ayub named only one in his "political autobiography": Maulana Abul Aala Maudoodi, founder and leader of Pakistan's major Islamic political party, Jamaat-i-Islami. Four years after Ayub's downfall, in 1972, it was in consultation with Maudoodi that Zulfikar Bhutto reopened the door to Islamization. Less noted for his Islamic piety, than for his political populism, Bhutto renamed Pakistan an "Islamic Republic" in his constitution of 1973, designated Islam as Pakistan's "state religion," and restricted the offices of head of state *and prime minister* to Muslims. He assured Maudoodi that no law repugnant to Islam would be passed under his constitution and that his "Islamic socialism" had "nothing in common" with Godless bolshevism,[34] nor with heresy. The ongoing campaign of orthodox *ulama* against the Ahmadiyya was capped when Bhutto declared them to be "non-Muslims." In 1974, he blended domestic populism with a foreign-policy shift to entente with the oil-rich Muslim states of the Middle East by presiding over an "Islamic summit" in Lahore.

The army chief appointed by Bhutto and his successor, General Zia, had Bhutto hanged. For all his Islamic and anti-Indian rhetoric and in spite of his last ditch attempt to woo Punjab's landlords, Bhutto was still a dangerous man. A populist politician was a danger to Pakistan's coalition of dominant classes. Whatever his capital crime, the crime behind the crime of Sindh's great landlord was class treason. Zia finished Bhutto, but refined his populist, ad hoc Islamization into policy. General Zia commanded a self-proclaimed "army of Islam." That was how he legitimated its coup of 1977. If generally taken with a pinch of salt, that legitimation had become increasingly creditable to Zia's officer corps, at least. Its intake, over the years, had come less and less from the sons of landlords, who generally carried their faith lightly. More and more, the army's officers were recruited from sons of the middle classes, to whom Islam was a weightier matter and who accepted religious instruction as part of their officers training.

General Zia was one of them. No one doubted the sincerity of his faith. The *ulama*, specifically the Sunni *ulama,* were, of course, delighted with his coup and were its greatest supporters. Zia's entente with the *ulama* was predicated on a complementarity of interests. The *ulama's* primary concern was with the observance of *shariah* injunctions, particularly, with regard to its sumptuary, personal, and penal codes. Zia catered to these, and employed *ulama* in policing them. With secular social issues—the concentration of wealth and power in Pakistan, general poverty and illiteracy, the paucity of health services and facilities for modern education, corruption, for example—the *ulama* were not particularly concerned. And here, Zia maintained the status quo: "the 'religious demands' of the Islamic groups [i.e., *ulama*-led parties and associations] were of such a nature that they could be easily incorporated and adjusted into the existing social and political relations."[35] No less than General Zia have his elected successors followed this pattern. There has been some backsliding on Islamization, to be sure. But both Benazir and Nawaz treated the *ulama* with caution and were wary of treading on their toes. Musharraf is not their friend, but he is reluctant to antagonize them. Constitutionally, the *shariah* remains the supreme law of the land. The religious parties, of which there are many, often at war with one another, do poorly in popular elections. But their "street power," their capacity to provoke violent mischief, to wage sectarian warfare, to rabble-rouse, is factored into every politician's calculations.

In February 1999, for example, riots led by the Jamaat-i-Islami and its student wing neither stopped the visit to Lahore of the Indian prime minister, Atal Bihari Vajpayee, nor interrupted negotiations between him and his host, Nawaz Sharif. But the riots were a further embarrassment to a Pakistani government already embarrassed by its apparent inability to maintain domestic order. In their thousands, the rioters fought pitched battles with police, virtually captured some of the city's neighborhoods, destroyed property, caused injury to hundred of people, closed roads and enforced the closure of businesses and public transport, delayed official proceedings, and stoned the cars of visiting dignitaries.[36] Except at the polls, where it has failed, the capacity of religious parties to convince Pakistanis to accept their "Islamic state" is untested but, quite reasonably, feared. In Islamabad, martial law notwithstanding, a month or so after the army's coup in 1999 and under General Musharraf's nose, *mujahidin* attacked U.S. and UN offices *with rockets* in retaliation for UN sanctions against the Taliban regime in Afghanistan.

In response to the fear, Nawaz moved to preempt it. In 1998, he put forward a scheme for what appeared to be, for lack of a better description, a civil theocracy. His proposed "Fifteenth Amendment" to Pakistan's constitution would have invested "the federal government and, in effect, the prime minister, with exclusive and unfettered powers to interpret and enforce *shariah*. . . ."[37] The amendment is certainly a dead letter now. Still, it is suggestive not only of Nawaz's disinclination to parliamentary democracy, but of a general politicians' fear of *ulama*.

In the interstices of the history of selective Islamization by Pakistan's politicians, civilian and military, there is, in part, a positive design. It is of nation-building. Obstructing Pakistan's path to nationhood, to the development of a national consciousness, and meant to be overridden by faith, are provincialism—or, more exactly, Islamabad's failure to deal successfully with provincialism—and India.

India's relatively successful management of a larger field of ethnolinguistic provincialism may be usefully juxtaposed to Pakistan's relatively unsuccessful management of a smaller field of ethnolinguistic provincialism. To be sure, there are many differences between the two cases. But I believe that among the crucial ones were, in India, a political party operating within the framework of parliamentary democracy, and, in Pakistan, neither the party nor the framework.

Because they were operating within the framework of parliamentary democracy, Congress hierarchs in the 1950s and 1960s had to decide either to accede to widespread, popular demands for the reorganization of Indian states on ethnolinguistic lines, or not to accede and put at risk Congress's "one-party dominance." They acceded. They did not seriously consider an alternative to parliamentary democracy. India over the years has evolved into a stable multination state of ethnolinguistic provinces, of "nation-provinces." It is because of this successful integration of nationalism and provincialism in its great Hindu-majority heartland that India can afford, economically and politically, to repress secessionist and unwanted provincial movements on the heartland's fringes: in the tribal states of the northeast, perpetually; sporadically among Assamese in Assam; for a while amongst Sikh ultras in Punjab; among Gorkhas on the West Bengal–Sikkim border; and, most notably and intractably, in Kashmir.

No less than Nehru, Jinnah and his lieutenants feared a threat to their infant nation-state from the centrifugal force of latent but long-lived and culturally entrenched ethnolinguistic provincialism. To contain these forces, Pakistan's rulers chose repression in the east and, from 1955 to 1970, the repressive amalgamation of its provinces in the west into "one unit," West Pakistan, dominated by Punjab. Ways other than repression *might* have been chosen, *might* have been considered, if Pakistan's rulers had had some alternative: if they had been working through a political party that was committed to operating within the framework of parliamentary democracy.

Repression cost Pakistan more than half its country in 1971. Now, almost thirty years after the secession of Bangladesh and the scrapping of "one unit," the growth of a national Pakistani identity is still being retarded by unnegotiated and unresolved provincialism. Provincialism's fuel is "Punjabi domination." Muhajir provincialism in urban Sindh, Sindhi provincialism in rural Sindh, Baluchi provincialism: all are fuelled by hostility to the preeminent position of Punjab and Punjabis in Pakistan's political life.[38] For want of any institution in which a political will might work to make it otherwise, a demographic reality—that Punjabis make up about 60 percent of Pakistan's population—has become a political fact, "Punjabi domination." The army, it should be noted, ostensibly Pakistan's national institution par excellence, is widely regarded in its minority provinces as a Punjabi army and an army of Punjab. General Musharraf, a Muhajir from Delhi, may succeed in changing this perception. But I doubt it. He is an institutional dictator. The generals to whom he is "responsible," their officers, and *jawans* are, as ever, overwhelmingly Punjabi.

Insofar as Islam has been used as an antidote to provincialism, as an instrument of national integration, it has been demonstrably unsuccessful. The bond of faith was inadequate to hold together East and West Pakistan. Nowadays, over 95 percent of Pakistan's population is Muslim. So, virtually all its domestic violence, including the long-running reign of the bomb and the gun in Karachi, is perpetrated by Muslims on Muslims and suffered by Muslims. The most serious attempt to use Islamization as a nation-building device was General Zia's. But Islamization, like Christianization or Judaization, is most likely to take sectarian form. Zia's Islamization was appropriate to the faith of Sunnis, Pakistan's largest sectarian group of Muslims. To the faith of Shiahs, the minority sect of Pakistani Muslims, Zia's Islamization was offensive and marginalizing. Its legacy to this day is an increase in the spread, incidence, and intensity of Sunni–Shiah sectarian violence. Sunni zealots want Shiahs, like Ahmadiyyas, declared to be "non-Muslims." *Fedayin* of both sects regularly and publicly murder one another and strafe and bomb each other's mosques, even at prayer times. Islamization, in sum, has had no effect on ameliorating ethnolinguistic strife in Pakistan, and it has exacerbated sectarian turmoil.

Particularly in the "new nations" of Asia and Africa, nation-building elites have imagined and invented walls to separate "us" from "them." In Pakistan, "they" are Indians. And between "us" and "them" the great wall is Kashmir. It is Pakistan irredenta. It represents the continuation of the "Pakistan" movement: a movement of Muslim unity. It embodies the unfinished work of Islam on the subcontinent. It is a daily reminder of the perfidy and untrustworthiness of Hindu India. Kashmir rightly belongs to "us," but it has been stolen by "them."

One day each year, the shops and offices in Pakistan's cities are officially closed to commemorate the struggle against Indian "occupation" of Kashmir. Hardly a day passes when Pakistanis are not reminded in their media of Kashmir. For a country that has been largely unsuccessful in integrating its provinces into a national whole, in developing a national identity, the issue of Kashmir is meant to transcend provincialism to mark a defining line between "us" and "them." It traces the lines of Islam and "communalism." It cuts across the cultural unity of Indians and Pakistanis. What distinguishes "us" from "them," and even from Muslims among "them," is that "we" are a Muslim nation-state, a *millet*, obliged in faith to support the *jihad* of the *ummah's* fragment in Kashmir, to redeem it from the tyranny and repression of a regime of Hindu infidels in Delhi.

There are hardliners ready to turn slogans into action. Mostly they are military officers and *mujahidin*-organizing *ulama*. Apparently, the Kargil fiasco was their collaborative effort. I have no doubt but that theirs was a serious attempt to establish a strategically significant Pakistani bridgehead in Indian Kashmir.[39] In his first broadcast as Pakistan's "chief executive," and in the usual code for military collaboration between his army and *mujahidin,* General Musharraf "made it clear that Pakistan would continue to support with moral, political and diplomatic backing militants seeking independence of Kashmir from India."[40]

Western pressure on General Musharraf to "restore democracy" is best understood as encouragement to restore civilian government. The civilian members of Pakistan's coalition of dominant classes are, in general, no more inclined than their military partners to "restore" democracy, but they are more likely to write-off Kashmir, in fact if not in rhetoric, and to get on with it—and to get on doing business with India. Thus, they are less likely than the generals to threaten, with missiles and patronized *mujahidin*, the status quo and relative political stability in South Asia and, more widely, in Central Asia.

The best two-thirds of the princely state that was Jammu and Kashmir before 1948 is now the Indian state of that name, and India will never surrender it. Pakistan has neither the military force nor the diplomatic influence to compel India even to discuss Kashmir. That is the fact of the matter, and India's military and diplomatic victory in the Kargil War has only made it, at once, more certain and, to the Pakistani army, more futilely vengeful. In reaction to Kargil, the Indian government will increase its defense spending by almost 30 percent, or by about U.S.$3 billion—in itself, more than Pakistan's entire military budget.[41]

About 60 percent of Kashmir's population is Muslim, and if a plebiscite were ever held among them they would almost certainly vote to take Jammu and Kashmir out of the Indian Union and either into Pakistan or, more likely, to independence. For India, that would be not only a loss of strategically important territory, but an ideological defeat. It would cast a shadow on India's claim to secular statehood and its Muslim minority's acceptance of that claim's validity. It might encourage Hindu zealots to spark a terrible bout of anti-Muslim rioting in

India. India will not hold a plebiscite. In the half-century that has elapsed since Nehru promised to hold one, he and his successors have found any number of reasons for not keeping his promise. The emergence in Indian politics of the BJP as a major player and *Hindutva* as a major theme add considerably to the unlikelihood of New Delhi even considering a plebiscite in Kashmir. It is, after all, home to the Lord Siva, and places holy to Hindu pilgrims lie in Kashmir's mountains. Members of one of Hinduism's great Brahmin castes, the caste from which the Nehru–Gandhi dynasty springs, the Kashmiri Pandits, have been driven from their villages by *mujahidin*—and the BJP is committed to their return.

Brigades of *mujahidin,* who took over what began as a Kashmiri movement against the *Dilli durbar,*[42] are now fighting Pakistan's proxy war in Kashmir. But they are unlikely to win it, *mujahidin* victories in Afghanistan notwithstanding. India is too determined to hold Jammu and Kashmir, regardless of the human and material costs. India will not be bled into giving up Kashmir. The situation in Kashmir resurfaced briefly as an issue for the "international community" when India and Pakistan gate-crashed the club of nuclear powers in 1998, and again with the Kargil War. But in spite of Pakistan's best diplomatic efforts, it has failed to "internationalize" the question of Kashmir. The position of the world's major powers, including Pakistan's erstwhile Cold War friends, is that the question is a matter for negotiations between India and Pakistan. That is to say, the major powers accept the status quo. India may, if pressed, return to talking about Kashmir, but it will always say the same thing: Jammu and Kashmir is a state of the Indian Union, no less than are Uttar Pradesh and Tamil Nadu. The insurgency in Kashmir is India's domestic concern and, as such, not a matter for international mediation. Indeed, to the "international community" in general, Kashmir is old and tired business. New and frightening business is "international [*mujahidin*] terrorism," and Pakistan is a culprit.

Finally, there is a negative design in Islamization. Simply, it is to preempt the power of the *ulama.* The president of Pakistan, a ceremonial position postnullification of the "Eighth Amendment," is an *alim* (one of the *ulama*), and *ulama* have served as ministers in Pakistani governments; however, as a class they are not partners in Pakistan's coalition of dominant classes, nor do the partners want them. General Musharraf does not want them. The members of his postcoup government and its National Security Council are military officers and bureaucrats. Among them are two women—but no *ulama.* In his earliest photo opportunities as Pakistan's chief executive, General Musharraf chose two distinctly "un-Islamic" poses: one with his smiling wife (and family), and another holding his pet dogs.[43] Photos, of course, are messages, and Musharraf's messages to the *ulama* are clear: "I am not one of you, and my government is not yours." By and large, the personal and professional proclivities of the partners in Pakistan's coalition of dominant classes are secular. However decorated by professions of faith, they speak and understand the language of secularity. Not always in step, to be sure, they march to the same drummer. They do not want partners who march to God's drummer. They do not want a *shariah* state. Much less do they want a *shariah* state governed by *ulama*.

But Pakistan is in crisis. Muslim ultras regularly demonstrate their "street power" in the barbarity of sectarian violence. Ethnolinguistic turmoil persists. Drug-traffic vendettas and ordinary criminal thuggery seem beyond government's ability even to contain. Perhaps this will change under military rule, perhaps not. It did not change in Karachi before the 1999 coup, although the city was under virtual military rule. There is a growing awareness among ordinary people of the enormity and generality of the wastefulness and corruption of Pakistan's rulers and ruling classes, even to their political top. The state has been bankrupted by them. But under Nawaz, they were held to account only with political selectivity by a special Accountability Commission, which was itself suspect. Perhaps this will change under Musharraf—but, as I have already suggested, it may not. The general has been loath to investigate cases of corruption within the army's officer corps on which he relies for support, or within the judiciary on which his regime and its ordinances depend for secular legitimation.

The promise of Pakistan's restoration to solvency apparently depends on Islamabad's acceptance of International Monetary Fund "conditionalities." Their stringencies would be felt most painfully neither by landlords, nor industrialists, nor generals, nor elite bureaucrats but by ordinary people. The spectre for the partners in Pakistan's coalition of dominant classes is of *ulama* offering to Pakistanis another way, an Islamic way, a way whose guides and governors will be the doctors of Islam: Pakistani equivalents of Imam Khomeini and Mullah Mohammed Omar.[44] The Islamic parties in alliance with their major constituency, organizations of shopkeepers, have emerged as the most vocal and active opponents of the military regime. The *ulama* do not want a Pakistani Mustafa Kemal Ataturk. They do not want to be dictated to by "salaried agents" of international financial institutions. They want a return to Friday as the weekly holiday in Pakistan. They want all the "Islamic clauses" of the 1973 constitution incorporated into the Provisional Constitutional Order under which the military rules. They want the army "to form a civilian caretaker government of honest and pious people and return to the barracks. . . ." Shopkeepers do not want tax reforms that will compel them to pay taxes.[45] Against this opposition, selective and cooptative Islamization and beating the Kashmir drum are the army's tried-and-true tactics to preserve the Pakistan that belongs to it and its coalition partners, to keep the *ulama* from the gates.

"Colonialism" in Bengal

The pre-Partition "Punjab tradition" pertained to one local, colonial administrative system in a vast empire whose captains prudently varied the contours of bureaucratic authoritarianism to fit the varying social landscapes of the empire's provinces. The "Punjab tradition," a synergy of bureaucratic authoritarianism and the rural hegemony of great landlords, was particular to Punjab. Its West

Pakistani legatees attempted to transform the tradition into an imperial regime whose metropolis was Punjab and whose "jewel in the crown" was eastern Bengal. It did not work. In Punjab, the Raj had confirmed landlords in their positions as the countryside's "natural leaders," and there was virtually no tradition of representative institutions and popular politics. In East Pakistan, Pakistan's Bengal, small-holding peasant hostility to their landlords had a long history, and the experiences of representative institutions and popular politics among Muslims had their longest and most successful history in the Indian Empire.

Parliamentary democracy was the instrument of Bengalis. They were not only the majority of Pakistanis, but en mass the only Pakistanis who belonged to a popularly based political party, and the only Pakistanis whose leaders were attuned to competitive parliamentary politics and successful in them. From a parliamentary democracy whose majority were Bengalis, West Pakistan's coalition of dominant classes had everything to lose: jobs, rank and salaries, perks, "rents," *izzat*, military command, spoils of the American alliance, the industrialists' milch cow, the security of great landlords in their holdings.

For want of a popularly based, national political party, West Pakistan's coalition of dominant classes was incapable of striking a bargain with Bengali politicians or even of attempting to coopt the upper strata of Bengali professionals and *jotedars.* The political instrument of the Punjabi–Muhajir elite of the west was repressive force, and they used it to counter the threat of parliamentary democracy from the east. Repression, of course, was less likely to produce national integration than to integrate Bengal into Pakistan as the west's satrapy. But that was preferable to the integration of the west into Bengal's parliamentary democracy. Thus, the hegemony of West Pakistan's coalition of dominant classes, the renovated "Punjab tradition," was extended to all of Pakistan. For eastern Bengal, it bore in miniature all the political, economic, and cultural hallmarks of imperialism.

Pakistan's capital cities were always in its western metropolis. Originally, the national capital was in Karachi—western Pakistan's largest and most industrialized city and Punjab's Arabian Sea entrepôt. In the mid-1970s, Pakistan's capital was shifted to the new city of Islamabad, on Punjab's northern border, and adjacent to the army's "capital," its headquarters in Rawalpindi. The demand, first raised in 1954 by a United Front of Bengali political parties, for headquartering Pakistan's minuscule navy in East Pakistan was never acceded to. Throughout South Asia, capital cities are prizes for their populations and those of their hinterlands. Scarce resources are concentrated in capital cities, and they are centers of political, bureaucratic, and symbolic power.

Professional politicians were the most active political class in eastern Bengal. It was they who regrouped in a United Front shortly after Partition and wiped the Muslim League from Bengali politics in the provincial elections of 1954. In a matter of months, the results of these elections were nullified, and the United Front government was dismissed by the Centre and replaced in power under the

India Act of 1935 by an appointed governor, a West Pakistani bureaucrat. Then, to make assurances doubly sure, to keep Bengali politicians from fishing in the troubled provincial waters of Sindh and Baluchistan, where there was considerable resentment against "Punjabi domination," the government in 1955 amalgamated Pakistan's western provinces into one unit, West Pakistan. By putting paid to parliamentary democracy for a decade—in effect, doing way with competitive party politics—Ayub's coup of 1958 precluded the Bengalis from fishing at all and prohibited their politicians from participation in politics.

In the bureaucratic authoritarianism consolidated by Ayub, Bengalis were at a distinct disadvantage. They were hardly represented in the coalition of dominant classes sustained and served by Ayub's domesticated and revised "Punjab tradition." In the elite bureaucracy and, particularly, in the army's officers corps, Bengalis were a tiny and ineffectual minority. At the center of Pakistan's bureaucratic politics in the mid-1950s, in the central secretariat there were 734 senior bureaucrats holding the rank of undersecretary or above. Of these, 42 were Bengalis—less than 6 percent. In the army, there were 897 officers of the rank of major or above. Of these, 15 were Bengalis—less than 2 percent—and almost all were majors.[46]

The great landlords of Punjab and Sindh had no counterpart in Bengal, no landlords to share, support, and sympathize with their interests. By migrating to India at the time of Partition, the great landlords of Bengal, who were by and large Hindus, reduced considerably the concentration of land-holding in Bengal's eastern districts. It was further reduced by the East Bengal provincial assembly in 1951. Moreover, first the provincial Muslim League and then the constituent parties of the United Front all subscribed to various schemes of redistributive land reforms. In its 21-point election manifesto, the front itemized the "abolition of *all* rent-receiving interests in land . . . without compensation," and the "distribution of . . . surplus land among the landless peasants."[47] For Maulana Bhashani, at least, "*all*" meant in all of Pakistan.

As for Pakistan's industrialists:

an astonishing 96 per cent of industrial investments were owned by people who either settled in or came from West Pakistan. Concentration of governmental expenditure in West Pakistan, the availability of managerial and technical skill among refugee businessmen settled in West Pakistan, the location of export–import licensing authorities and financial institutions in Karachi manned by non-Bengalis—all these led to the concentration of industrial power in West Pakistan. *West Pakistan's industrial entrepreneurs, unwilling to cede any portion of their monopolies to East Bengali businessmen, lent full support to the West Pakistani ruling elite.*[48]

East Bengal was the source of capital accumulation meant for the industrialization of West Pakistan—facilitated by government, but by and large in the hands of private capital. Much of what was meant to be industrialization was (and still is) trading. By 1960, West Pakistan's big businessmen were "earn[ing] windfall profits," by using an overvalued rupee to buy imported goods for local sale.

Bengali farmers, who produced Pakistan's major export, jute, got less than the market price for it. In turn, they paid more than the market price for products of the west's tariff-protected infant industries and its resold imports. Thus was East Pakistan's surplus transferred to the west—over the years, amounting to billions of rupees. The government's development expenditure, including foreign aid, went overwhelmingly to the west. Central government employment was overwhelmingly in the west. Per capita income was anywhere between 30 and 60 percent higher in the west than it was in the east. In the later years of his regime, Ayub Khan addressed his government's attention to these "regional imbalances." Nonetheless, they worsened, probably due to the consequences of the India–Pakistan war of 1965 and the growth of private investment in the west.[49]

To the injury of their economic exploitation of Bengal, Pakistan's Punjabi and Muhajir rulers added the insult to Bengalis of cultural contempt. Indeed, the United Front of 1954, which finally evolved into the movement for an independent Bangladesh, was first galvanized by the insistence of Pakistan's rulers that Urdu and only Urdu would be Pakistan's "official language." For the Bengali middle classes, this denigration of their language was, to be sure, an insult, and it also threatened to be injurious to their prospects for government employment. The Quaid and his lieutenants were adamant: Bengali was a Hindu language. It was symbolic of the degradation and exploitation of Bengal's Muslims by the Hindu *bhadralok*. It was emblematic of the corruption visited on Islam by the Hinduized Muslims of Bengal. Its very script embodied Hindu eroticism and "polytheism."

When he was president of a united Pakistan, Ayub Khan summed up the situation, in a fine reminder that "orientalism" was (and is) not a perspective on the Oriental "other" exclusive to the use of Occidental observers. Thus, Ayub informs the readers of his "political autobiography" that in contrast to the "successive conquering race[s]" which inevitably left their "traces" in the area of West Pakistan, his eastern Bengali countrymen:

probably belong to the very original Indian races. . . . [U]p to the creation of Pakistan they had not known any real freedom or sovereignty. They have in turn been ruled either by the caste Hindus, Moghuls, Pathans or the British. In addition, they have been and are still under considerable Hindu cultural and linguistic influence. As such they have all the inhibitions of down-trodden races and have not yet found it possible to adjust psychologically to the new-born freedom. Their popular complexes, exclusiveness, suspicion and a sort of defensive aggressiveness probably emerge from this historical background. . . .[50]

In sum: as long as East Bengal was part of Pakistan, parliamentary democracy was out of the question. The west's antidemocratic coalition of dominant classes was unwilling to risk it. Pakistan had no national political party which might have operated within the framework of parliamentary democracy to protect the coalition's interests even as it worked to integrate the Bengalis into Pakistan. East

Bengal was part of Pakistan for the first quarter century of its existence—more than enough time for the west's coalition of dominant classes to consolidate and consolidate their hegemony. It was lost in the east, of course, with East Pakistan's secession. But that barely shook the hegemony of Pakistan's dominant coalition at home. Its concession after 1971 to parliamentary democracy was to tolerate Bhutto's show of it for a few years and, after General Zia's death, to play it as a charade, from 1988 to 1999.

Imperial Dependence

The consolidation of the Muhajir–Punjabi imperium in eastern Bengal was only an effect of Pakistan's post-Independence debut in international politics as a U.S. client state. Its cause was fear of India. In 1955, a Pakistani scholar put it succinctly: "The only guarantee of our survival was military aid from the United States."[51] Its price was Pakistan's formal enlistment in the ranks of America's Cold War allies. Particularly reliable allies, in the estimation of American officials, were that "small group of British-trained administrators and military leaders" who were in the 1950s increasingly and openly assuming political power in Pakistan.[52]

The Cold War was Pakistan's opportunity. Nehru refused to join India to the Western alliance led by the United States. Beneath the moral veneer of his assertions of "non-alignment" was a clear geopolitical understanding of the post-Partition, post–Second World War subcontinent. India would be its dominant power only if the subcontinent did not become a Cold War arena, only if the United States and the Soviet Union were kept out as major players. For the United States, on the other hand, the Cold War's arena was the globe, and the subcontinent was located on the periphery of an "international communism" whose proclivity to expand into the "free world" had to be "contained." Pakistan was less concerned with containing the communist menace than with countering the threat of a dominant India. Its alliance with the United States was meant to preclude that dominance. It was for Pakistan an alliance of complementary interests: with the United States in preference to the Soviet Union, in part because of the ideological and personal preferences of Pakistan's rulers and in part because Washington had more to offer.

Pakistan joined the South East Asia Treaty Organization (SEATO) in 1954 and thereby lent itself to Washington's attempt to "internationalize" its military intervention in Vietnam. By joining the American-sponsored Baghdad Pact (later CENTO) in 1955, Pakistan agreed to become a salient on the American ring of "containment" around the great Sino-Soviet landmass: ruled by communists who were directed from the Kremlin and bound to expand beyond the Soviet empire's borders. The Ayub government signed a mutual defence treaty with Washington in 1959. From a base close to the Pakistani city of Peshawar, American planes took off on reconnaissance missions over the Soviet Union. For these Cold War services to the United States, from 1954 to 1965 Pakistan received military hardware worth more than a billion dollars.[53] After Israel and Egypt, Pakistan was the greatest recipient of American aid.

Again, these billions given by Washington to fight the menace of "international communism" were taken by Pakistan to even the balance of military force between it and India. Which it did—at least, in the context of the "short, sharp war" of 1965. A collateral, though by no means insignificant, benefit of American aid was weighting the scales in Pakistan's domestic politics further in favor of the west's coalition of dominant classes and against Bengal. Yet Pakistan's Punjabi–Muhajir rulers got less than they wanted from their American patrons. Certainly, in Washington, at least until the beginning of the Kennedy administration in 1960, India was publicly scorned for its "neutralism," its unwillingness to take its stand with the "children of light"[54] in the post–Second World War Armageddon. But even so, in the assessments of American policymakers, India was intrinsically the linchpin of international politics on the subcontinent. Inherently its major power, the "largest democracy in the world," and notwithstanding its "non-alignment," India was America's fond hope for a model of development in the "third world" alternative to communism in China. So Pakistan, a tactical base in the Cold War, never replaced or even equaled India in Washington's global, Cold War estimations. India received no military aid from the United States until its disastrous border war with China in 1962. But to Pakistan's displeasure, from 1957 "non-aligned"/"neutralist" India received more economic aid from Washington—though not in per capita terms—than its Pakistani ally.[55]

From Washington's assessment of India's inherent importance, there followed the second and culminating Pakistani displeasure with its American ally. The United States would not support Pakistan's position on Kashmir. Washington would not hold India to Nehru's promise to the United Nations to agree to hold a plebiscite in Kashmir in order to determine its ultimate disposition. The turning point for Pakistan in its career as an American ally was the Sino–India border war in 1962. At no time before or since has New Delhi been more vulnerable to having such a promise wrung from it. The price for Washington's military assistance! The pay-off to its Pakistani allies! But the Americans would not do the wringing—that would add additional injury to the injury of arming Pakistan's enemy. Washington would remain "neutralist" on the issue of Kashmir. General Ayub was furious. But he was not imprudent. Without inviting the Americans out, he began to invite the Chinese in.

Pakistan's relationship with Beijing was not entirely vitiated by Islamabad's Cold War alliance with the United States. China's policymakers appreciated Pakistan's fear of India and had complementary concerns of their own about New Delhi. Rather than negotiate a reasonable settlement of its disputed borders with China, for example, India chose, first, to go to war, and then, after being beaten, to turn to Beijing's archenemies—the United States and the Soviet Union—for military assistance. However badly it fared in 1962, India was the only county in Asia with the potential to challenge China. An enemy's enemy is a friend. From this mutual understanding, Pakistan received China's economic and military aid, a settlement of Azad Kashmir's border with that of China's troubled Xinjiang province, and unequivocal diplomatic support for Pakistan's position on Kashmir. The culmination of Pakistan's entente with China, according to Ayub's foreign minister, Zulfikar Bhutto, was a clear warning to India during its 1965 war with Pakistan that if Indian forces attacked East Pakistan, a Chinese army would come to its defense. Probably for fear of an increase in Chinese influence on the subcontinent, the Soviet Union's rulers brokered an armistice between India and Pakistan at Tashkent in 1966 and began to mend their fences with Islamabad.

Pakistan's entente with China and its cordial relations with the Soviet Union displeased the United States, but so low in Washington's order of foreign-policy priority was South Asia that its relationship with Pakistan was not notably affected. Besides, the Cold War was changing, and, coincidentally, it was changing to Pakistan's advantage. Its rulers facilitated America's rapprochement with China, in return for which a grateful President Nixon ordered American policymakers to "tilt" toward Pakistan in its Bangladesh War with India in 1971.[56] Washington gave its qualified support to the preservation of Pakistan's "territorial integrity" and, in a futile attempt to intimidate the unintimidateable Indira Gandhi, it sent a naval task force led by one of its great aircraft carriers to anchor in the Bay of Bengal. But the United States did not come into the war. Nor—probably for fear of a clash with the Soviet Union, then recently allied to India—did China. Postwar, Pakistan's ambitions, abetted by China, among others, to become a nuclear power strained its friendship with Washington. But for ten years from 1979, General Zia's Pakistan served as Washington's "front-line" state—arming, training, and directing various armies of *mujahidin*—in America's proxy war with the Soviet Union in Afghanistan. In return, and to India's intense displeasure, Pakistan supplied itself, one way or the other, with billions of dollars' worth of state-of-the-art American arms.

In sum, the thread that winds itself through this sketchy outline is Pakistan's policy of bringing makeweights onto its side of the subcontinental balance of power. In part, as I have indicated above, this was a dictate of prudence—to survive India's alleged ambition to strangle Pakistan at birth. In part, it was an attempt to garner support for Pakistan's stand on Kashmir. In part, until 1971, it was a means of strengthening the hold of the west's coalition of dominant classes on Pakistan's domestic politics. More generally, it was a way of giving credence to the "two-nation" theory that legitimated Pakistan—to vindicate its claim to being a nation equal to India. It was the smaller, but in no way the lesser, successor state of the British Indian empire. The greatness of nations is, after all, not measured in the extent of the landmass that they occupy nor the census counts of their populations. So, in some ways Pakistan was the more equal republic of the "Indo-Pakistan subcontinent"[57]—for example, in its Islamic faith, the glory of Mughal rule, and the gallantry of Muslim soldiers.

But the reality that lurked behind Pakistan's alliances with the United States, and its entente with China, began to intrude post–Cold War. By every conventional, mundane measure of a state's importance in international politics—population, armed forces, strategic location, industrialization, and so forth—Pakistan is less equal than India. For their own reasons, Washington and Beijing may or may not have consciously encouraged Pakistan's illusion of equality, they may or may not have saved Pakistan from being reabsorbed or trifled with by India. But there is no doubt that Pakistan's great friends served the interests of its coalition of dominant classes in the west and thereby contributed to Pakistan's nondevelopment as a parliamentary democracy and even to the nondevelopment in Islamabad of a financially responsible, developmentally oriented, competent, and honest authoritarianism.

What else have they contributed? American and Chinese bluster was unsuccessful in helping Pakistan preserve its territorial integrity against the secessionist movement in eastern Bengal. They were unsuccessful in helping Pakistan to sustain its position on the Kashmir question against India's unequivocal answer to it. China's technological assistance may have been successful in encouraging Pakistan's illusion of equality by helping it to respond to India's nuclear tests in 1998 with tests of its own. However, India's tests were motivated not by its fear of Pakistan, but by Delhi's unsettled relations with China. India wants to be a member of the nuclear power "club" because China is a member and because "great powers" have nuclear arsenals. Apart from Pakistan's quixotic quest for international recognition as India's equal, the only plausible explanation for Islamabad's economically ruinous program of nuclear weapons development is that it provides a shield behind which Pakistan can pursue its proxy war in Kashmir and against any prospective Indian threat to desist or else. But is it Pakistan's nuclear shield that keeps such a threat from being made? I doubt it. India poses no nuclear threat to Pakistan—it does not have to. New Delhi wants only to keep the Kashmir that it already holds, and it can hold it without nuclear weapons or the threat of their use. It did so during the Kargil War. With the end of the Cold War, the United States has come to recognize India as South Asia's "managerial power."[58] Even after the Kargil War, and its specter—largely imaginary—of a nuclear holocaust on the subcontinent, neither the United States nor any of its allies are willing to take steps to "internationalize " the Kashmir issue. It is, they continue to insist, a matter to be solved through bilateral negotiations between India and Pakistan. Their support, in a word, is for the status quo.

The Cold War victory for Pakistan has been in Afghanistan. As a consequence of its service as Washington's "front-line" state in its proxy war with the Soviet Union in Afghanistan, coupled with the ethnic and religious turmoil that succeeded the Soviet Union's retreat, Islamabad has probably laid to rest the specter of "Pakhtunistan." Its source was Afghanistan's Pathan (Pakhtun) majority, whose tribesmen's long-standing demand was for an Afghan province or separate state of their own, to be partially carved from Pakistan's north. But the price of victory has been high. Thanks to its military intelligence agency's support of the Taliban *mujahidin*, Pakistan's coalition of dominant classes now has a state ruled by Muslim zealots on its border. Religious parties in Pakistan have been inspired by Taliban's apparent triumph in Afghanistan, and their "street power" has been augmented from the arsenal of modern firearms in the Afghani *jihad*. The heroin trade, which was a major source of funding for the various armies of *mujahidin* in Afghanistan's civil war, has become a major export industry in Pakistan and a domestic scourge. Neither Pakistan's support of the Taliban nor its stand on Kashmir has endeared Pakistan to its erstwhile Cold War great friends.

Once again, and to what unknown effect or motivation, a ruler of Pakistan has turned to the "Muslim world." It will be the "cornerstone" of General Musharraf's foreign policy, he said. His first trip abroad as Pakistan's chief executive, a fortnight after his coup, was to Riyadh to confer with the king and crown prince of Saudi Arabia.

BANGLADESH

As in love and war, there is a certain universality of experience in politics. From his familiarity with them in post–Second World War, Soviet-dominated eastern Europe, Milan Kundera has given us a finely drawn caricature of politics which coincidentally captures their likeness in Bangladesh:

People are always shouting they want to create a better future. It's not true. The future is an apathetic void of no interest to anyone. The past is full of life, eager to irritate us, provoke and insult us, tempt us to destroy or repaint it. The only reason people want to be masters of the future is to change the past. They are fighting for access to the laboratories where photographs are retouched and [to the archives where] biographies and histories [are] rewritten.[59]

Politics in Bangladesh is mired in the past. Fighting to "destroy or repaint" it are two major parties in a crowded field of many minor parties and their multitude of factions. At this writing, the ruling party in Dhaka is the Awami League. It is led by Sheikh Hasina Wajed, daughter of the martyred "Father of the Nation," Sheikh Mujibur Rahman. In 1975, he with members of his entourage and immediate family were murdered in a military coup. Now, "across the barricades," on the opposition's front bench in the Jatiya Sangsad, the national parliament, sits the leader of the Bangladesh National Party (BNP)—and Sheikh Hasina's enemy and predecessor as prime minister—Begum Khaleda Zia. She is the widow of the general who, after a series of coups, succeeded Mujib, came to power in the bloody aftermath of his murder, and was at least complicit in the exoneration of his assassins, if not in the masterminding of his assassination.

Or conversely: While Sheikh Mujib sat out the War of Liberation in a Pakistani jail, Khaleda Zia's husband, General Ziaur Rahman, was one of the war's great military heroes. On the field of battle in 1971, Zia led his "Z Force" in the fight against the Pakistani army, and it was he who broadcast the message of Bangladesh's liberation to his countrymen. As Bangladesh's leader, prime minister, then president from 1975 to 1981, when he too fell to yet another army coup,

Zia brought order and stability from the chaos of Mujib's misgovernment. Now, "across the barricades" from Zia's widow, on the Jatiya Sangsad's treasury bench, sits her enemy, Sheikh Hasina—political heiress of the man who, to be sure, organized and articulated his country's demand for freedom, but then betrayed it: to megalomania and India.

Certainly, the past remains "full of life" in the politics of India and Pakistan, as it does in politics elsewhere and generally. But, in few places, I think, is the past so apparently intrusive into the present as it is in Bangladesh, nor so lowering over the future. Two threads wind together through Muslim Bengal's political past in British India and Pakistan and tie them to Bangladesh's political present. The threads, which we can separate only for the purposes of analysis, are an insistence upon autonomy and an ideological commitment to parliamentary democracy as *the* legitimate system of government. As we trace their windings through Bangladesh's unhappy career as East Pakistan, we see—with the benefit of hindsight, to be sure—that the adoption of a renovated and colonial "Punjab tradition" by West Pakistan's coalition of dominant classes doomed the Pakistan of 1947. The threads were knotted in 1970–71. East Bengal vindicated its demand for autonomy by a parliamentary democratic triumph, and then, after the War of Liberation, it established for Bangladesh a parliamentary democracy—but failed to sustain it. We want here to account for that failure, to recount—rather than repaint—the relevant past, and to fill with our guesses the future's apathetic void.

Autonomy

Below is an excerpt from what is known as the "Pakistan Resolution." The resolution was adopted in March 1940 at the Lahore session of the All-India Muslim League. It was a momentous occasion: the birth of "Pakistan." To mark it, a *minar* (tower) was subsequently raised on what had been the session's venue.

no constitutional plan would be workable in this country or acceptable to Muslims unless it is [so] designed ... that geographically contiguous units ... in which the Muslims are ... a majority, as in the North Western and Eastern zones of India, should be grouped to constitute *independent states in which the constituent units shall be autonomous and sovereign.*[60]

At the request of Jinnah, the Quaid-i-Azam, the resolution was moved by none other than Fazlul Huq, Muslim India's only elected premier, leader of a Muslim League government in Bengal, and by far the most popular politician in the largest Muslim-majority province in British India. A year later, the Quaid had Huq expelled from the League. At issue between the two politicians was Huq's unwillingness to submit the Bengal Provincial Muslim League (BPML) and its government to Jinnah's dictates. Presumably, the plain meaning of the emphasized clause above was understood by both Huq and Jinnah.

Through the combined efforts of Jinnah loyalists and British officials, Huq was forced from Bengal's premiership in 1943. For the Quaid, Huq was too much his own man—a left-leaning provincial populist. For the British, he was insufficiently anti-Congress. He was succeeded by Jinnah's lieutenant in Bengal. But that "reliable wealthy knight"[61] was not the choice of the BPML, and it soon shunted him aside in favor of H. S. Suhrawardy, a prominent Calcutta lawyer and a major figure in the successful reorganization of the BPML as a popular political party. Suhrawardy enjoyed his colleagues' confidence but not the Quaid's.

In 1946, the "Pakistan Resolution," as it was moved by Fazlul Huq, was the centerpiece of the BPML's overwhelmingly successful election campaign. It captured virtually all of the provincial assembly's Muslim seats. A month after the election, however, in April, and over the heated protests of the powerful and popular general secretary of the BPML, Abul Hashim, a Muslim League convention in Delhi "amended" the Pakistan Resolution to provide for "[one] *sovereign independent state of Pakistan.*" Less than three weeks later, and to Jinnah's great embarrassment, Suhrawardy and Abul Hashim issued a joint statement in favor *not* of one Pakistan as their preferred outcome of the subcontinent's impending partition, but rather of "[one] *sovereign independent united Bengal.*"[62] In the rush of things, that preference was lost. But the sentiment that animated it was not.

In Pakistan's first year, Jinnah's personal and repeated insistence that Urdu and Urdu alone would be Pakistan's official language was enough to mobilize against the regime in Karachi the Bengali professional middle class, in particular, and its apprentices-cum-generational opponents, university students. Language in Bengal, as in France, for example, is a critical and sensitive component of "communal" identification and consciousness. For both the Bengali professional middle class and university students, the Quaid and his Muslim League government's rejection of Bengali as an official language side-by-side with Urdu was an affront. Bengali was, after all, the language of Pakistan's majority. Moreover, the Quaid's rejection of Bengali was an injury to that majority's middle class: a career obstacle. Competence in the official language is, of course, a requisite for white-collar government employment. Government is a major employer on the subcontinent, and government employment is a source of job security and can be a cornucopia.

The initial impetus to the post-Partition autonomy movement in east Bengal was provided by this "official language issue." It—coupled with the Centre's stacking of the BPML's leadership with Bengalis whose political base was in Karachi and Karachi's stacking of the bureaucracy in Bengal with Punjabis and Muhajirs—led to the discrediting of the Muslim League in East Pakistan and the League's decimation in the 1954 provincial elections. The "21-point" election manifesto of the victorious United Front highlighted its demand for provincial autonomy. Other multiple-point manifestos followed—proclamations of the end-lessly fissioning, fusing, and proliferating political parties and factions in eastern Bengal. Whatever their disagreements with one another, however, all—save those of the Islamists—agreed on the demand for provincial autonomy.[63] From 1966, the six-point program of Sheikh Mujib's Awami League refracted these demands to a pinpoint.

Provincial autonomy was *the* demand. It was *the* demand on which the Awami League won its landslide victory in the Bengali provincial elections of 1970. Having virtually monopolized the poll in Bengal, the AL emerged as the ruling party not only in East Pakistan's provincial assembly but in Pakistan's National Assembly. It was *the* demand that held the AL's factions and its allied parties and their factions together. It was *the* demand on which Mujib could not compromise. It was *the* demand that Pakistan's coalition of dominant classes would not accept lest they lose it all to the AL's parliamentary majority. It was *the* demand that was vindicated in the War of Liberation from which the republic of Bangladesh emerged.

Today, the demand still echoes in Begum Khaleda Zia's and her partisans' fulminations against the ghost of Mujib, his daughter, and the AL for allegedly reducing a victorious Bangladesh to India's satellite. Or conversely, the Awami League echoes the charge that General Zia's successors would abandon Bangladesh to the machinations of "pro-Pakistani fundamentalists": collaborators with Islamabad's army in the slaughter, rape, and plunder of Bengali civilians that preceded, provoked, and accompanied the War of Liberation.[64]

Parliamentary Democracy

From 1937, it was not parliamentary democracy yet, but parliamentary politics that was the instrument used first in Bengal by Fazlul Huq and his Krishak Praja Party, and then by the BPML to prise political power from the Hindu *bhadralok*. It was through the parliamentary democratic election of 1954 that the United Front sent to Pakistan's rulers in the west an unambiguous message of East Pakistan's disaffection and its demand for autonomy. Karachi's nullification, in effect, of that election brought into sharp contrast the political capabilities of west versus east. The west had the guns. The numbers were in the east. On the one side, there was an authoritarian civilian–military bureaucracy ruled through a renovated "Punjab tradition"; on the other, popular politicians who challenged that rule through a system of parliamentary democracy. Only in such a system was the Bengali majority in Pakistan a political asset. Only within a system of parliamentary democracy could east Bengal realize its demand for provincial autonomy. For Pakistan's Bengalis, the connection between provincial autonomy and parliamentary democracy was established from 1954, and confirmed in 1970–71.

Mujib returned to Bangladesh in triumph after the War of Liberation. He had become the revered Bangabandhu—the friend of Bengal, the "Father of the Nation," an icon and an oracle. The "four pillars" of *Mujibbad* (Mujibism)—nationalism, democracy, socialism, and secularism: the Bangabandhu's projection of himself in ideological terms and his Word to AL exegetes—was to be

Bangladesh's creed. With noblesse oblige appropriate to the occasion, Mujib surrendered his wartime title of president and assumed only the role to which the AL's victory in the 1970 elections entitled him. He became his country's first prime minister, the leader of the majority party in what had been the provincial assembly of East Pakistan and became Bangladesh's Jatiya Sangsad. In its constitution of 1972, Mujib recommitted Bangladesh to parliamentary democracy and reconfirmed it in popular elections to the Jatiya Sangsad in 1973. But it did not last for long—nor did Mujib.

According to Rounaq Jahan, and plausibly, Sheikh Mujib's political plan was to replicate in Bangladesh India's variant of the Westminster model—a "one-dominant party" parliamentary democracy.[65] Mujib was no less a charismatic leader than Nehru, and, for the sake of argument, he was no less ideologically committed to the construction of a parliamentary democracy dominated by its ruling party. But the Bangabandhu lacked the constructive wherewithal. He lacked both a well-organized political party and his Indian counterpart's control over it, and he was unable to exercise Nehru's control over the state's bureaucracy or its army. The AL was a movement rather than a party: an agglomeration of parties and their factions, and further fragmented during the War of Liberation. University students, who were the most active political group in east Bengal and without whose movement there would have been no Bangladesh, were armed and, except for those loyal to the AL, beyond the Bangabandhu's control. The civil bureaucracy was factionalized, between those who served in Bangladesh's Indian capital-in-exile, Mujibnagar (Mujib city), during the War of Liberation and Bengali Muslim "collaborators" who continued during the war to work for the civil service of Pakistan. The Bangladesh army, which loomed large after its victory in the War of Liberation, had developed only during the war. It was not a disciplined armed force but, rather, an agglomeration of factionalized, politically competitive, and ideologically opposed corps of regulars and irregulars, "freedom fighters" and repatriated soldiers from Pakistan, and officers and mutinous *jawans*.

Mujib's fate was sealed not only by his misgovernment and in its wake corruption, "crony capitalism,"[66] gangsterism, lawlessness, famine, shortages, and inflation, but by his "second revolution" of 1975. It was "revolution" from a precarious top and it failed. Parliamentary democracy was ditched by the Bangabandhu in favor of a one-party, private-army-reinforced dictatorship. He was murdered a few months later. A series of military coups and countercoups followed. The two generals who succeeded Mujib, in 1975 and 1982, Zia and H. M. Ershad, acknowledged the long-standing acceptance in eastern Bengal of parliamentary democracy's legitimacy by using it as a mask. Both soldiers reinvented themselves as civilian leaders of political parties, which they created and which still exist, and largely through these they manipulated semblances of parliamentary democracy.

Ershad was finally overthrown in 1991 by an unrelenting and apparently interminable popular movement in support of a return to substantive parliamentary democracy. Elections were held under the aegis of a civilian caretaker government, and Zia's party, the BNP, was returned to power. In 1996, this time in response to mass agitation led by the AL, elections for the Jatiya Sangsad were held again under a caretaker government, and Mujib's daughter led his AL back into power. Thus, Bangladesh passed what I earlier called my "acid test" for parliamentary democracy: the party that had been elected to power surrendered it to the party that defeated it at the polls. But the pass is tentative at best. Uncertainty fills the interstices of this brief narrative, and the future of parliamentary democracy in Bangladesh is by no means secure.

An Apathetic Future?

Throughout this work, I argue that parliamentary democracy's building blocks in India, crucial and mutually supporting, have been two decades of "one-party dominance," land reform that favored landed peasantries; adult franchise; and substantially empowered provincial legislative assemblies. We can locate parliamentary democracy in Bangladesh at some point midway between India's success in establishing it and Pakistan's failure.

In all their countries, the subcontinent's population majorities live in their villages. A sine qua non of parliamentary democracy, then, is its rural existence. In Bangladesh, that existence is nominal. Adult villagers are enfranchised, but they have no assemblies in which to legislate in their own interests. Bangladesh's political system is urban-centered, and its rural voters are little more than "vote banks" of Dhaka's parties. Under these circumstances, it may be a fool's errand to pursue a discussion of parliamentary democracy, as I have already suggested. Still, an end to the argument here would sacrifice to "the hobgoblin of little minds"[67] our attempt to understand what *might be* democratic political development in Bangladesh, its developmental possibilities. Better to press on.

The abolition of the Permanent Settlement and land reforms that favored landed peasants, *jotedars,* were on the Krishak Praja's agenda from 1937 and a contentious issue of Bengali Muslim League politics from them. Initially, land reforms in eastern Bengal were a by-product of the flight of Hindu landlords to India and their abandonment of their lands at the time of the subcontinent's partition. In 1950, land reform laws, similar to those in India, officially abolished rent-receiving interests in land and put a ceiling on landownership. In his attempt to enlist landed farmers as his "basic democrats" in East Pakistan, Ayub raised the land ceiling. But this was to little avail. Successor to the *jotedars,* in post-Partition Bangladesh, was a class of "surplus farmers." But it disappeared into the subdivision of small holdings. Between 1960 and 1984, the percentage of farm acreage held by large farmers decreased from 46 to 26 percent; the percentage of the total number of farm holdings held by large farmers decreased from 10 percent to 5 percent. The number of small farmers increased from 52 to 70 percent, and the number of landless or near-landless rural households increased from about 17 percent in 1951 to about 57 percent in 1983–84.[68]

Again, only among Bengalis in pre-Partition subcontinental Muslim politics was there in composition and organization a coalition of politically dominant classes which was similar to Congress's and, as such, favorable to the development of parliamentary democracy. The coalition was led by the professional middle class, and its partner in the countryside was the class of *jotedars*. Between these two classes there had long been a one-way movement of social mobility. Eastern Bengal possessed only minuscule classes of Muslim landlords, industrialists, and well-established professional men from whose families it might recruit its bureaucrats, lawyers, doctors, journalists, teachers, engineers. They were recruited from the good families of *jotedars*. After Partition, there was a flight from East Pakistan of Hindus, who had made up most of eastern Bengal's professional and business classes. Many of their successors were West Pakistanis; they in turn fled after the War of Liberation. The positions vacated by these migrations were filled by the sons of *jotedars*. With the advent of a national government in Dhaka, public-sector industrialization, and government-patronized and foreign-aid-subsidized capitalism, the *jotedars* as a class virtually disappeared into the urban professional and business classes.

What they left behind was a largely impoverished and illiterate peasantry. There is little economic or social distinction between one peasant family and another—little relative deprivation or affluence on which to base the political mobilization of peasants, as they have been mobilized in India, one group against another. Social classes are hardly apparent. Not only are the vast majority of farm families poor, but there is little to distinguish them from the tiny minority of their neighbors who are "rich." There is no longer anything in the Bangladeshi countryside comparable to caste, that great Indian institution of democratic political mobilization. There have been no "farmers' movements"—mass movements in protest against the allocation of government resources or the "terms of trade" between "the countryside" and "the city"—in Bangladesh as there have been in India.

Local government in the countryside is subservient to the government in Dhaka and manipulated by it and by the party opposed to that goverment. Competition for local office in the countryside is frequently fierce, sometimes murderous. But it is directed by the city's political parties and their factions. It is by becoming their clients that better-off peasant families serve their interests. In competition with the urban-centered AL and BNP, General Ershad turned to the countryside and tried to develop a system there of political councils. But these were meant to provide his "civilianized" regime with a rural support base, reminiscent of Ayub's "basic democracies," rather than to empower autonomous institutions of local self-government.

If today the countryside is virtually disenfranchised, nevertheless there is no structural barrier to its enfranchisement tomorrow. Those apparently immovable obstacles to parliamentary democracy's development in Pakistan's countryside—great landlords—do not exist in Bangladesh. There is no rural partner for a "marriage of iron and rye." Even landlords' successors—peasant proprietors of large holdings, landed patrons of landless clients—are thinner on the ground in Bangladesh than they are in India. Today, the urban professional and business classes form Bangladesh's coalition of politically dominant classes. They are committed, if not ideologically then with resignation, to parliamentary democracy. There is probably no alternative to it in Bangladesh—none acceptable to those classes. It is at least possible that, in future, an urban middle-class party will, like Ershad's Jatiya Party, but more successfully, galvanize parliamentary democracy's competitive dynamic in the countryside by looking to it not merely for votes but for allies. Certainly, this would be a more difficult political task in Bangladesh than it has been in India, where villagers are more differentiated by class and by caste, community, and "community." But I have no doubt that political imagination can do the job in Bangladesh. It did in India. Before and after Independence, much of the differentiation among people and virtually all of the political meaning given to it—"scheduled tribes," religious "communities," "Pakistan," OBC, Dalits—have been works of imagination and invention.

The Awami League movement for provincial autonomy and, relatedly, parliamentary democracy in Pakistan was not unlike the Congress movement for *swaraj* in British India and the Muslim League movement for "Pakistan." All were legitimated by the ideology of nationalism and directed by charismatic leaders. All were "action groups" rather than corporate bodies. All presented detailed plans of a "new society" from which their political opponents— "Britishers," Hindus, Punjabis, and Muhajirs—would be excluded. All were incubated by educated townsmen and spread by them into the countryside.[69] Congress evolved from a movement into "one-dominant party" and then a party among parties. The "Pakistan" movement all but ended with the establishment of Pakistan. But, the AL movement fragmented in Bangladesh into what might be called movement parties. By this, I mean parliamentary democratic political parties that compete for power as if they were movements. What lies at the heart of parliamentary democracy's arrested development in Bangladesh is, I believe, this movement-party characteristic of its politics.

The movement parties led by the AL and the BNP are both agglomerations of factions and factionalized parties. They have only this in common: they want political power and, the "acid test" elections of 1996 notwithstanding, they mistrust the exercise of power by the opposing party. It is not the ordinary, healthy mistrust that democratic politicians have of one another—of promises made to be broken, of commissions of inquiry whose conclusions are predetermined, of "economic modelling" based on political calculations, and so forth. Rather, it is a profound mistrust of the opposing party's commitment to seek, retain, and surrender power according to some mutually agreed-upon parliamentary democratic "rules of the game." For want of them, violence in general and the *hartal* (general strike) in particular are permanent features of political life in Bangladesh.

The government will not part from office, so the mistrust has it, or hold elections that it might lose unless it is forced to do so by extra-parliamentary action, *hartal.* It will stoop to treason in order to hold on to power in Dhaka. In a nutshell, provided by the BNP's Khaleda Zia: her sworn enemy, the AL government, has prepared "a blueprint to stay in power permanently and make Bangladesh subservient to [India]."[70]

The longer the government is in power, the more likely it is to stay permanently, the less likely it is to relinquish office, and the more difficult it will be for a *hartal* to dislodge it. Elections are plebiscites that vindicate the ideology of the winner's movement and remove the loser's legitimate right to govern. The loser's legitimate right to govern is vindicated by a successful *hartal,* a general strike that forces the government from office, a plebiscite by other means. The characteristic conception by movements, in general, of politics "in terms of friend–foe relations"[71] is manifest in Bangladesh's parties.

The development of parliamentary democracy in Bangladesh is impeded less, I think, by proliferating parties and factions than by their aggregation into movement parties rather than election-oriented coalitions of parties. Although any number of parties compete in Bangladesh's parliamentary elections, only six secured at least one seat in 1996. Ninety-eight percent of the seats went to three major parties, and the Awami League won a clear majority of the seats. By contrast, thirty-eight parties, divided into two electoral coalitions and "others," secured at least one seat in India's 1999 parliamentary elections, and no party won a clear majority of the seats.

As in Bangladesh the faction rather than its inclusive party is the basic unit of political competition in India. But political coalitions in India, as distinguished from movement parties in Bangladesh, compete for political power according to some generally agreed-upon parliamentary democratic "rules of the game" and confidently expect their opposing coalitions to do so too. Albeit with some tolerable measure of fraud and violence, it is in their mutual interests, they believe, to abide by the rules. Their opponents are members of their "political community." They are in the same game, and there is no game without rules. They want to win elections, but they are willing to lose them and even surrender power. The game will continue tomorrow. And who knows? Tomorrow may be the lucky day for some faction to switch to another party, or for some party to align itself with another coalition.

Rules and beliefs are, of course, learned and confirmed by experience. From my own observations of elections in India, it seems self-evident that the parliamentary democratic "rules of the game" and their acceptance as legitimate take some learning by a population the majority of whom were only yesterday cultivators "subject" to noncultivating rulers who were born to their *gaddis* or seized them. In Bangladesh, the learning and experiential curves have been comparatively short and flat. Compare them to India's! The popular movement for *swaraj* in India preceded by roughly thirty years the popular movement for autonomy in Bangladesh. Both as a movement and a party, Congress had an organizational base that the AL had not. India had held four general elections and Congress governments had been unseated in a number of Indian states by 1970 when the

AL triumphed in Pakistan's first general elections and was then denied office by military force. Indians, under the tutelage of "one-party dominance," in transition from elite parliamentary politics to parliamentary democracy, were learning to trust the parliamentary democratic game. East Bengalis were learning that the regime in West Pakistan could not be trusted. And they were learning how to organize their mistrust into a determined and uncompromising movement for autonomy. While Bangladesh was being ruled by generals from 1975 to 1991, India held seven parliamentary elections, Congress was voted out of power twice at the Centre in favor of opposition party alliances, and "one-party dominance" disappeared from state politics.

In the hands of its consolidator, General Ziaur Rahman, the army coup of 1975 took the form of a movement counter to Mujib's aborted "second revolution." Like the AL, the BNP was a movement party. It sought to reinvent nationalism in Bangladesh by discrediting the nationalist credentials of the AL. Thus, "we" became "Bangladeshis," no longer "Bengalis"—no longer parts of a cultural whole shared with Indian Bengalis. "They," in juxtaposition to whom "we" identify ourselves as a nation, are no longer Pakistanis. That was yesterday. Today, "they" are Indians—determined to subvert Bangladeshi nationalism, steal the Ganges water vital to our agriculture,[72] make us their satellite state. "Bengalis" are Indians and Hindus. "We," or more than four-fifths of us, are Muslims. "We" define ourselves as Muslims. "We" reject the secularism of *Mujibbad*. Under Zia's regime, the Islamic parties that had collaborated with Pakistan's army during the War of Liberation were rehabilitated. This reinvention of nationalism in Bangladesh was rewarded by diplomatic recognition to Dhaka from Islamabad and from the capitals of other Muslim countries. Like Pakistan, and no less futilely, Bangladesh enlisted Islam in nation-building.

To Zia's reinvention of Bangladesh, the AL of the martyred Mujib responded by reaffirming *Mujibbad*: not necessarily in the literal meaning of its slogans, but as the prophet's embodiment in his Word. We need not take the prophet's words literally to believe in his prophethood. In Bangladesh, the war of the Words was on. The language of competing party movements was ideological, although their actions were frequently violent. It was and is a war not for Bangladesh's autonomy or independence, but over national identity. Who are "we"? Not in relationship to anything intrinsic to "us"—"Bangladeshis" and "Bengalis" in Bangladesh are, after all, the same people—but rather in our relationship to some party movement that defines "us."

University students, the most active political "class" in Bangladesh, are in the front line. The university student movement, which had provided the autonomy movement with its shock troops, without which there would have been no Bangladesh, broke into its factions and their fragments after the War of Liberation and Mujib's failed "second revolution." They were "Bangladeshis" and "Bengalis," Islamists and leftists in fragments—all now armed with the war's leftover weapons. The fragments came together briefly and decisively in the movement that forced General Ershad from office in 1991 and preceded the restoration of parliamentary democracy. But student movements have not been conducive to the conservation and development of parliamentary democracy in Bangladesh. It is largely students who provide Bangladesh's warring parties with the marchers in their processions, their slogan shouters, enforcers of their *hartals*, and their "musclemen." In addition, student movements in Bangladesh, as elsewhere, "tend to be authoritarian, intransigent, violent,. . . susceptible to charismatic dominance . . . [and] . . . the cult of *machismo*," entrapped in the "dualism of intellectual elitism and popular mysticism."[73]

Given this bleak accounting of the war of movement parties in Bangladesh, are there any indications in it of hope for parliamentary democracy's future development in Bangladesh? There are some. But the indicators are mixed. So, for example, the AL and the BNP have agreed on this "rule of the game": The government resigns before parliamentary elections are held, and they are then conducted by a neutral caretaker government. The rule is appropriate to parliamentary democratic politics in Bangladesh. By far the greatest holder of the country's resources is the government in Dhaka. There are no great private fortunes in Bangladesh as there are in India, nor even agglomerations of small fortunes, to fund a credible election campaign against the government in power. There are no provincial governments with resources for use in the election campaigns of parties in opposition to the government in Dhaka. By agreeing to the rule, both parties have accepted the possibility of losing power at the polls. Two elections have been held under this rule, and the contending parties agreed afterward to their results. In 1991, the AL expected to win the elections, but it lost them and allowed the BNP to form a government. In 1996, the BNP lost the elections and surrendered government to the AL. After both elections, of course, the losing side reverted to *hartal* in order to stay in the game.

In 1998, the AL government refused to surrender power to a neutral caretaker government before holding elections for local bodies. That was not part of the rule, Sheikh Hasina argued. A *hartal* led by the BNP ensued. At this writing, the *hartal* has blossomed into a BNP-led movement for new *parliamentary* elections. It wants "this corrupt and anti-people [Awami League] party . . . [to] be dislodged from power *immediately*"[74]—before the end of the five-year term for which it was elected and in spite of its holding a clear majority in the Jatiya Sangsad. So, while there is a Bangladeshi amendment that does apply to the "rules of the game," some of the old rules apparently are no longer applicable.

I am indebted to my colleague Shamsul I. Khan for the suggestion that one of the driving forces behind Bangladesh's *hartals* is its "crony capitalism"—the product of the flood into post-Liberation Bangladesh of billions of dollars of foreign aid and investment, much of it into the funnel of government patronage in an economy largely dominated by government. Thus, cronies of the party out of power are unsure of their ability to survive long separation from the trough of political patronage, and they are fearful of the competitive advantage that long access to the trough is likely to confer on their competitors by cronies of the party in power. Five years is half a decade in "crony capitalism." In order to secure the source of their prosperity, reduce their dependence on politicians and bureaucrats and their obligations to them, and hedge their bets in the war of movement parties, any number of businessmen have gone into politics.

"The *nouveau riche* class" (i.e., "crony capitalists"), "well understanding how they had been created by political power, . . . [want] to have political power for themselves." And they have it. The dominant group in both political parties—on their backbenches and in their ministries—is composed of businessmen.[75] While it may certainly be in the immediate interests of some of them to support particular *hartals,* businessmen *as a class* are penalized by *hartals*—by the closure of economic activity.[76] The penalty is shared by serving bureaucrats, who collect a "rental" income for facilitating the business of business, and retired bureaucrats and military officers who have used their government connections to make a second career in the business of business. Estimates of the cost of *hartals* to the Bangladesh economy vary. The AL government's exaggerated estimate is that the *daily* cost to direct production of a successful *hartal* is approximately U.S.$800 million.[77] More realistically, *The Far Eastern Economic Review* costs the sixty days of opposition party *hartals* from 1996 to March 2000 at more than U.S.$100 million in "lost production and exports."[78] The eminent economist Rehman Sobhan wants more "serious empirical work . . . to ascertain the extent to which *hartals* . . . actually inhibit investment and production and exports. . . ."[79] However, no one, so far as I know, doubts but that *hartals* are bad for business. But no one can predict the emergence of an organized and effective business and business-related *class* opposition to *hartals.*

A seasoned practitioner of the *hartal* in opposition, the AL in government offered the BNP in opposition a pact in 1998 to ban the *hartal* as a political weapon. Begum Khaleda Zia, of course, refused the offer out of hand. Sheikh Hasina, she said, "cannot be trusted" not to run roughshod over an opposition that had renounced the use of *hartal*, nor to keep her promise to renounce the use of *hartal* when the AL is returned to the opposition benches.[80] More recently, after government and opposition parties failed to agree on a "consensus" candidate for the post of Chief Election Commissioner, the BNP and its allies refused to accept the government's appointment as legitimate.[81] Thus, Khaleda Zia has signaled her threat not to accept the results of the next parliamentary elections should her BNP and its allies lose them. But these events are more likely to delay rather than end the fight for generally acceptable rules of the parliamentary democratic game in Bangladesh. The fight go on. The rule of holding parliamentary elections under neutral caretaker governments, for example, was finally adopted in 1996 only after bruising battles between the governing BNP and the AL opposition.

Sheikh Hasina could not be trusted in 1998 because more than a decade before she unilaterally quit an all-party anti-Ershad *hartal.* In the ideology of mistrust, a decade is not a long time. Over the BNP opposition's uproar, one of Sheikh Hasina's first acts in office in 1997 was to give constitutional standing to her father's status as "Father of the Nation."[82] The title had been bestowed on Mujib by convention twenty-seven years earlier. In 1998, Hasina ordered the arrest and trial of a group of men who were allegedly involved in the 1975 murders of her father and family members and other AL figures. Among those arrested were politicians of the BNP. The latter responded with the threat of a *hartal* and the accusation that Sheikh Mujib's murder was the result of a conspiracy hatched within the AL itself.[83] And so it goes. Again, the political debate in Bangladesh is largely over repainting the past. But it is highly personalized repainting—of two men's political careers by the daughter of one and the widow of the other. It is unlikely, I think, to survive their inevitable departures from politics. The conflict between them assumes an ideological cover, but, like paint, it is a surface cover. It has no base, no grounding in class or status group conflict.

Both parties are dominated by the same people: urban, educated, English-speaking, "modernist" (as distinguished from "fundamentalist") Muslim, business, and professional class. Again, divided into movement parties, they form the coalition of dominant classes in Bangladesh. I do not think that many of them give much consideration to whether they are "Bengalis" or "Bangladeshis," and, I suspect, their successors will give the matter even less consideration. That quintessential Hindu *bhadralok literatus*, Rabindranth Tagore, enjoys the same iconic standing in Dhaka as he does in Calcutta. Other than in political debate, I do not think that many of the businessmen and professionals of the AL and the BNP share their party leaders' zeal to vindicate the political legacies of a dead father and a dead husband.

India's assigned role in Bangladesh's politics has been to sort out Zia's "Bangladeshis" from Mujib's "Bengalis." In 1997, India signed a second treaty with the AL government to close the one major outstanding issue between the two countries and a major source of anti-Indian hostility in Bangladesh: the diversion at the Farakka Barrage in West Bengal of the Ganges's flow to Calcutta's harbor and away from Bangladesh's fields. Bangladeshis (more than Bengalis) rail from time to time against India's alleged dictation of the treaty's terms to a supine AL and against New Delhi's bullying in general, real and imagined. But unlike Islamabad, Dhaka accepts, however reluctantly, India as the subcontinent's "managerial" power. India is still central to the BNP's demonology, now over "land transhipment rights" granted to India by the "anti-national" AL government. However, following the settlement of the water-sharing issue, there is really no major outstanding, unresolved conflict between Dhaka and New Delhi. There is nothing remotely comparable to the issue of Kashmir. In sum, the ideological conflict that fuels the war of the movement parties in Bangladesh is itself running out of steam.

Finally, the succession of military coups and countercoups in Bangladesh from 1975 to 1982 were not those of a centrally commanded and disciplined army but, rather, of factions in a politicized and undisciplined army. Nowadays, the officers and men of the Bangladesh army are well provided for, to be sure. But the army, as such, is not a political contender. It is looked to by virtually no one in Bangladesh as the ultimate instrument standing ready to bring order out of domestic political chaos. It has never enjoyed the institutional veto power in Bangladesh that the army had in Pakistan under the "Eighth Amendment." It has never enjoyed the conventional veto power in Bangladesh's politics that the army has always enjoyed in Pakistan's. The army's commanders are not partners in Bangladesh's coalition of politically dominant classes. The Bengalis were never cultivated as a "martial race" in British India, and the army enjoys considerably less prestige and presence in Bangladesh than it does in Pakistan. Pakistanis are told that their army is in the same league as India's. Bangladeshis know that theirs is not. Further military intervention into Bangladesh's parliamentary democratic politics is not, of course, impossible, but in the foreseeable future it is improbable. Even more improbable is "revolution from below."

Students have an anomalous relationship to parliamentary democracy. On the one hand, the internecine and violent warfare between student factions, the employment of students by political parties as their enforcers and "musclemen," the stashed automatic rifles in student hostels, the degradation of university education by student politics—all do no service to the development of parliamentary democracy in Bangladesh. On the other hand, students are probably parliamentary democracy's "reserve army." A student movement was largely responsible for toppling the Ershad dictatorship in 1991 and restoring parliamentary democracy. No event would more likely mobilize another massive, united student movement in defence of parliamentary democracy than a military coup.

The Islamic parties have had some of their thunder stolen by the BNP's explicit rejection of Sheikh Mujib's "secularism" and the AL's backsliding. As in Pakistan, the major parties are fearful of the collective "street power" of the Islamic parties. But they are minor players at the polls. In the 1996 elections for the Jatiya Sangsad, the major Islamic party, Jamaat-e-Islami, contested 300 seats to win 3 of them and 8 percent of the popular vote. So, while parliamentary democracy is not served by the Islamic parties, it is not threatened by them either. And their presence is a reminder to both "Bengalis" and "Bangladeshis" of their mutual interest in the preservation of parliamentary democracy.

NOTES

1. Dietrich Rueschemeyer, Evelyne Huber Stephens, and John D. Stephens, *Capitalist Development and Democracy* (Cambridge: Polity Press, 1992), p. 9.

2. A *biradari* is a patrilineal kinship group, a "brotherhood."

3. See discussion of the 1940 Lahore "Pakistan Resolution" later in this chapter.

4. In Sindh, where the Muslim League was virtually nonexistent before the 1946 elections, a government that was Muslim League in name came to power afterward, but it was hardly popularly based. Ayesha Jalal characterizes pre-partition Sindhi politics thus: "In Sindh, politics was a term dignifying power struggles between rival landlord factions." *The State of Martial Rule* (Cambridge: Cambridge University Press, 1990), p. 159.

5. "Moth-eaten" was Jinnah's description.

6. He ended his last indefinite fast, to bring communal peace to India's riot-torn capital, only on the Indian government's assurance that it would release the cash assets that it owed to Pakistan and was withholding.

7. Chaudhri Muhammad Ali, *The Emergence of Pakistan* (Lahore: Research Society of Pakistan [first impression], 1973), p. 175.

8. Ibid., p. 371; emphasis added.

9. Reproduced in Aminur Rahim, *Politics and National Formation in Bangladesh* (Dhaka: University Press, 1997), pp. 257–258.

10. Hasan Zaheer, *The Separation of East Pakistan: The Rise and Realization of Bengali Muslim Nationalism* (Dhaka: University Press, 1994), p. 34.

11. Rangalal Sen, *Political Elites in Bangladesh* (Dhaka: University Press, , 1986), p. 124. There were separate seats for Hindus.

12. Government of Pakistan, *Report of the Land Reforms Commission* (1959), Appendix 1, quoted in Iftikhar H. Malik, *State and Civil Society in Pakistan* (London: Macmillan, 1997), p. 91.

13. "Asia 1994," *Far Eastern Economic Review*, p. 184.

14. This is his title in the international and Pakistani press. In the army, he is (or was) General Pervaiz.

15. Asad Sayeed, of the Pakistan Institute for Labor Education and Research, quoted by Siddarth Varadarajan, "A Wary Nation Ponders over Its Political Future," *Times of India*, internet edition, 23 November 1999.

16. "Basic democracy" was the name of the scheme: see discussion later in this chapter.

17. Akmal Hussain, *Poverty Alleviation in Pakistan* (Lahore: Vanguard Books, 1994), p. 4.

18. Akmal Hussain, "Land to the Tiller: First Step Towards Democracy," *The News on Friday* (Lahore), 8 December 1995, p. 20.

19. "Lords of Misrule," *Far Eastern Economic Review*, 20 May 1999, pp. 22–29. This tallies with the information that I have received in conversations in Lahore with informed Pakistanis, most authoritatively Akmal Hussain and Najjam Sethi. See also Malik, *State and Civil Society in Pakistan,* p. 88, and Omar Noman, *The Political Economy of Pakistan 1947–85* (London: KPI, 1988), p. 127.

20. Masud Mufti, "Our MNAs [members of national assemblies] and MPAs [members of provincial assemblies] Are Bigger Than Our Constitution" (no publication details). The author is a leading Pakistani journalist.

21. Ibid.

22. Shahid Javed Burki, "Is Pakistan's Past Relevant for Its Economic Future," *Pakistan: 1997*, edited by Craig Baxter and Charles H. Kennedy (New Delhi: HarperCollins, 1998), p. 34, endnote.

23. www.transparency.de.

24. *New York Times*, internet edition, 6 March 2000.

25. VVIP: an Asian distinction between those who are merely important and those who are truly important.

26. The term may be—and by the British was sometimes—used contemptuously: a shyster.

27. Chaudhri Muhammad, *The Emergence of Pakistan*, p. 239.

28. Maulana Abul Ala Maudoodi, leader of the Jamaat-i-Islami, quoted in Lawrence Ziring, *Bangladesh from Mujib to Ershad: An Interpretive Study* (Dhaka: University Press, 1992), p. 26.

29. W. W. Hunter, *Indian Musalmans* (reprinted Delhi: Indological Book House, 1969).

30. Leonard Binder, *Religion and Politics in Pakistan* (Berkeley, CA: University of California Press, 1961), chap. 11, and Keith Callard, *Pakistan* (New York: Macmillan, 1957), chap 6.

31. For details of its structure, see Karl von Vorys, *Political Development in Pakistan* (Princeton, NJ: Princeton University Press, 1965).

32. Another name for *ulama,* and sometimes used disparagingly on the subcontinent.

33. Mohammad Ayub Khan, *Friends Not Masters: A Political Biography* (New York: Oxford University Press, 1967), chap 11.

34. Stanley Wolpert, *Zulfi Bhutto of Pakistan* (Delhi: Oxford University Press, 1993), p. 206.

35. Mumtaz Ahmad, "Revivalism, Islamisation, Sectarianism and Violence in Pakistan," *Pakistan 1997,* edited by Craig Baxter and Charles H. Kennedy (New Delhi: HarperCollins, 1998), p. 106. For my analysis of Zia's Islamization, in general, I am particularly indebted to this article.

36. Ziaullah Niazi and Asif Shazad, "Cop Killed, 100 Hurt in Lahore," *The News* (Lahore), internet edition, 21 February 1999.

37. "Betraying Jinnah," *The News* (Lahore), internet edition, 12 October 1998.

38. Nawaz Sharif, whose brother was chief minister of Punjab and who was particularly partial to Punjabi underlings, exacerbated this hostility. "Living Like a King—Sharif's Litany of Abuses," *The News* (Lahore), internet edition, 24 October 1999.

39. Specifically, to destroy the Indian army's ability to use the road from Srinagar Jammu and Kashmir's capital to Leh, the major town in western Kashmir.

40. "Pak Announces Troop Reduction along Border," *Times of India*, internet edition, 18 October 1999.

41. *New York Times*, internet edition, 6 March 2000.

42. Literally, the government in Delhi. The expression is used nowadays to suggest the government's remove from "us"—as in "those people" in Washington/Albany/Sacramento, etc.

43. Based on their understanding of the Quran, Muslims, in general, regard dogs as inappropriate house pets.

44. Mullah Mohammad Omar is leader of the Taliban movement in Afghanistan.

45. *The News* (Lahore), internet edition, 22 May and 4 June 2000. A Turkish army officer, Ataturk, was the founding father of Turkey as a secular republic in 1923 and, afterwards, a no-nonsense secularizer of Turkish society.

46. Talukder Maniruzzaman, *The Bangladesh Revolution and Its Aftermath* (Dhaka: University Press, 1988), p. 7.

47. Quoted in Sen, *Political Elites*, p. 120; emphasis added.

48. Maniruzzaman, *The Bangladesh Revolution*, p. 8; emphasis added.

49. Zaheer, *Separation of East Pakistan,* chap. 2.

50. Ayub Khan, *Friends*, p. 187.

51. Mushtaq Ahmad, *The United Nations and Pakistan* (Karachi: Pakistan Institute of International Affairs, 1955), p. 140.

52. Quoted in Zaheer, *Separation of East Pakistan*, p. 72.

53. Talukder Maniruzzaman, *Politics and Security of Bangladesh* (Dhaka: University Press, 1994), p. 119.

54. From the title of a 1944 treatise on the moral basis of political democracy, written by the leading American Protestant theologian Rienhold Niebuhr. *Children of Light and Children of Darkness* (New York: Scribner's Sons, 1944).

55. S. M. Burke and Lawrence Ziring, *Pakistan's Foreign Policy*, second edition (Karachi: Oxford University Press, 1990), p. 255.

56. "Texts of Secret Documents on Top-Level Discussions of Indian–Pakistan War," *New York Times*, 6 January 1972, pp. 15, 18.

57. So called in the works of many Pakistani writers.

58. Mohammad Ayoob, "India in South Asia: The Quest for Regional Predominance," *World Policy Journal,* Winter 1989–90, vol. 12, no. 1.

59. Milan Kundera, *The Book of Laughing and Forgetting* (London: Penguin, 1983), p. 22.

60. Quoted in Syed Razi Wasti, *Muslim Struggle for Freedom in British India* (Lahore: Book Traders, 1993), p. 370; emphasis added.

61. W. C. Smith, *Modern Islam in India*, quoted in Sen, *Political Elites*, p. 56.

62. Sen, *Political Elites*, chap. 3; emphases added.

63. For an exhaustive accounting, see Shamsul I. Khan, S. Aminul Islam, and M. Indadul Haque, *Political Culture, Political Parties and the Democratic Transition in Bangladesh* (Dhaka: Academic Publishers, 1996).

64. *The Daily Star* (Dhaka), internet edition, 28 March 1998, "Grand Rally at Central Shaheed Minar."

65. Rounaq Jahan, *Bangladesh Politics: Problems and Issues* (Dhaka: University Press, 1987).

66. I prefer this wonderfully descriptive alliteration, applied to Indonesian capitalism during the Soeharto era, although it is not generally used to describe much the same phenomenon in Bangladesh.

67. "A foolish consistency," according to Ralph Waldo Emerson.

68. Khan, Islam, and Haque, *Political Culture*, p. 17.

69. For a good discussion of movements see, the articles entitled "Social Movements" by Rudolf Heberle and Joseph R. Gusfield, *International Encyclopedia of the Social Sciences*, Vol. 14, edited by David L. Sills (New York: Macmillan, 1968), pp. 438–452.

70. *The Daily Star*, internet edition, 28 October 1999.

71. Heberle and Gusfield, "Social Movements."

72. See the discussion of the Farakka Barrage later in the chapter.

73. Lewis S. Feuer, *The Conflict of Generations: The Character and Significance of Student Movements* (London: Heinemann, 1969), chap. 5.

74. Begum Kahaleda Zia, quoted in the *Daily Star* (Dhaka), internet edition, 2:251, 5 May 1999; emphasis added.

75. Maniruzzaman, *Politics and Security*, chap. 6.

76. There is some survey evidence to support this proposition and a number of "express[ions] of concern" from business houses and associations about the frequency of *hartals*. *Daily Star* (Dhaka), 1:70, 21 October 1997 and 1:111, 1 December 1997. There is a "Petition against Hartal in Bangladesh" on the internet. It is to be presented to all political parties and newspapers once it receives 1,500 signatures. It now has about 1,000 signatories, most of whom are expatriate Bangladeshis—a valuable source of remittances and, potentially, investments.

77. Kazi Alauddin Ahmed, "The Cry of the Hour," *Daily Star*, 25 November 1998, p. 4.

78. 9 March 2000, p. 17.

79. "Overview," *Experiences with Economic Reform: A Review of Bangladesh's Development 1995* (Dhaka: University Press, 1995), p. 55.

80. *The Bangladesh Observer*, 26 November 1998, p. 1.

81. *The Daily Star*, internet edition, 23 May 2000.

82. *Dawn* (Lahore), 20 February 1997, p. 17.

83. *The Hindu*, internet edition, 12 October 1998.

6

Does Parliamentary Democracy Matter?

The assumption underlying this book is that parliamentary democracy is not only a political system but a political system, with social effect. My guide is John Rawls's *A Theory of Justice.*[1] Like his, my assumption is that parliamentary democracy, however flawed, is the one political system among others best able to deliver social justice: fair treatment to its citizens. And with Rawls, I assume that the delivery of this social justice is the primary, legitimating function of parliamentary democracy.

Two questions arise: First, is this assumption substantiated, even in some small measure, tentatively, hopefully, in a comparative study of political development on the subcontinent? I believe that it is. That, I think, is clear in some of what I have already written and in what I add in summary below. Second, how to proceed? I want first to make some comparisons—or more exactly, to add to the comparisons that I have already made—of the post-Partition careers of those parts of the British Indian empire that were divided in 1947: Punjab into most of what is now Pakistan and the Indian states of Punjab and Haryana; the eastern districts of Bengal that are now Bangladesh and the Indian state of West Bengal. Finally, I want to say some things, in general, about parliamentary democracy and social justice in India, Pakistan, and Bangladesh.

THE PUNJABS

Our basic text is a comparative study of agricultural development in Indian and Pakistani Punjab written by Holly Sims in 1988. Four decades earlier, when the subcontinent was partitioned, she tells us:

Pakistan got the rich agricultural lands of West Punjab, whose agricultural growth rates and yields . . . were higher than those of [Indian] East Punjab during the forty years preceding Independence. Pakistan also received 80 percent of the province's irrigation facilities and most of its rural roads and power grids.[2]

But what eastern Punjab got, its gift from Partition, was a province of few great landlords and a government sympathetic to the interests of cultivating proprietors. The Sikh and Hindu farmers of eastern Punjab were, in the main, cultivating small-holders. Families of Sikh and Hindu refugees from West Punjab, many of them prosperous peasants there, were settled on small-holdings in the east; these were generally, smaller than their holdings in the west from which they had fled.[3] So, the first "land reforms" in Indian Punjab, a leveling of proprietorship, were a consequence of Partition. Congress, which was barely present in pre-Partition Punjab, extended its *raj* from India's center to post-Partition Punjab. The usual pattern of land reforms followed. Great estates and noncultivating landlords as a class virtually disappeared in the 1950s. A rough-and-tumble parliamentary democracy appeared at the provincial level, and in Punjab it became, par excellence, the instrument of cultivating proprietors.

Now, fifty years on, Indian Punjab has surpassed Pakistani Punjab not only in every measure of agricultural productivity, but also in every related indicator of human welfare. The incidence of poverty in the villages of Indian Punjab is negligible.[4] Not so in the west. In the east, "the category of pure tenants (without landownership) has completely disappeared." In Pakistani Punjab, 19 percent of the land area is cultivated by tenants who own no land.[5] Every village in the east is electrified and serviced by a paved road. Not so in Pakistani Punjab. In Indian Punjab, the rate of literacy is twice that of Pakistani Punjab. Tube-well ownership and cooperative society membership are more general in the east than in the west. The same Green Revolution commercialized agriculture in the both Punjabs. But the inputs requisite to participation in this revolution, including credit, are more equitably available in the east than in the west.[6] Their availability has turned holdings that were previously marginal into viable, albeit hardscrabble, farms. More equitable relations of sharing have developed between proprietors and sharecroppers under Green Revolution conditions. Agricultural labor is better paid in Punjab than in any other part of India. In spite of caste on the one hand and the theological egalitarianism of Islam on the other, traditional rituals symbolizing social distances between classes have survived less well in Indian than in Pakistani Punjab. Hindu Dalits are increasingly assertive in Indian Punjab, and untouchability among Sikhs has virtually disappeared. In comparison to Pakistani Punjab, then, Indian Punjab is virtually a model of how parliamentary democracy can shape agricultural prosperity into some semblance of social justice.

How, then, can we account for the Khalistan Movement, which racked Indian Punjab during the 1980s? Ostensibly, it was a secessionist movement for the establishment of an independent, sovereign Punjab in which the *khalsa* (the Sikh community) would rule. Its denouement in 1984 was, first, the invasion of Amritsar's Golden Temple by Indian army troops to blast out the secessionists whose leader had made this Sikh holiest-of-holy places his headquarters and sanctuary, and, second, the subsequent assassination by her Sikh bodyguards of the Indian prime minister, Indira Gandhi, who had ordered the invasion. For a while thereafter, things went from bad to worse. Many ordinary Sikhs who were not *khalistanis* were nonetheless outraged at the sacrilege of a military assault on their *Durbar Sahab* (the Golden Temple), and refused the Indian government's support in its repair. In Delhi neighborhoods where Sikhs are concentrated, there was a murderous anti-Sikh riot led by a handful of Congress politicians and their hooligans. The Khalistan Movement was momentarily revived. But by the end of the decade, a combination of brutal police repression and equally brutal response from *khalistani* militias, bred of their waning popular support, saw their movement fragment and collapse.

In the light of Punjab's post-Independence history as one of India's most successful provincial parliamentary democracies, what sense can we make of the Khalistan Movement? We need to think about what it was and what it was not. In part, it was a continuation of an old story: the Sikh fear that, without the protection of a political border, the *khalsa* and the *panth* (the faith) risk reabsorption into Hinduism. The Khalistan Movement was an extreme expression of this fear. As it metastasized, its leadership drifted over time from moderates in the Sikh religious-"communal" party, the Akali Dal, into the hands of a murderous, anti-Hindu Sikh cleric, Sant Jarnail Bindranwale, and his disciples. Police repression, of course, accelerated the drift. The Khalistan Movement was in part the provider of a materially and psychically rewarding occupation for *goondas*: lumpen young men. Relatedly, perhaps, the movement was driven by feelings of relative deprivation. While the Green Revolution had been generally beneficial in Punjab, it had been particularly and disproportionately beneficial to the well-to-do. As such, it substantially increased the economic and social distance between them and the less well-to-do. Of all Indian religions, Sikhism is perhaps the most egalitarian in its élan. So, those who were relatively deprived suffered insult as well as injury. The well-to-do farmers who, as Akalis and Congressmen, dominated Punjabi politics compounded the injury by serving themselves to government largesse for agricultural development at the expense of providing industrial development to enhance the employment prospects of the sons of the relatively deprived.

The Khalistan Movement was not a popular movement. Its popularity was at times exaggerated by popular reactions to its repression, by stories of "encounters" staged by police in order to murder *khalistanis* and anyone else who got in the way, and by the movement's enthusiastic support from expatriate Sikh communities, most notably in the United Kingdom. But its lack of support in Punjab finally doomed it. Sikhs were confronted, on the one side, by a disarray of Jat

Sikh ultras who were certain to lose the war and were in desperation turning feral—supporting themselves by brigandage and extortion, executing Sikh "collaborators," and so forth. Certain to win the war was a Jat Sikh police force led by an unyielding Jat Sikh chief and supported by Indian paramilitary and military forces. The Sikhs chose not only the winning side but, I believe, the better game. For almost a decade now, they have resumed their lives as one of India's most prosperous, vibrant, and politically active "communities." A rump of the Khalistan Movement survives in Pakistan as a resource for troublemaking in India and a monument to the alleged hypocrisy of "secularism" in Hindu India. But there, in Punjab, apart from the occasional pay-back assassination by *khalistani* diehards, the movement has virtually disappeared.

THE BENGALS

In power since 1977, the longest-serving state government in India is the Left Front in West Bengal led by the Communist Party of India-Marxist. In 1997, the front won its fifth straight election for the West Bengal legislative assembly. Jyoti Basu, parliamentary leader of the CPI-M in West Bengal, has been the state's chief minister since the front was first elected to power. In his eighties now, he is the longest-serving chief minister in any Indian state. Like Basu, leaders and cadres of the CPI-M are, in general, *bhadralok*. Like Basu, any number of them were refugees from Pakistan's East Bengal. They fled leaving their interests as *zamindars* and rentiers behind them. Even before Partition, these same interests of *bhadralok* in western Bengal were gradually eroded by the rise to rural dominance of the landed peasantry and finally demolished by the Congress government's abolition in 1953 of the Permanent Settlement's *zamindari* system. Deprived of their rental income from the countryside, the *bhadralok* have focused their sights, and with notable success, on the urban careers that first opened to them in British India. As they were then, so they are now: West Bengal's and one of India's most notable professional middle classes.

Particularly notable for us is that West Bengal's *bhadralok* are one regional middle-class and upper-caste grouping whose political dominance has been unchallenged to date by OBC and/or Dalit politicians and their parties and factions. To this feat, the CPI-M's *bhadralok* have contributed in no small measure. They have done so by recruiting a rural constituency through land reforms that are, with Kerala's, more favorable than any other in India to the interests of the countryside's underclasses. But just how favorable and to which underclasses is a matter of great contention.

At the one extreme, for example, G. K. Lieten argues that the CPI-M–led Left Front government has substantially reallocated both social honor and income in the West Bengal countryside. The CPI-M's sustained efforts to bring the countryside's underclasses, including Dalits, into dominant positions in West Bengal's *panchayati raj* system has encouraged their "empowerment": "The tendency to look for external support of patrons has, by and large, been replaced by confidence in organised solidarity."[7]

This newfound, Left Front-sponsored confidence and solidarity has contributed, clearly but in some unspecified ways, to discrediting the moral basis of caste hierarchy and even to the disappearance of the "practice of untouchability."[8] In response to the interests and instructions of their political masters, West Bengal's civil servants and police have demonstrated a new solicitude for the lowly and poor, and there has been a marked reduction in the abuses visited on them by their caste and class betters. Under the Left Front government, the right of West Bengal's rural underclasses "to exist as human beings has finally been recognised."[9]

As to the reallocation of income, Lieten argues that West Bengal under the CPI-M's government was the only state in India that overfulfilled its original land-redistribution targets and that West Bengal's poor account for "almost half of the land redistribution beneficiaries in the country." Wages for agricultural laborers also began to increase under the Left Front government, and there "has actually been a downward trend in the relative number of agricultural labourers, a trend very much unlike what has been observed in the rest of India."[10] "Operation Barga," the program of tenurial rather than redistributive land reform for which the CPI-M is best known, "has accorded to most . . . sharecroppers a guaranteed and heritable access to their plots, and has largely done away with [their] interlocking of dependence [on cultivating proprietors for security of tenure, wage labor and credit]."[11] Moreover, CPI-M government programs to increase the availability of fertilizer and HYV seeds to small peasants and sharecroppers has increased West Bengal's agricultural productivity and, through this, benefited the rural underclasses.

In sum, "short of a struggle for independence from the Republic of India," and within its "socio-economic formation [which] remains fundamentally capitalistic," the CPI-M's rural reforms have gone about as far as they can go:[12] "higher productivity and a better deal for small peasants, [sharecroppers] and agricultural labourers have combined to reduce . . . extreme poverty and to reverse the . . . process [of ongoing and increasing rural misery]."[13]

Ross Mallick disagrees. He challenges every one of Lieten's conclusions.[14] The CPI-M base in the countryside is a coalition of poor and the middle peasants. The latter are clearly dominant. It is they and not the poor and despised who control the *panchayats*. There has been no social reform under the Left Front government. "Ideas about pollution and untouchability are the same as elsewhere in India."[15] There has been no economic reform in favor of the poor. No more than the Congress government before it has the CPI-M government "carried out [any] significant land reforms since *zamindari* abolition."[16] There have been no more redistributive land reforms in West Bengal under the CPI-M government than there have been in other states in India under the government of bourgeois parties. And no less than these parties has the CPI-M failed the poor as a "developmental channel." With regard to agricultural wages, "the Communists have not made any noticeable impact . . . , despite claims to the contrary."[17]

At one with the rest of the CPI-M's rural reforms, "the prime beneficiaries of Operation Barga" have been middle peasant sharecroppers rather than the "poorest *bargadars* [sharecroppers]." The majority of the poorest are Dalits and tribal people, too dependent on their peasant proprietor landlords for wages and credit to register their legitimate claims to tenurial security.[18]

In sum, the CPI-M "experiment in West Bengal is now widely regarded by knowledgeable observers as a failure." It need not have been. There "was sufficient scope within the Indian constitution for reforms conducive to communist growth in a revolutionary direction, [but] these reforms were not undertaken." The only set of policies the Left Front followed with "single minded devotion" involved those policies that would keep it "in power at all costs."[19]

In support of their almost diametrically opposed positions, both Lieten and Mallick[20] marshal the extensive bibliographies of other scholars and elaborate arrays of statistical evidence. But that is not our concern. Underlying their contradictory arguments there is an area of agreement among Lieten, Mallick, and the scholars and journalists whose works they cite. And that is our concern. We are not concerned—not directly, at least—with what the CPI-M has or has not done in Bengal. We are concerned directly with what the party is and is not.

The CPI-M in West Bengal is not a revolutionary party. It is a parliamentary democratic party. It holds office by virtue of winning elections. Like other regional non-Congress parties, and even Congress itself (in Gujarat, for example), it wins elections by piecing and holding together a rural constituency of diverse groups. These are, in general, of lesser socioeconomic status than the constituency that sustained its Congress predecessor in West Bengal. The Left Front's apparently unshakeable electoral strength is in the countryside. Like other regional parties that have used the competitive dynamic of parliamentary democracy as their vehicle to power, the CPI-M is constrained in what it can and cannot do by calculations appropriate to a parliamentary democratic party operating within a system of parliamentary democracy in India. With apparent success over the past twenty-two years, the CPI-M has been able to maintain parliamentary democracy's "delicate balance" between "pressures from subordinate classes and threat perceptions . . . of economic elites."[21] In the Indian countryside, that balance is a particularly delicate one because subordinate classes are so dependent for their livelihoods on economic elites.

Ironically, those characteristics that we associate with communist parties— tactical flexibility within the framework of a strategic ideology, organizational skills, and discipline—have made the CPI-M a successful parliamentary democratic party in West Bengal. Indeed, it has become West Bengal's "one-dominant party," reminiscent of Congress: "The Left Front effectively embrace[s] all classes except for the tiny minority of the very biggest landowners, leaving no class enemies or entrenched interests to fight against."[22]

The CPI-M has not "refused to implement a transition to socialism."[23] It has never contemplated such a transition. The CPI-M is a reformist, parliamentary democratic party. The Left Front implemented reforms to capitalist agriculture that Congress put on the books but could not (or would not) implement because they were contrary to the interests of its upper-class and higher-caste rural constituency. Jyoti Basu outlined his party's position in terms that need little translation even for the noncommunist reader. Merely substituting "parliamentary democracy" for "capitalist system" will do. So, at the onset of the Left Front's regime in 1977, Basu praised his colleagues. They

were not fools but rational and sensible people. They understood that this was not a socialist country, that its socio-economic life was regulated by the capitalist system. Hence their state government would have to proceed with a policy and programme within the constraints of the capitalist system and coexist with capitalists and landlords.[24]

A good systematic comparative study of "agrarian structure and productivity" between Bangladesh and West Bengal has been made by the Bangladeshi scholar Bimal Kumar Saha.[25] Along with many scholars cited by Lieten and Mallick, Saha's evaluation of the CPI-M's performance in absolute terms is somewhere at midpoint between theirs. In terms relative to the prevailing situation in the Bangladeshi countryside, however, Saha's evaluation of the Left Front's rural reforms in West Bengal is favorable. Thus, while at the time of Partition the degree of differentiation and inegalitarianism was higher among the peasantry of western Bengal than among the peasantry of the east, "now exactly the reverse exists":

In respect of technological and structural (capitalist) transformation, West Bengal [is] now. . . ahead of Bangladesh. For Bangladesh the overwhelming direction of the agrarian economy appears to be toward stagnation in production levels and growing polarisation and mass impoverishment. In West Bengal, the principal thrust is . . . to insure the continued viability of small peasant cultivation with [a] somewhat . . . increasing tendency . . . [toward] productivity through state subsidies and village level organisation.[26]

The tenancy, credit, and labor markets for the poor are "more exploitative in Bangladesh than in West Bengal" where "a large part of government activity is focused on sharecroppers and agricultural labourers through tenancy regulations . . ., employment generation and institutional credit. . . ."[27] In the absence "of any such effective measures" in Bangladesh, peasant proprietors "can evict any [sharecropper] at any time," who after bearing all the costs of production cannot afford to be pressured into paying more than the "customary fifty percent" of his produce. For credit, too, the Bangladeshi sharecropper is at the mercy of peasant proprietors who have become the countryside's chief moneylenders: "pure tenants [and sharecroppers] are not allowed to take institutional loans while landowners can get credit against the total amount of owned land though they operate only part of it."[28]

The voters in West Bengal's countryside apparently do not accept Mallick's verdict of "failure" on the Left Front's "experiment" in West Bengal. In any case, it is apparently less of a failure, if we are to believe Saha (and I see no reason not to), than Pakistani and Bangladeshi "experiments" with rural reform in eastern Bengal. Lieten's claim for the CPI-M's "success" in West Bengal's countryside is hardly extravagant. Under the Left Front government, the poor "have attained a tolerable level of poverty"[29]—no more than that. After twenty-two years of government in a state with one of the subcontinent's poorest countrysides, could we have expected more from a communist party turned party of parliamentary democratic reformism? I do not think so. It may be, as I suggested earlier, that in India's socially differentiated, inegalitarian, and small-holding rural society, social justice in the form of radical redistributive land reform could only be delivered by an authoritarian regime. But even if we could choose such a regime for India—and fortunately we cannot—it would, as a matter of social justice, be incumbent upon us to balance the possibility of regime-imposed redistributive land reforms against the costs of authoritarianism. The history of our century suggests that those costs would more than likely be high.

INDIA, PAKISTAN, AND BANGLADESH

For whatever it is worth, the United Nations publishes annually a league table of human development. A comparison of India and Pakistan based on standard-of-living indicators compiled and refined in the UN's Human Development Index (HDI) of 1998 suggested that the two states were about equal among "low human development" countries. India's rates of literacy and education were notably higher than Pakistan's, and Pakistan's per capita GDP was notably higher than India's. The HDI values of the two countries were about equal—shamefully equal. Of 174 countries listed, Pakistan was 138th and India 139th. Bangladesh lagged behind both India and Pakistan in all indexed items and in their cumulative value. In 1999, India was promoted to 132nd position on the index, ahead of Pakistan—still at 138th. Bangladesh fell further behind: from 147th in 1998 to 150th.[30] In the 2000 index, the relative positions of the three countries was much the same as it had been in 1999, except that India had moved slightly ahead.[31]

Again, half a century ago what is now the largest part of Pakistan was the most highly developed agricultural part of a generally impoverished subcontinent. Except for eastern Bengal, all of the impoverishment went to India. Thus, recent Human Development Indexes suggest that while the progress of human welfare in India's villages is hardly satisfactory, it has been more general than in Pakistan's.

But even assuming that this suggestion is correct, we can hardly attribute such progress to the development of parliamentary democracy in India and its nondevelopment in Pakistan. Even in India, where parliamentary democracy at the provincial level is general, human development is not. Compare, for example, on the one hand Punjab, where agricultural development has been relentlessly pursued, and on the other hand Bihar, where, I am reliably informed, development—as the UN Development Program defines it—is simply not on anyone's political agenda.[32] Bangladesh's uncertain parliamentary democracy has had no positive effect—possibly no effect at all, or even a negative effect—on its human development.

Perhaps the development of parliamentary democracy in India, its uncertain course in Bangladesh, and its nondevelopment in Pakistan should be placed in a wider comparative framework—though even there our observations can only be speculative, subjective, tentative, and inconclusive. But, in summation, I think that they are worth making. A convenient prototype is provided for us by Rueschemeyer, Stephens, and Stephens:

At the one extreme, there are cases where formally democratic processes barely modify the distribution of power and economic resources. At the other end of the spectrum, the actual political power of the many has over time made a real difference in the distribution of scarce social and economic resources—of income and wealth, of power and influence, of honour and respect—and thus also in turn improved the bases of political equality.[33]

If, for the sake of argument, Pakistan occupies any place at all on this spectrum, it is at "the one extreme," and stuck there. Its "formally democratic processes" are fairly well limited to periodic elections since 1988, in which voters get to choose a government of civilian politicians from competitive factions of their country's coalition of politically dominant classes. The winning faction governs until the army tires of it, as it did in 1999. Again, no Pakistani government has ever been voted out of power. All have been removed either directly or indirectly by the army. Periodic elections in Pakistan have had no discernible effect on "the distribution of power and economic resources." They remain as firmly as ever in the hands of the homogenizing, albeit factionalized, coalition of landlords, industrialists, generals, and elite bureaucrats. And this is no more likely to be changed by military rule from 1999 than it was by military rule from 1977 to 1988. In response to international pressure to "restore" parliamentary democracy, General Musharraf has referred dismissively to it as a "label" that he will reaffix in the army's own good time[34]—in three years, perhaps. Indeed, even as a system of government with no regard to its social effect, parliamentary democracy in Pakistan has never been much more than a label.

The most politically significant social change over the past two decades or so in Pakistan has been the changing social origins of army officers, "from the landed elite to a wider base in the urban middle strata and the . . . class of . . . capitalist farmers."[35] But in no way is this is a consequence of parliamentary democracy, but rather of expanding, remunerative career opportunities opening to the sons of landlords and of other upper-class families. The change has increased the military's autonomy from the society of landlords but has strengthened its connections to institutional Islam—hardly a change for the parliamentary democratic better! What the *ulama* and the army share is a lack of commitment to parliamentary democracy and a hard line on Kashmir. As a class, none were more initially welcoming of General Musharraf's coup—as they were of General Zia's coup before it—than the *ulama*. Unlike Zia's coup, however, Musharraf's has not been carried out by a general in command of his self-proclaimed army of Islam. His messages to the home front have made that clear. But while they have dampened the *ulama's* enthusiasm for military rule, their aversion to parliamentary democracy is undiminished and their wariness of the "so-called establishment" of civil and military bureaucrats has increased. Under General Musharraf, they threaten to impose order on the "status quo." Apparently, the "Islamic revolution"—a "true Islamic order"—will emerge only from chaos.[36]

In what was then East Pakistan, parliamentary democratic elections in 1970 presaged such fundamental changes in "the distribution of power and economic resources" that the elections' results had to be vindicated in a war of secession and accommodated in an independent Bangladesh. But political democracy soon gave way to erratic military rule. Parliamentary democracy at this writing is only a decade old in Bangladesh. And while its legitimacy is questioned by none of the real contenders for political power, they have yet to agree on a set of rules that will allow the game to proceed productively for their country or even to their mutual advantage. Less as a result of parliamentary democracy than of the establishment of a Bangladeshi state, the major social changes in recent years have been the disappearance of the *jotedars* into the urban middle classes and, relatedly, the symbiotic development of parliamentary democratic politics and the "crony capitalism" of a new class of Bangladeshi entrepreneurs. For the vast majority of Bangladeshis who live in the countryside, parliamentary democracy has yet to make any "real difference in the distribution of scarce social and economic resources." The "political power of the many" has not been enhanced by a parliamentary democracy that is dominated by urban interests. There are institutions of local self-government in the countryside, but they lack substantive and autonomous authority to vindicate the countryside's concerns, either as a region or of any of its classes. We might place parliamentary democracy in Bangladesh "at the one extreme," but in comparison to parliamentary democracy in Pakistan it is more than a label and there is no antidemocratic coalition of dominant classes to keep it from inching along the spectrum.

In India, parliamentary democracy has put down its roots into the countryside. In these terrains of *Homo hierarchicus,* parliamentary democracy was revolutionary in conception—and, relatedly, in its inherent competitive dynamic—but reformist in practice. Beginning at the one extreme, it changed the "distribution of [agrarian] power and economic resources" away from noncultivating great landlords and in favor of land-holding farmers and dominant and twice-born castes. This was the political sea-change in the development of parliamentary democracy. In combination with a capitalist economy, parliamentary democracy redistributed "income and wealth" to produce one of the world's largest middle classes, variously estimated on the criteria of purchasing power as somewhere between 10 and 20 percent of the Indian population, rural and urban. One of the world's great "bourgeois revolutions" of the second half of the twentieth century occurred (and is still occurring) in India.

From that point, however, parliamentary democracy moved little during India's early decades of Congress's "one-party dominance." Over the past twenty years or so, however, democratic processes have begun to move across the spectrum. Most notably, "power and influence, . . . honour and respect" have been substantially redistributed; "income and wealth," less so. From 1967, the erosion in India's states of Congress dominance and its final disappearance has been both cause and effect of the proliferation of provincial parties, which are largely representative of local OBC interests and have become major contenders for power in *panchayati raj* and state government.

During his brief tenure as India's non-Congress prime minister in 1989–90, V. P. Singh thrust the interests of the OBC into the national political agenda. In accordance with recommendations of the Mandal Commission, he ordered the reservation of a substantial proportion of positions in central government service for OBC castes. In the chaos that followed, V. P. Singh lost his majority and Congress returned to power in 1991. But in spite of the efforts of upper castes to close it, the door to "mandalization" only opened more widely. The 1996 parliamentary elections were contested by three coalitions: Congress and its allies, the BJP and its allies, and the National Front–Left Front. The last of these, renamed the United Front, was largely a coalition of provincially based, subordinate-class political parties. Of the three coalitions it won the highest percentage of the popular vote (28.5 percent), and of the twenty-one ministers in the first United Front government more than half belonged undisputedly either to OBC or Dalit castes.[37] The United Front collapsed as a government in 1998 and has since dissolved as a coalition. Nowadays, OBC politicians and parties swim in the Indian political mainstream. If not the BJP itself, most of the provincial parties that constitute its majority in the parliament elected in 1999 are representative of OBC interests. Dalits lag behind; however, in the state in which they are best organized, Uttar Pradesh, their party, the Bhujan Samaj Party, won 14 seats in 1999 compared to 4 in the parliamentary elections of 1997–98. If they can maintain that unity, they stand a better chance of playing a major roll in India's largest state and even at its center. And that is good news for Dalits.

To be sure, the redistribution of "power and influence, . . . honour and respect" in the daily life of Indian villagers has lagged behind its redistribution in political arenas. But there is no doubt that these arenas impinge on daily life, and that there is a growing awareness of their impingement. By enhancing its power and influence in the *panchayati raj* institutions in its district, an OBC caste enhances its power and influence in its villages. It becomes increasingly difficult for villagers to deny at least a modicum of honor and respect to a Dalit caste if its votes are important to its state government: "Political empowerment has set in motion a process of change in social relations evident in the breakdown of caste barriers in urban areas, and the attenuation of caste restrictions and much greater social interaction between upper and lower castes in rural areas."[38]

In the West, where increasing inequality of wealth and income is hidden behind an increasing observance of the etiquette of social equality, we may have forgotten or repressed the memory of the pain to those among us who were treated as pariahs and underestimate the intensity of their aspirations for social equality. "At the heart of political change [in India], V. P. Singh pointed out, was the urge" for self-respect for people who have been oppressed by pure caste for centuries. The individual wants respect for his or her person and identity. For some this aspect is not important, but for those who suffer indignity every day, who suffer disrespect as a human condition, it is more hurtful than poverty.[39]

What more can we say of parliamentary democracy's impact on the redistribution of income and wealth in India? Land reforms, inspired by the Congress Party and implemented by state legislative assemblies dominated by cultivating proprietors, redistributed income and wealth: downward from landlords to these farmers and upward to them from rural underclasses—marginal farmers, sharecroppers, subtenants, landless laborers. In caste terms, the major beneficiaries of this redistribution were dominant and twice-born castes. Smaller, OBC farmers also profited from land reforms, although not to the same extent as they did from *panchayati raj* and the Green Revolution. The latter's inputs, it should be noted, were distributed not by an authoritarian government according to some "elite. farmers strategy," as in Pakistan, but by provincial parliamentary democratic governments whose members and constituencies were increasing from the OBC. The "creamy layers" of its castes—cultivating proprietors—were the primary and immediate beneficiaries of this income redistribution. But it has given impetus to the OBC quest for political power and increased access via "mandalization" to the professions and government service. These are sources of prestige, power, influence, and remittance income for OBC farm families. Across party and state lines, "mandalization" has become the general rule in India

Compensatory discrimination has been the route of income redistribution to Dalits, largely through government service, and more narrowly based than wealth and income redistribution to the OBC. It is from this narrow base, however, that the leadership has come, as in the Bhujan Samaj Party of Uttar Pradesh, for example, for the increasing social and political assertiveness of Dalits. But they are still the poorest of the poor. For these Dalits and other deprived groups (most Muslims, for example), I do not see much hope of any further redistribution of wealth and income in the countryside. Land reforms that favored cultivating proprietors, divisions into smaller holdings of proprietorship amongst their heirs, Green Revolution transformations of marginal into viable land holdings, and the increasing political influence of OBC caste farmers have all increased the constituency opposed to any further land reforms. Tenurial reforms, consonant with commercial farming—the CPI-M's "Operation Barga," for example—are at least theoretically possible. But there must be a will. And such reforms are on the agendas of no governing or major opposition parties save the communist parties, which have become effectively provincialized in Kerala and West Bengal.

Substantial, further redistribution of income and wealth in India will come, I believe, from the development of industry, including agro-industry. Industrialization has been laggard in India, not least because the necessary transfer of resources from agriculture to industry has been impeded by a rural-centered, cultivating-proprietor-dominated parliamentary democracy. But that urbanization is growing rapidly, and industrialization slowly but surely, there is no doubt. One quarter of India's population lives or works in its towns and cities, and mostly in its largest cities. In the factory sector, largely concentrated in these large cities, employment has trebled since 1960, fixed capital has increased one-hundred-fold, gross output is seventy-five times greater, and value added is more than fifty times greater.[40] No one doubts but that the material and human resources in India are more than adequate to its further industrialization.

Because of the growing linkages between the farm and the factory—through remittance income and agro-industry, for example—the farmers' movements of the 1980s, which championed the interests of the "countryside" versus the "city," are less likely to recur. Problems abound, however, in the "city": the interests of public-sector industries and their employees versus the interests of the private sector in an era of "privatization"; the interests of small business versus the interests of the great Indian conglomerates supported by the ideology of "economic rationalism"; the interests of Indian industry as opposed to the forces of "globalization"; and, as ever, the interests of labor versus those of capital and institutionalized corruption and nepotism versus the public interest. Parliamentary democracy, within whose framework most of India's political conflicts have been successfully negotiated, may yet negotiate its industrialization. But those who look to see it done rapidly are likely to be disappointed.

NOTES

1. Oxford: Clarendon Press, 1972.

2. Holly Sims, *Political Regimes, Public Policy and Economic Development: Agricultural Performance and Rural Change in the Two Punjabs* (New Delhi: Sage, 1988). See also, Sucha Singh Gill, "Political Economy of Agricultural Development in Two Punjabs," *Economic and Political Weekly*, 11 March 1989.

3. John R. Westley, *Agriculture and Equitable Growth: The Case of Punjab-Haryana* (Boulder, CO: Westview, 1986).

4. H. S. Shergill and Gurmail Singh, "Poverty in Rural Punjab: Trend over Green Revolution Decades," *Economic and Political Weekly*, 30:25, 24 June 1995, pp. A80–83.

5. Gill, "Political Economy."

6. "Terrorism" in Punjab during the 1980s is generally attributed, at least in part, to the lack of industrial development sufficient to provide employment for young men of marginal farm families who were relatively deprived in the successful development of capitalist agriculture. Ibid.; Promode Kumar, "Violence in Punjab," *Seminar*, October 1995, pp. 55–58.

7. G.K. Lieten, *Continuity and Change in Rural West Bengal* (New Delhi: Sage, 1992), p. 279.

8. Ibid., p. 251.

9. Ibid., p. 285.

10. Ibid., pp. 51, 139.

11. Ibid., p. 276.

12. Ibid., p. 193.

13. Ibid., p. 201.

14. Ross Mallick, *Development Policy of a Communist Government: West Bengal since 1977* (Cambridge: Cambridge University Press, 1993).

15. Ibid., p. 81.

16. Ibid., p. 47.

17. Ibid., p. 74.

18. Ibid., p. 53.

19. Ibid., pp. 3, 212, 214.

20. It should be noted that much of the data from Government of India sources which Mallick uses to sustain his argument were gathered either before the CPI-M came to office or in its early years in office.

21. Dietrich Rueschemeyer, Evelyn Huber Stephen, and John D Stephens, *Capitalist Development and Democracy* (Cambridge: Polity Press, 1996), p. 223.

22. Mallick, *Development Policy*, p. 209.

23. Ibid., p. 211.

24. Quoted in Lieten, *Continuity and Change*, p. 21.

25. Bimal Kumar Saha, *Agrarian Structure and Productivity in Bangladesh and West Bengal: A Study in Comparative Perspective* (Dhaka: University Press, 1997).

26. Ibid., p. 170.

27. Ibid., p. 166.

28. Ibid., p. 166.

29. Lieten, *Continuity and Change*, p. 276.

30. After substantial refinement, the indexed items in 1998 were life expectancy, education, and GDP. The HDI Value is the sum of these divided by three. http://www.undp.org/HDI/html.

31. Ibid., year 2000.

32. Conversation with Shaibal Gupta; see also Saba Naqvi Bhaumik, "Yadavs in the Pit," *India Today*, 4 October 1999, pp. 11–12.

33. Rueschemeyer et al., *Capitalist Development,* p. 297.

34. *Times of India*, internet edition, 9 November 1999.

35. Akmal Hussain, "The Dynamics of Power: Military, Bureaucracy and the People," *The Daily News* (Lahore), 16 July 1992, p. 11.

36. "Qazi [Husain Ahmed, Jamaat-I-Islami chief] Asks Rulers to Cut Stint in Power," *Dawn*, internet edition, 15 November 1999.

37. Interjit Badhwar, "United Front: Pitfalls and Promises," *India Today*, 30 June 1996, pp. 20–26, and Harinder Baweja, "Changing Face of Parliament," ibid., pp. 24–26.

38. Zoya Hasan, *Quest for Power*, p. 163.

39. Quoted in ibid., p. 164.

40. A convenient compilation of such statistics is the annual *Statistical Outline of India*, published in Mumbai by Tata Services Limited.

Bibliography

Some of the works cited below appear in the notes, some do not. Some of the works cited in the notes—particularly those that are only the sources of specific references—do not appear below. In the works cited here, I have, in general, but with several notable exceptions, preferred more to less recent publications; books to journal articles; edited collections to their separate pieces; more to less comprehensive studies; and variety to consistency in ideological or theoretical underpinning and methodology. In works that span two or more of the categories listed below—"The Subcontinent before Partition" and "India," for example—I have cited them where they have been most useful to me. So readers will have to do some fossicking. Those in search of even further reading may find it in the bibliographies of the works cited below, or in the comprehensive *Bibliography of Asian Studies,* published as a delayed annual by the Asian Studies Association, Ann Arbor, Michigan; the latter is also available online through library subscription. Amazon.com is a good source for recent and not so recent book titles. *Asian Studies Review, Asian Survey, India Today, Economic and Political Weekly, Far Eastern Economic Review, Journal of Asian Studies, Modern Asian Studies, Pacific Affairs, South Asia,* and *South Asia Research* are some of the usual sources of articles about South Asia. Any number of newspapers from the subcontinent are online (search for "all the world's newspapers").

Works of Theoretical Relevance
and General Subcontinental Reference

Anderson, Benedict. *Imagined Communities.* London: Verso, 1991.

Bailey, F. G. *Stratagems and Spoils: A Social Anthropology of Politics.* New York: Schocken, 1969.

De Bary, Wm. Theodore, et al., eds. *Sources of Indian Tradition.* New York: Columbia University Press, 1958.

Dobb, Maurice. *Studies in the Development of Capitalism*, revised edition. New York: International Publishers, 1963.

Etienne, Gilbert. *Rural Change in South Asia: India, Pakistan, Bangladesh.* New Delhi: Vikas, 1995.

Gerth, H. H., & Mills, C. Wright, eds. and trans. *From Max Weber: Essays in Sociology.* New York: Oxford University Press, 1958.

Hamilton, Richard F. *The Bourgeois Epoch: Marx and Engels on Britain, France and Germany.* Chapel Hill, NC: University of North Carolina Press, 1991.

Hutton, J. H. *Caste in India*, 3rd edition. London: Oxford University Press, 1961.

Inden, Ronald. *Imagining India.* Oxford: Blackwell, 1990.

Kumar, Dharma, with Desai, Megnad, eds. *The Cambridge Economic History of India, Vol. 2, c. 1757–1970.* Cambridge: Cambridge University Press, 1981–82.

Lasswell, Harold. *Politics: Who Gets What, When and How.* New York: Meridian Books, 1958.

Moore, Barrington, Jr. *Social Origins of Dictatorship and Democracy.* Boston, MA: Beacon Press, 1966.

Mujeeb, M. *The Indian Muslims.* New Delhi: Munshiram Manoharlal, 1985.

Myrdal, Gunnar. *Asian Drama.* abridged edition, ed. Seth R. King. New York: Vintage, 1972.

Phadnis, Urmila. *Ethnicity and Nation-Building in South Asia.* New Delhi: Sage, 1989.

Rawls, John. *A Theory of Justice.* Oxford: Clarendon Press, 1972.

Raychaudhuri, Tapan, & Habib, Ifran, eds., *The Cambridge Economic History of India, Vol. 1, c. 1200–1750.* Cambridge: Cambridge University Press, 1981–82.

Robinson, Francis, ed. *The Cambridge Encyclopedia of India, Pakistan, Bangladesh, Sri Lanka, Nepal, and the Maldives.* Cambridge: Cambridge University Press, 1989.

Rueschemeyer, Dietrich; Stephens, Evelyne Huber; & Stephens, John D. *Capitalist Development and Democracy.* Cambridge: Polity, 1992.

Said, Edward. *Orientalism.* New York: Random House, 1979.

Shanin, Teodor. *Peasant Societies.* Harmondsworth: Penguin, 1973.

Schwartzberg, Joseph E. *An Historical Atlas of South Asia.* Chicago, IL: University of Chicago Press, 1978.

Skocpol, Theda. *States and Social Revolutions: A Comparative Analysis of France, Russia and China.* Cambridge: Cambridge University Press, 1979.

Smith, W. C. *Islam in Modern History.* New York: Mentor, 1959.

Sobhan, Rehman. *Agrarian Reform and Social Transformation: Preconditions for Development.* Dhaka: University Press, 1993.

Walker, Benjamin. *The Hindu World*, 2 vols. New York: Praeger, 1968.
Wehler, Hans-Ulrich. *The German Empire*, trans. Kim Traynor. Leamington Spa: Berg Publishers, 1985.
Wolf, Eric R. *Peasants*. Englewood Cliffs, NJ: Prentice-Hall, 1966.

The Subcontinent before Partition

Ahmad, Qeyamuddin. *The Wahhabi Movement in India*, 2nd revised edition. New Delhi: Mahohar, 1994.
Ahmad Khan, Muin-ud-Din. *History of the Fara'idi Movement in Bengal, 1818–1906*. Karachi: Pakistan Historical Society, 1965.
Ansari, Sarah F. D. *Sufi Saints and State Power: The Pirs of Sind, 1843–1947*. Cambridge: Cambridge University Press, 1992.
Anstey, Vera. *The Economic Development of India*. London: Longmans, Green, 1957.
Barrier, Norman. *The Punjab Alienation of Land Bill of 1900*. Durham, NC: Duke University Commonwealth Studies Center, 1966.
Bessaignet, Pierre, ed. *Social Research in East Pakistan*. Dacca: Asiatic Society of Pakistan, 1960.
Broomfield, J. H. *Elite Conflict in a Plural Society: Twentieth Century Bengal*. Berkeley, CA: University of California Press, 1968.
Chandra, Bipan, et al. *India's Struggle for Independence*. New Delhi: Penguin, 1989.
_____. *Nationalism and Colonialism in Modern India*. Hyderabad: Orient Longman, 1979.
Chatterji, Joya. *Bengal Divided: Hindu Communalism and Partition 1932–1947*. Cambridge: Cambridge University Press, 1994
Chaudhuri, Nirad C. *The Autobiography of an Unknown Indian*. London: Hogarth Press, 1991.
Darling, Malcolm. *The Punjab Peasant in Prosperity and Debt*. Bombay: Oxford University Press, 1947.
Gilmartin, David. *Empire and Islam*. London: I. B. Tauris, 1988.
Gopal, Ram. *Indian Muslims: A Political History, 1858–1947*. London: Asia Publishing House, 1959.
Gordon, Leonard A. *Bengal: The Nationalist Movement 1876–1940*. Delhi: Manohar Book Service, 1974.
Gupta, Shiv Kumar. *Arya Samaj and the Raj (1875–1920)*. New Delhi: Gitanjali Publishing House, 1991.
Hamid, Abdul. *Muslim Separatism in India: A Brief Survey 1858–1947*. Lahore: Oxford University Press, 1971.
Hardy, Peter. *The Muslims of British India*. Cambridge: Cambridge University Press, 1972.
Harun-or-Rashid, *The Foreshadowing of Bangladesh: Bengal Muslim League and Muslim Politics 1936–1947*. Dhaka: Asiatic Society of Bangladesh, 1987.
Hunter, William Wilson. *Indian Musalmans*. Reprinted Delhi: Indological Book House, 1969.
Jalal, Ayeshi. *The Sole Spokesman: Jinnah, The Muslim League and the Demand for Pakistan*. Lahore: Sang-e-Meel Publications, 1992.

Jones, Kenneth W. *Arya Dharma: Hindu Consciousness in 19th-Century Punjab.*
    Berkeley, CA: University of California Press, 1976.
Lahiri, Pradip Kumar. *Bengali Muslim Thought 1818–1947.* Calcutta: K. P Bagchi,
    1991.
Low, D. A., ed. *The Political Inheritance of Pakistan.* London: Macmillan, 1991.
Markovits, Claude. *Indian Business and National Politics, 1931–1939.* Cambridge:
    Cambridge University Press, 1985.
Mason, Philip. *A Matter of Honour: An Account of the Indian Army, Its Officers and
    Men.* London: Jonathan Cape, 1974.
Menon, V. P. *The Story of the Integration of the Indian States.* Bombay: Orient
    Longmans, 1961.
Minault, Gail. *The Khilafat Movement: Religious Symbolism and Political Mobil-
    ization in India.* New York: Columbia University Press, 1982.
Neimeijer, A. C. *The Khilafat Movement in India, 1919–1924.* The Hague: Martinus
    Nijhoff, 1972.
Pandey, Gyanendra. *The Construction of Communalism in Colonial North India.*
    New Delhi: Oxford University Press, 1992.
Qureshi, Ishtiaq Husain. *The Muslim Community of the Indo-Pakistan Subcontinent,
    610–1947.* 'S-Gravenhage: Mouton, 1962.
Robinson, Francis. *Separatism among Indian Muslims: The Politics of the United
    Provinces' Muslims 1860–1923.* Delhi: Oxford University Press, 1994.
Sarkar, Sumit. *Modern India 1885–1947.* Madras: Macmillan, 1983.
Seal, Anil. *The Emergence of Indian Nationalism.* Cambridge: Cambridge Univer-
    sity Press, 1971.
Siddiqui, Kalim. *Conflict, Crisis and War in Pakistan.* London: Macmillan, 1972.
Singh, Khushwant. *A History of the Sikhs*, 2 vols. Delhi: Oxford University Press,
    1963, 1966.
Smith, Vincent A. *The Oxford History of India*, 3rd edition, ed. Percival Spear.
    London: Oxford University Press, 1961.
Stein, Burton. *A History of India.* Oxford: Blackwell, 1998.
Stokes, Eric. *The Peasant Armed: The Indian Revolt of 1857,* ed. C. A. Bayly.
    Oxford: Clarendon Press, 1986.
Van den Dungen, P. H. M. *The Punjab Tradition.* London: Allen & Unwin, 1972.
Wasti, Syed Razi. *Muslim Struggle for Freedom in British India.* Lahore: Book
    Traders, 1993.
Wolpert, Stanley. *A New History of India*, 4th ed. New York: Oxford, 1993.
Woodruff, Philip [Philip Mason], *The Men Who Ruled India*, 2 vols. New York:
    Schocken, 1964.
Yadav, K. C., & Arya, K. S. *Arya Samaj and the Freedom Movement, Vol. 1, 1875–
    1918.* New Delhi: Manohar, 1988.

India

Béteille, André. *Society and Politics in India.* New Delhi: Oxford University Press,
    1997.
Björkman, James Warner, ed. *Fundamentalism, Revivalists and Violence in South
    Asia.* Riverdale, MD: Riverdale Company, 1988.

Brass, Paul R. *The Politics of India since Independence*, 2nd edition, Cambridge: Cambridge University Press, 1995.

_____. *Ethnicity and Nationalism: Theory and Comparison*. New Delhi: Sage, 1992.

Chakrapani, C., & Vijaya Kumar, S., eds. *Changing Status and Role of Women in Indian Society*. New Delhi: M. D. Publications, 1994.

Chaudhri, D. P., & Das Gupta, Ajit K. *Agriculture and the Development Process: A Study of Punjab*. London: Croon Helm, 1985.

Chaudhuri, Pramit, ed. *Readings in Indian Agricultural Development*. London: Allen & Unwin, 1972.

Dumont, Louis. *Homo Hierarchicus*. London: Weidenfeld & Nicolson, 1970.

Gill, Sucha Singh, "Political Economy of Agricultural Development in Two Punjabs," *Economic and Political Weekly*, 11 March 1989.

Gough, Kathleen, & Sharma, Hari P, eds. *Imperialism and Revolution in South Asia*. New York: Monthly Review Press, 1973.

Hasan, Zoya. *Dominance and Mobilisation: Rural Politics in Western Uttar Pradesh 1930–1980*. Delhi: Sage, 1989.

_____. *Quest for Power: Oppositional Movements and Post-Congress Politics in Uttar Pradesh*. New Delhi: Oxford University Press, 1998.

Hazell, Peter B. R., & Ramaswamy, C., eds. *The Green Revolution Reconsidered: The Impact of High-Yielding Rice Varieties in South India*. Delhi: Oxford University Press, 1991.

India, National Commission for Scheduled Castes and Scheduled Tribes, *Report 1998*.

Kapur, Rajiv A. *Sikh Separatism: The Politics of Faith*. London: Allen & Unwin, 1986.

Khanna, B. S. *Panchayati Raj in India*. New Delhi: Deep & Deep, 1994.

Khanna, Girija, & Varghese, Mariamma. *Indian Women Today*. New Delhi: Vikas, 1978.

Kishwar, Madhu, & Vanita, Ruth, eds. *In Search of Answers: Indian Women's Voices from Manushi*. London: Zed Books, 1984.

Kohli, Atul. *Democracy and Discontent: India's Growing Crisis of Governability*. Cambridge: University of Cambridge Press, 1991.

Kothari, Rajni. *Politics in India*. New Delhi: Orient Longmans, 1970.

Kumar, Promode. "Violence in Punjab," *Seminar*, October 1995, pp. 55–58.

Lieten, G. K. *Continuity and Change in Rural West Bengal*. New Delhi: Sage, 1992.

Mallick, Ross. *Development Policy of a Communist Government: West Bengal since 1977*. Cambridge: Cambridge University Press, 1993.

Masselos, Jim, ed. *India: Creating a Modern Nation*. Delhi: Sterling, 1990.

Mathew, George, ed. *Status of Panchayati Raj in the States of India 1994*. New Delhi: Institute of Social Sciences, 1995.

Mendelsohn, Oliver, & Vicziany, Marika. *The Untouchables: Subordination, Poverty and the State in Modern India*. Cambridge: Cambridge University Press, 1998.

Menon, V. P. *The Story of the Integration of the Indian States*. Bombay: Orient Longmans, 1961.

Morris-Jones, W. H. *The Government and Politics of India*. London: Hutchinson University Library, 1964.

Nayar, Baldev Raj. *Minority Politics in the Punjab*. Princeton, NJ: Princeton University Press, 1966.

Reddy, G. Ram, ed. *Patterns of Panchayati Raj in India*. Delhi: Macmillan, 1977.

Rudolph, Lloyd I., & Hoeber, Susanne. *The Modernity of Tradition: Political Development in India*. Chicago, IL: University of Chicago Press, 1984.

_____. *In Pursuit of Lakshmi: The Political Economy of the Indian State*. Chicago, IL: University of Chicago Press, 1987.

Shergill, H. S., & Singh, Gurmail. "Poverty in Rural Punjab: Trend over Green Revolution Decades," *Economic and Political Weekly*, 30:25, 24 June 1995, pp. A80–83.

Sims, Holly. *Political Regimes, Public Policy and Economic Development: Agricultural Performance and Rural Change in the Two Punjabs*. New Delhi: Sage, 1988.

Singh, Gopal, ed. *Punjab: Past, Present and Future*. Delhi: Ajanta Publications, 1994.

Srinivas, M. N. *Social Change in Modern India*. Berkeley, CA: University of California Press, 1966.

Stern, Robert W. *Changing India*. Cambridge: Cambridge University Press, 1993.

_____. *The Process of Opposition in India*. Chicago, IL: University of Chicago Press, 1970.

Weiner, Myron, ed. *State Politics in India*. Princeton, NJ: Princeton University Press, 1968.

Westley, John R. *Agriculture and Equitable Growth: The Case of Punjab-Haryana*. Boulder, CO: Westview, 1986.

Zelliot, Eleanor. *From Untouchable to Dalit: Essays on the Ambedkar Movement*. New Delhi: Manohar, 1996.

Pakistan (including East Pakistan until 1971)

Abbot, Freeland. *Islam and Pakistan*. Ithaca, NY: Cornell University Press, 1968.

Ahmad, Mushtaq. *The United Nations and Pakistan*. Karachi: Pakistan Institute of International Affairs, 1955.

Ahmed, Akbar S. *Resistance and Control in Pakistan*. London: Routledge, 1991.

Ahmed, Manzoorudin, ed. *Contemporary Pakistan: Politics, Economy and Society*. Karachi: Royal Book Company, 1980.

Ayub Khan, Mohammad. *Friends Not Masters: A Political Biography*. New York: Oxford University Press, 1967.

Baxter, Craig, & Kennedy, Charles H., eds. *Pakistan: 1997*. New Delhi: HarperCollins, 1998.

Binder, Leonard. *Religion and Politics in Pakistan*. Berkeley, CA: University of California Press, 1961.

Callard, Keith. *Pakistan*. New York: Macmillan, 1957.

Chowdhury, Subrata Roy. *The Genesis of Bangladesh*. London: Asia Publishing House, 1972.

Hussain, Akmal. *Poverty Alleviation in Pakistan*. Lahore: Vanguard Books, 1994.

_____. "The Dynamics of Power: Military, Bureaucracy and the People," *The Daily News* (Lahore), 16 July 1992, p. 11.

Hussain, Mushahid, & Hussain, Akmal. *Pakistan: Problems of Governance.* New Delhi: Centre for Policy Research, 1993.

Jalal, Ayesha. *The State of Martial Rule.* Cambridge: Cambridge University Press, 1990.

James, William E., & Roy, Subroto, eds. *Foundations of Pakistan's Political Economy: Towards an Agenda for the 1990s.* Karachi: Oxford University Press, 1992.

Khan, Asghar, ed. *Islam, Politics and the State: The Pakistan Experience.* London: Zed Books, 1985.

Korson, J. Henry, ed. *Contemporary Problems of Pakistan.* Boulder, CO: Westview Press, 1993.

Malik, Iftikhar H. *State and Civil Society in Pakistan.* London: Macmillan, 1997.

McGrath, Allen. *The Destruction of Pakistan's Democracy.* Karachi: Oxford University Press, 1996.

Muhammad Ali, Chaudhri. *The Emergence of Pakistan.* Lahore: Research Society of Pakistan, 1973.

Noman, Omar. *The Political Economy of Pakistan 1947–85.* London: KPI, 1988.

Rizvi, Hasan-Askari. *The Military and Politics in Pakistan 1947–86.* Lahore: Progressive Publishers, 1987.

Samad, Yunis. *A Nation in Turmoil: Nationalism and Ethnicity in Pakistan 1937–1958.* New Delhi: Sage Publications, 1995.

Siddiqui, Kalim. *Conflict, Crisis and War in Pakistan.* London: Macmillan, 1972.

Vorys, Karl von. *Political Development in Pakistan.* Princeton, NJ: Princeton University Press, 1965.

Waseem, Mohammad. *Politics and the State in Pakistan.* Islamabad: National Institute of Historical and Cultural Research, 1994.

Wolpert, Stanley. *Zulfi Bhutto of Pakistan.* Delhi: Oxford University Press, 1993.

Zaidi, S. Akbar, ed. *Regional Imbalances and the National Question in Pakistan.* Lahore: Vanguard Books, 1992.

Bangladesh

Anisuzzaman. *Creativity, Reality and Identity.* Dhaka: International Centre for Bengal Studies, 1993.

Feuer, Lewis S. *The Conflict of Generations: The Character and Significance of Student Movements.* London: Heinemann, 1969.

Heberle, Rudolf, & Gusfield, Joseph R. "Social Movements," *International Encyclopedia of the Social Sciences*, Vol. 14, ed. David L. Sills. New York: Macmillan, 1968.

Jahan, Rounaq. *Bangladesh Politics: Problems and Issues.* Dhaka: University Press, 1987.

Khan, Shamsul I., Islam, S. Aminul, & Haque, M. Indalul. *Political Culture, Political Parties and the Democratic Transition in Bangladesh.* Dhaka: Academic Publishers, 1996.

Kochanek, Stanley A. *Patron–Client Politics and Business in Bangladesh.* Dhaka: University Press, 1993.

Maniruzzaman, Talukder. *Politics and Security of Bangladesh.* Dhaka: University Press, 1994.

_____. *The Bangladesh Revolution and Its Aftermath.* Dhaka: University Press, 1988.

Puchkov, V. P. *Political Development of Bangladesh 1971–1985.* New Delhi: Patriotic Publishers, 1989.

Rahim, Aminur. *Politics and National Formation in Bangladesh.* Dhaka: University Press, 1997.

Saha, Bimal Kumar. *Agrarian Structure and Productivity in Bangladesh and West Bengal: A Study in Comparative Perspective.* Dhaka: University Press, 1997.

Sen, Rangalal. *Political Elites in Bangladesh.* Dhaka: University Press, 1986.

Sobhan, Rehman. *Bangladesh: Problems of Governance.* New Delhi: Centre for Political Research, 1993.

Ullah, Mahbub. *Land, Livelihood and Change in Bangladesh.* Dhaka: University Press, 1996.

Wood, Geoffrey D. *Bangladesh: Whose Ideas, Whose Interests.* Dhaka: University Press, 1994

Zafarullah, Habib, Taslim, M. A., & Chowdhury, Anis, eds. *Policy Issues in Bangladesh.* Dhaka: University Press, 1994.

Zaheer, Hasan. *The Separation of East Pakistan: The Rise and Realisation of Bengali Muslim Nationalism.* Dhaka: University Press, 1994.

Ziring, Lawrence. *Bangladesh from Mujib to Ershad: An Interpretive Study.* Dhaka: University Press, 1992.

Index

ABOUT THE AUTHOR

Robert W. Stern is a Senior Research Fellow at Macquarie University in Sydney, Australia. For more than thirty years his professional life has centered on the study of modern South Asia. He is the author of four books, including *Changing India* (1993), and a number of articles.